Russell Hoban/Forty Years

Children's Literature and Culture
Volume 15
Garland Reference Library of the Humanities
Volume 2214

Children's Literature and Culture

Jack Zipes, *Series Editor*

Russell Hoban/ Forty Years

Essays on His Writings for Children

Edited by
Alida Allison

Garland Publishing, Inc.
A member of the Taylor & Francis Group
New York & London
2000

Published in 2000 by
Garland Publishing, Inc.
A member of the Taylor & Francis Group
29 West 35th Street
New York, NY 10001

PS
3558
.O336
Z86
2000

10   9   8   7   6   5   4   3   2   1

Library of Congress Cataloging-in-Publication Data
Russell Hoban/forty years : essays on his writings for children / [edited by]
    Alida Allison
      p.   cm. — (Garland reference library of the humanities ; v. 2214.
    Children's literature and culture ; v. 15)
    Includes bibliographical references and index.
    ISBN 0-8153-3185-1 (hardcover : alk. paper) — ISBN 0-8153-3799-x
      (pbk. : alk. paper)
      1. Hoban, Russell—Criticism and interpretation   2. Children's stories,
    American—History and criticism.   I. Allison, Alida.   II. Garland reference
    library of the humanities ; vol. 2214.   III. Garland reference library of the
    humanities. Children's literature and culture; v. 15.

PS3558.O336 Z86 2000
813'.54—dc21
                                                                   99-047805

Cover photo by Tana Hoban

Credits appear on page 219.

Printed on acid-free, 250-year-life paper.
Manufactured in the United States of America

To Russ, my favorite author, and Byron, my favorite husband

Contents

Series Editor's Foreword

Dedicated to furthering original research in children's literature and culture, the Children's Literature and Culture series includes monographs on individual authors and illustrators, historical examinations of different periods, literary analyses of genres, and comparative studies on literature and the mass media. The series is international in scope and is intended to encourage innovative research in children's literature with a focus on interdisciplinary methodology.

Children's literature and culture are understood in the broadest sense of the term *children* to encompass the period of childhood up through late adolescence. Owing to the fact that the notion of childhood has changed so much since the origination of children's literature, this Garland series is particularly concerned with transformations in children's culture and how they have affected the representation and socialization of children. While the emphasis of the series is on children's literature, all types of studies that deal with children's radio, film, television, and art are included in an endeavor to grasp the aesthetics and values of children's culture. Not only have there been momentous changes in children's culture in the last fifty years, but there have been radical shifts in the scholarship that deals with these changes. In this regard, the goal of the Children's Literature and Culture series is to enhance research in this field and, at the same time, point to new directions that bring together the best scholarly work throughout the world.

Jack Zipes

Russell Hoban's books defy classification. Illus. Nicola Bayley.

Introduction

ALIDA ALLISON

The *New York Times* calls Russell Hoban a novelist whose work is "fiercely imagined."[1] "He's the most interior man I've ever met," says a friend. Originality, interiority, and an uncompromised commitment to what his character Manny Rat calls "fings vat simply cannot be figured out"[2] describe an author equally well respected in the over-boundaried worlds of children's and adults' literatures. Many of Hoban's "children's books" are so labeled because they are short and they are illustrated. But *The Sea-Thing Child* (1972, 1999), *La Corona and the Tin Frog* (1979 and soon to be reissued), *The Marzipan Pig* (1986), and many of Hoban's more than sixty books for children defy genre and reading-level pigeonholes. They are works of art that simply happen to be short and to be illustrated. Hoban has often said that the only difference between his works for children and his writings for adults is the "child's narrower frame of reference." Thus many essays in this volume discuss Hoban's works for adults alongside those determined by publishers to be for children. Because of the intelligence and sophisticated humor of Hoban's characters as they grapple with their realities, his writing appeals on an intellectual level as rare in adults' books as in children's. For the depth, resourcefulness, and receptivity of his characters implies, by extension, similar characteristics in his readers, young and old. Many of Hoban's stories are "mind-trips," and if there are readers who don't want to go along, that's no concern of the author's. Far from dummying anything down—from ideas to syntax and vocabulary—Hoban implies through the quality of his books that his readers are not only quite capable of understanding his stories but will also recognize similar experiences in their own lives, at whatever stage they may be in. His plots probe rock-bottom relationships, the ones that really count—relationships between us and other people, of course, but more importantly, relationships between us and ourselves.

Hoban's contribution to literature is honored in this book of essays. The variety of analytical viewpoints as well as nationalities of contributors speaks to the richness and singularity of Hoban's body of writing, ranging from his first picture book, the 1958 *What Does It Do and How Does It Work?*, to the Whitbread Award–nominated 1996 Young Adult novel *The Trokeville Way*. In addition, there are his eight novels for adults, the most recent being *Angelica's Grotto;* a score of superb essays collected in *The Moment under the Moment* (1994) and *The Hoban Omnibus* (1999); two librettos, including *The Second Mrs. Kong,* which debuted at the Glyndebourne Opera House in 1994 and subsequently toured Europe; and several books of poetry, such as *The Last of the Wallendas* (1997). There are also his occasional appearances at universities and public readings, and a good number of published interviews. Now in his mid-seventies and apparently indefatigable despite some ups and downs with health, Hoban typically works on several projects simultaneously, writing late at night.

Because Hoban has lived thirty years in Britain, which he still associates with "courage and good writing," the expatriate Pennsylvanian is often mistaken for an Englishman. Indeed, he "loves writing about London," its weather, its neighborhoods, its Underground stations and bridges. Nevertheless, born in 1925, Hoban is the child of Jewish immigrants to America and of the generation and general background of Norman Mailer, Joseph Heller, Bernard Malamud, and Saul Bellow. But, unlike them, except for essays, he seldom writes about the first half of his life in America, about the Depression, about World War II, or about politics and the big outside world in general. Hoban's father died when Russell was eleven. He dropped out of Temple University during his first semester and never went back to college, married young, and fought in Italy. Returning to the States, he and his wife Lillian began to raise a family, which they moved to Connecticut while Hoban worked with art and words in New York City. He freelanced illustrations and articles, was on the staff of a major advertising agency (like another verbally playful children's author, Dr. Seuss), and found he liked to write better than he liked to draw. But it was what he calls a "fluke" that in the late 1950s, he and his drawings were introduced to Ursula Nordstrom at Harper & Row. He soon became a self-supporting children's book writer.

Forty years ago, Hoban was just publishing his first books for children. Garth Williams, the renowned illustrator of *Charlotte's Web,* turned Frances into a badger in the very successful (and still in print) *Bedtime for Frances,* Hoban's second picture book. Before long, with his wife as illustrator, Hoban was publishing two, sometimes three books a year, a feat that he continues. Many of the Hobans' books are now standards on lists of reviewers' best books: for example, *The Mouse and His Child* (1967), the five Frances books, *Emmet Otter's Jug Band Christmas* (1971), *How Tom Beat Captain Najork and His Hired Sportsmen* (1974), and *The Pedalling Man and Other Poems* (1968, 1990). What lifts Hoban's domestic, reassuring books of the 1960s above any number of picture books of the same period is the quality of Hoban's writing. His ear for dialogue, his eye for scene, the unobtrusive presence he scripts for the patient parents, the ingenuity with which characters like Herman the Loser solve their problems make for books that fully engage the reader's ear, eye, and attention. These early Connecticut countryside books are unambiguous in assuming and affirming the wholeness of the nuclear family, even when they are as irreverent as *The Little Brute Family* (1966) and *Dinner at Alberta's* (1975, but written earlier). But even the Brutes are redeemable; at the book's end, they have renamed themselves the Nice Family. The sloppy Arthur improves his manners, winning the lovely Alberta. In *Charlie the Tramp* (1966), all on his own, the charming Charlie comes home after testing the boundaries of what he wants to do with his life. In *Harvey's Hideout* (1969), a quarrelsome brother and sister compromise over their proprietary concerns. In *The Story of Hester Mouse* (1965), the diminutive rodent manages against all odds to find happiness as a writer.

Thirty years ago, approximately, Hoban leaped from writing what he has since called "little didactic, pleasant cautionary tales" no more than "twelve pages of manuscript long" to writing complex adult novels, such as *Kleinzeit* (1974) and *Turtle Diary* (1975). Hoban's first novel, *The Mouse and His Child,* brought him broad acclaim from critics who hadn't known "he had such a novel in him." At about the same time, having left Connecticut with his family anticipating a long stay in London, "when the dust cleared," as he puts it, he remained in England while his wife and four children returned to the States. It was a time in his life when he says he saw "everything I love going off in a different direction." Written at this time, Hoban's first adult novels establish a basic theme of his repeated twenty-five years later in *Mr. Rinyo-Clacton's Offer* (1998): "You think about a possibility and all of a sudden an actuality has you by the throat."

As established in these novels, Hoban's main characters are the kind who, young or mature, undergo personal crises, episodes of personal loss followed by quests to reconfigure meaning in their lives, people who are not quite comfortable in themselves. But in their striving for "fidelity," faithfulness to the essence of things (including themselves), they connect with secondary characters who are comfortably situated within themselves. Examples are the albatross in *The Sea-Thing Child,* Bundlejoy Cosysweet in *How Tom Beat Captain Najork and His Hired Sportsmen,* Nurse in *Kleinzeit,* or George in *Turtle Diary,* with whom the uncomfortable-in-himself William G. has this exchange:

> "How do you stay cheerful?" I said. (William G.)
> "I don't mind being alive," he said. (George) (p. 161)

But at no time during or since his own crisis did Hoban stop writing children's books. Those of the 1970s and early 1980s develop and express new relationships—with others, with his own mind, and with his writing, expanding now into new genres. In the early 1970s, Hoban married Gundul Ahl; they still live in London, where they have raised three sons. He has said that, for whatever reason, it was not until he had moved to London that he was able to write adult novels. Children's books of this period, like his adult novels of the time, are vigorous testings of the bounds of reality and explorations of new kinds of connections. Characters in *La Corona and the Tin Frog* lyrically long for each other and for self-expression, eventually breaking out of the conventional closed ending. The anti-didactic *How Tom Beat Captain Najork and His Hired Sportsmen* and *The Dancing Tigers* (1979) empowered children before the word "empowerment" entered academese. In *Ace Dragon, Ltd.* (1980), the flight of fantasy becomes literal. *They Came from Aargh!* (1981) is one of a series of books in the early 1980s that drew upon the antics of Hoban's three young sons, while *Flat Cat* (1980) is an offbeat monosyllabic romp in cartoon form. *The Rain Door* (1986) and *Jim Hedgehog and the Lonesome Tower* (1988) acknowledge the youngster's interior life, while *Monsters* (1989) pushes the outer limits of experience and empowerment.

Ultimately, however, temporal categories are conveniences only, for amid the tidy scaffolding of the decades crop up singular expressions of Hoban's genius, children's books as diverse as *The Sea-Thing Child,* with its mythopoetic, metaphysical tone, *The Pedalling Man and Other Poems,* and *Ponders* (1988), a spoofy collection of pondside play, puns, and improbable characters such as Starboy Mole (these animals have up to forty tentacles on their noses). Hoban has written the gamut, from Easy Readers and counting books to profound essays about childhood and children's authors such as Kipling, Wilde, and the Grimm Brothers. Consistently over the years, however, Hoban has been able to retain and restate through his characters the regard he has for letting things be themselves, his admiration for things that are effortlessly themselves— such as stones, seashells, certain trees, undomesticated animals like lions and sea turtles, and snippets of songs—potent presences that all the time send messages to receptive children and adults about how reality is connected, or "hooked-up." The child characters in Hoban's books question least the sources of—much less the actuality of—such messages. Thus they wind up flying on dragon's backs or conversing in lonesome towers with unusual women, or dispatching psychoanalysts who are themselves, unfortunately, unreceptive.

Hoban has seven children and many grandchildren. He has, for most of his adult life, been surrounded by children, an odd fact for a man so comfortable with silence and reflective time. While these familial surroundings have certainly figured into the versimilitude of Hoban's stories, his own recollections of childhood, including what he read, contribute to his writing equally or more. He is of the Beatrix Potter school of children's writers: "I write for the child in me." His essays on authors such as Stevenson and Andersen refer to a cherry tree he used both as a perch to read in and as a source of nourishment, but childhood is no sentimental idyll in his books. In *A Bargain for Frances* (1970), Frances must outwit the manipulative Thelma; the eponymous Herman and Harvey of their picture books deal with snide older sisters, Arthur of *Dinner at Alberta's* (1975), Nick of *The Trokeville Way* (1997), and Oliver in "Dark Oliver" (1989) all combat bullies. And in later children's stories, parents are far from the assets they are to Frances; they ignore, dither, deflate, or domesticate their children's experiences. With the best of intentions, Hoban's parents pressured him into doing great art, deflating for him the joy in what he had just done by pointing him toward what he would accomplish next. He calls this "uphill lean,"[3] and in many interviews and talks he emphatically states his objection to the tampering of parents and teachers with the openness of children.

Unlike the similarly anti-authorian Shel Silverstein and Roald Dahl, who also humorously depict nasty situations, Hoban's comedic bent is more philosophical than anarchistic or macabre, more dispassionate, deeper. In the opening pages of *The Marzipan Pig,* for example, three characters—a marzipan pig, a mouse, and a clock—are eaten or break, but the emphasis of the entire story is on the continuation of life rather than on its demise. At the book's end, Quentin Blake's hibiscus-loving mouse dances with total abandon on the moon-drenched Albert Bridge "and she [does] not," Hoban writes, "get eaten by the owl." For any given receptive individual, there is the possibility of reprieve, hope for a happy ending, or at least some improvement of one's lot. Hoban is pessimistic only about the human race in general.

There are many things that Russell Hoban is not. He is not an author of books with multicultural characters or themes, nor with foreign settings, nor, for the most part, with female protagonists. Families in Hoban's books are untouched by the complications of poverty, politics, unemployment, ill health, or race. His stories typically unfold through connected episodes in a mysterious, modern day, but innocuous London. While his books of the 1960s were neatly resolved, his more recent, more postmodern books purposefully merge the mundane and the extraordinary. For Hoban, it is the interior landscape that matters most.

Critics have pointed to *The Mouse and His Child*'s female elephant as a caricature of women as interior decorators as opposed to pursuers of self-winding and to the aproned Mum in many of his books as a poor model, since she merely stays home. In fact, there are many strong women in Hoban's books, for example, Mum is the authority in *The Flight of Bembel Rudzuk* (1982) and in the other four books illustrated by Colin McNaughton in the 1980s. The female seal in *The Mouse and His Child* is quite self-sufficient; she makes a conscious choice to stop her adventuring and join the family at the reconstructed doll house hotel the male characters win at the story's end. Applying a new sort of literary criticism to this classic book of Hoban's—evolutionary criticism that analyzes characters based on the activity of their "selfish genes"—to use Richard Dawkins's terminology—one could say that the elephant and the seal (or rather their genes) are the smartest characters in the book. While the males are out pursuing complete independence—which turns out to be illusory—or risking their lives fighting for territory and home, the females are feathering their nest. The maximum amount of energy is being expended by others in a manner from which the females can only benefit. I, for one, can easily imagine a future for the elephant and the seal in which they continue to run the family business, travel abroad, and "improve themselves." After all, the mice and the uncles' efforts to win back the house from the rats would have been illusory, too, had not the elephant, while cleaning house, disrupted Manny Rat's plan for revenge.

Indeed, that Hoban's books tend toward male protagonists is not a function of Hoban's gender insensitivity but rather the natural outcome of his doing most of his writing while he had three sons at home. At any rate, Hoban's response to most critics is that he can only write what's in him to write. As he wrote in 1972: "Whatever seas the writer is trawling in, he can only haul up in his nets the fish that swim there."[4]

Russell Hoban/Forty Years is a recognition by international scholars of the complexity of the fish in Russell Hoban's nets. The analytical perspectives of contributors to this volume vary greatly. Though most authors explore several of Hoban's books in their essays, I have presented their contributions in an order generally reflective of the chronology of the books they are discussing. Thus the first essay, written by Carole Scott, comments upon *The Twenty-Elephant Restaurant* (1977), among other Hoban books, in applying a Lacanian perspective to Hoban's work. Jamie Madden's essay follows, discussing the meaning of the monsters and machines that appear in many Hoban stories, including Hoban's first picture book, *What Does It Do and How Does It Work?* (1959). Martin Teitel's essay takes a philosophical look at the epistemological basis of the Frances stories of the 1960s and early 1970s. The next five essays focus upon *The Mouse and His Child.* John Stephens relates his experiences using the 1967 text with 1990s students and suggests ways in which the book can speak powerfully to our times. Maria Nikolajeva, on the other hand, discusses the literally timeless underpinnings of the story, referring her comments to work by Mircea Eliade. James Addison sees the work of William Blake as singularly important in understanding *The Mouse and His Child,* while James Carter compares the book to the movie version, and Staffan Skott sees the novel as an allegory of Jewish history. Dennis Butts's essay and mine following it investigate themes, images, and symbols in several of Hoban's books. Hoban's reception by the German reading public is the subject of Winfred Kaminski's essay. Closing the book, as it closes the century, a postmodern sensibility is applied by Christine Wilkie-Stibbs to *The Mouse and His Child* and several of Hoban's more recent picture books, and by Margaret Bruzelius, who probes both the meaning and the context of *The Trokeville Way* in her essay.

Russell Hoban has spent half his life writing. I asked him how it all began:

Q: Can we begin at the beginning?

A: Yeah, then we can fill in the middle and the end.

Q: Your first children's book came out in 1959, yet you never sought to be a children's author. You had met someone who worked at Harper and Row . . .

A: . . . and she suggested I show these big drawings on brown paper to Ursula Nordstrom, who was head of books for boys and girls. She liked them and she gave me the contract for my first book, which was *What Does It Do and How Does It Work?* I don't remember whether the first drawings I showed her had any captions, but it was understood from the beginning that I would do the text and the pictures. Then came *Bedtime for Frances* and then *The Atomic Submarine.*

Q: How did you get from *What Does It Do and How Does It Work?* to *Bedtime for Frances?*

A: It happened that a neighbor's child was very inventive with finding ways of stalling when it was bedtime. The idea interested me, and I just made up ways I thought were entertaining about a child who doesn't want to go to bed. The choice of animal was by Garth Williams, who illustrated it and had a very long career doing all kinds of cuddly animals. He fancied doing an animal like a badger for a change rather than a mole or a rabbit or a squirrel.

Q: How did your wife Lillian begin doing the art?

A: She had always wanted to be a children's book illustrator, so when I got my foot in the door at Harper's, I told them I wanted Lillian to do the next Frances book. She continued doing badgers.

Q: You've had so many illustrators. Would you say a word about how your books came together, like James Marshall and *Dinner at Alberta's?*

A: I think I'm right in remembering he did the illustrations when I'd already moved to London; I'd done the text before. So I never met James Marshall. I never met Garth Williams. I've met Nicola Bayley; in fact, I gave her the toys to work with for *La Corona and the Tin Frog.* Amelia Edwards at Walker Books showed me some of Clive Scrunton's work, and I thought he'd be very good for *Flat Cat.* He showed me what he had in mind and I liked what he did. The books I did with Colin McNaughton were a result of watching my sons Jake and Ben and Weiland frolicking around and drawing up the things they got up to. Colin did pictures that were fun and full of mischief and were very good with the text. Quentin Blake is the one with whom I've had the most long-term and amiable relationship. He's wonderful in making the pages turn right and in thinking of amusing ways of doing things. He's also a distinguished fine artist.

Q: When you look back on books like Frances from the perspective of thirty or forty years, do you have any thoughts other than they've provided a livelihood for you?

A: I'm profoundly grateful that they keep selling. But I wish to God that they wouldn't train teachers to instruct children that writers are real living people who want to get letters and answer them. When I was a kid, I loved to read Zane Gray, but it never occurred to me to want a letter from him or a lock of his hair. I read the books and that was the end of the transaction.

Q: It's not unusual for you to publish several books a year.

A: Oh, no. I usually have several projects going on at the same time. *Mr. Rinyo-Clacton's Offer* came out in the spring of 1997 with Jonathan Cape and *The Last of the Wallendas* in November of that year with Hodder Books. I call it poetry for all ages. Some of it is light verse, some of it is rhymed, it goes all over the lot. *The Pedalling Man and Other Poems* has been well received over the years because poems from it are always being used in anthologies. I'm curious to see how Wallenda will do.

Q: Its poem "Crystal Maze" is downright disturbing.

A: Well, halls of mirrors scare me.

Q: When your close friend author Leon Garfield died, you wrote "The Wall at All Hallows" for him. How did you two meet?

A: In 1970, in Exeter at a children's literature conference. He had read *The Mouse and His Child* and was enthusiastic about it. We became fast friends. We used to meet for lunch and read our work to each other. It's a funny thing about friendship; it doesn't have so much to do with the content of your conversations as with what goes on underneath it. That's how it was with Leon—we were best friends. There were people I've had better conversations with, but we just had that kind of hook-up.

Q: When you do children's books, do you have a particular sort of child in mind?

A: No. I know from experience that a certain kind of writing that I sometimes do will be promoted. It will say on the book jacket it's for an early reader or it's for six- to eight-year-olds. I just write what I write, and then the editors and publishers decide what market slot it's for. I write all different kinds of things. Some of them don't fit any market slot.

Q: Do you ever get sick of writing children's books, like your children's writer character Neara H. in *Turtle Diary*?

A: I sometimes get put off by the world of children's literature. Nowadays everything is marketing; for the whole world it's marketing. You can take an executive who was selling shoes last week and this week he's selling paintings. They figure out where there is a niche in the marketplace and ask, How do we push it? There aren't a lot of things being done for the love of the thing itself. There is a breed of young, college-trained editors who don't know doodleyshit and they're determined to impose their ignorance on you. They have, forgive me, taken a course in children's literature and have ideas, God help us. I had an experience with that when Lillian [his first wife and illustrator] and I were still together. Contrary to the usual procedure where we just sat down with Ursula Nordstrom and the production designer, we were put at a table with all kinds of new faces and there was this young person who said, "Well, the way I see this scene. . . ." I said, "The way *you* see it?" and we walked out.

Q: How would you respond to the criticism of some of your children's books?

A: There was a magazine a few years ago called *Spare Rib* that gave me hell because Frances's mother wore an apron and was busy in the kitchen, and the father came home from the office and read the newspaper. Well, what can I do? I'm a dinosaur.

Q: In *Riddley Walker,* you talk about "first knowing"—a kind of effortless knowledge that animals have, very different than human "cleverness." Do children have first knowing?

A: I think children start out with more than they end up with, generally. Look at one limited aspect of childhood, the drawings they do, the kind of drawing my son Weiland used to do. I'm looking at one tacked up to the wall right now. He was maybe five or six, before he had any ideas of correctness. It compares favorably with people whose prices are up in the many thousands. He can't draw like that now, and that happens with most kids. They have a kind of primal hook-up with things that they lose when they get older because they have no rational explanation of it and no rational applications of it. There is a classic kind of drawing kids do of a cephalopod, a big head with arms and legs coming out of it, before they know how to draw a proper body. That strange creature they draw is maybe one manifestation of what's called the collective unconscious.

Q: In *The Medusa Frequency,* you talk about "the world child." What is the world child?

A: Different people have different ways of conceiving something. My view is a pessimistic one. There is such a thing as a world child. There is the being of the world that will always be betrayed. It's in the latter stages of this betrayal right now. The world that's being left to my children and your children is a pretty shitty thing. It's a world that by degrees has become almost exhausted. . . . . The human race is, I think, a failed experiment.

Q: Revocable?

A: I think it's irrevocable. When the cockroaches take over, they're not going to build any cathedrals, but they're not going to do any harm.

Q: In your children's book *M.O.L.E.,* the surviving mole eats the last cockroach, so there may not be even cockroaches left.

A: [Laughs] That's right. I've told you before about this toy I used to have—the black box. Turn it on and a hand comes out and turns it off. That's a heavy metaphor.

Q: When you write for kids, do you feel compelled to leave an optimistic message? For example, in *La Corona and the Tin Frog,* the characters escape, and even in *M.O.L.E.,* you write that there is always another garden.

A: That's a limited message. That is, I feel for the individual there's always another garden. For the individual, there's always the breaking out of whatever cage or trap the person is in, into some kind of freedom. But in the wider view, for the world—no, I don't think there's any hope. The individual generally gets somewhere in his own world line just as the individual has to accept the fact he's mortal. I accept the fact that I am mortal.

Look at my physical state right now; it's pretty bad. Yet even with all that, there are times when I experience joie de vivre. I feel hooked up in a joyous way. I get a rush of feeling good. If you compare these physical states with mental ones, I think they're kind of parallel. I think that often the mental state we live in is a dragging along kind of thing that's far short of what we'd hoped for. Then there are times when there are exciting connections and you get hooked up with something. I don't expect much more than that.

Q: Though you enjoyed Oscar Wilde as a child, you criticize him in "Wilde Pomegranates" for pretentiousness, and you criticize Rudyard Kipling for insincerity.

A: I have changed my mind about Kipling. If he had written only a story called "The Devil and the Deep Blue Sea," I think there would be cause for celebration. In 1994, I had an operation and came out of the hospital and was very weak. It was summer and I sat out in the backyard and I had a paperback of Kipling's stories. One of them was called "The Devil and the Deep Blue Sea." It was about a tramp steamer that was always operating on the wrong side of the law. This would have been back in Kipling's time. The reason that in my weakened state there in the backyard I found that book so vivifying, so life-affirming, was the way Kipling had brought that engine, that crew, that steamer to life on the page. Before I was fully recovered, I dragged myself to the science museum with a camera and went around photographing steamers as close as I could to that period. I ordered about 100 pounds of books about steam navigation. I do this kind of thing from time to time, not that I'm ever likely to need the information as reference, but I get my kicks getting these surges of interest in something and acquiring all that I can about it at the time. Anyway, the experience reinforced my feelings about the literary art, that it is both life-affirming and life-sustaining. It's a good thing. We need it.

NOTES

[1]Benjamin DeMott. "2000 Years After the Berstyn Fyr." *The New York Times Book Review,* June 28, 1981, p. 18.

[2]Russell Hoban. *The Mouse and His Child.* (New York: Harper & Row, 1967), p. 162.

[3]Russell Hoban. "Time slip, uphill lean, laminar flow, place-to-place talking and hearing the silence." *Children's Literature in Education* vol. 9. November 1972, p. 44.

[4]Ibid., p. 40.

Acknowledgments

I am grateful to the College of Arts and Letters at San Diego State University (SDSU) for providing the travel funds for research, and to Russ and Gundul Hoban for their hospitality in London and especially for the unforgettable night at the Glyndebourne Opera House. My research assistant Cynthia McDaniel's generous help, reliability, and good company have been crucial to this book, as were the assistance of Jamie Madden and Terie Baylis. As usual, my colleagues Jerry Griswold, Lois Kuznets, and June Cummins provided valuable suggestions and support. Martha-E. Casselman, Michele Ryan, and Christy Torres of the Department of English and Comparative Literature office were also very helpful.

Thanks are also given to Jack Zipes, to Garland Publishing, to Tana Hoban for permission to use her photo of Russell Hoban, and to the British Film Institute for permission to reprint the still from the film *The Extraordinary Adventures of the Mouse and His Child.* The generosity of Quentin Blake, Nicola Bayley, and the estate of Lillian Hoban is also greatly appreciated

Finally, I would like to thank my friend and mentor Professor Emeritus Peter Neumeyer, who began the children's literature program at SDSU in the late 1970s. It was in Peter's unexcelled classes that I read my first Russell Hoban book, *The Mouse and His Child,* and there that I realized what joy could be found in reading—and teaching—children's literature.

The owl dances to see the taxi meter's violet glow. Illus. Quentin Blake.

List of Illustrations

Russell Hoban/Forty Years

Hoban's Street Performers

CAROLE SCOTT

The street performer is a significant figure in many of Russell Hoban's books. Naturally his showmen and women entertain, expressing their talents in a variety of forms including improvisational performance, formal plays, puppetry, music, and dance. But they are infinitely more than entertainers: in the tradition of Shakespeare's Fools, they introduce the characters within the books, as well as the reader, to new images, to new perceptions and ways of perceiving, and to new philosophies of life. As savants and philosophers, they turn the key that opens the gateway to new worlds. Through these characters, Hoban celebrates creativity as the driving force of life, and showpeople as guardians of the human spirit.

The spectrum of seriousness in Hoban's work ranges from whimsy to deep ritual import. The love-struck owl in *The Marzipan Pig,* smitten by the violet glow of the taxi meter, sings and dances in the street in his attempt to communicate with her, and quickly makes the 50p he needs for another taxi ride. In *The Trokeville Way,* Moe Nagic, the onetime magician, now reduced to playing his concertina in the street, holds the key to the psychological otherworld, entered through a painting, that challenges Nick Hartley to confront his fears. The Caws of Art's traveling theater performs "The Last Visible Dog," a play inspired by the philosophical questions permeating *The Mouse and His Child.* And the politico-religious Eusa Show ritually performed by the Eusa Men in *Riddley Walker* is a threatening performance in a dystopian world where a resurrected and distorted Punch and Judy show becomes a violent answer for the future. Though some of these performances may be accidental rather than intentional, an unexpected outcome of ordinary life's actions, they represent an integral part of Hoban's universe, his sense of reality. As he tells us in *The Twenty-Elephant Restaurant,* "Sometimes it's a one-man circus and sometimes it's a twenty-elephant restaurant. And that's life."

Jacques Lacan has some interesting and very relevant insights to offer that help us understand the significance of the performance arts in Hoban's work. Lacan perceives that the initial "jouissance" of life embodied in the mother-child relationship gives way to the sense of lack and loss that permeates human existence. As the mother once mirrored us, now the Other becomes the meaningful audience for our expression of who we are, and it is the gaze of the Other that reflects our being and gives us a sense of self. More than any other art form, performance art dramatizes the interaction between self and Other, for the audience reflects the emotions presented onstage back to the players, heightening the possibilities for recognition and misrecognition.[1] As Barbara Freedman asserts in her *Staging the Gaze: Postmodernism, Psychoanalysis and Shakespearean Comedy,* "The assumption of the mirror image in the construction of the ego is the primary misrecognition, which in turn is rehearsed in our demand that others see us as we would ourselves"[2] (32). In tales where image is important, recognition and misrecognition come strongly into play. Freedman discusses the "use of the other [in playing out] this misrecognition in narrative form" and explains that "Freud's various definitions of the ego—as a projection of the body surface, as a mechanism for identificatory processes, and as an object-turned-subject—are reread by Lacan as unfolding progressions in psychic functioning set into play by the spatial lure of the other's image"[3] (32).

In *Lacan and the Subject of Language,* Ellie Ragland-Sullivan similarly perceives performance as a relevant feature of Lacan's vision, suggesting that his sense of life itself may be conceived of as a "strange masquerade where we dance around each other, accommodating ourselves to others through monumental farces, the strangest of bedfellows, subject to intense contradictions, outrageous comedies, keeping the Other at arm's distance and blaming others instead"[4] (77). She also notes that Lacan's sense of the function of language is to create a system of rules that substitutes for desire and attempts to negotiate it, becoming "not only a field of decorative tautologies, but also a life preserver surrounding the real of lack and loss"[5] (2). Artists, above all, are through their work constantly trying "to recreate or somehow embody the lacks and losses they know only too well"[6] (74).

The Twenty-Elephant Restaurant provides a picturesque extended metaphor for the transformation of a drab meaningless life into a colorful and creative one through the expressive means of performance art. After fifty years of marriage, condensed into one six-line paragraph, a couple suddenly perceive their wobbly table (for years temporarily steadied with a matchbook) as the source of their problems of age and weariness and decide the husband should make a new one. Building the new table brings youth and vigor to him, and he boasts that the "table is really strong. It's steady as a rock. No matchbooks under that table." The ensuing dialogue leads to their new vision of life as performance.

> "Elephants could dance on that table."
>
> "How many?" said the woman.
>
> "Only one really," said the man. "I don't think there's room for two."
>
> "Oh," said the woman. "When you said elephants, I thought you meant more than one."
>
> "One to a table, I'd say," said the man. . . .
>
> "Where would we get the elephants?" said the woman.
>
> "Advertise in the Classified Section," said the man. "Elephants wanted for table work. Must be agile."
>
> "Then we'd have to pay them," said the woman.
>
> "If people paid to see them dance, then we could pay the elephants," said the man.
>
> "How do you know they'll be worth paying to see?" said the woman. "Maybe they won't be good enough dancers."
>
> "We could open a restaurant," said the man. "The elephants could wait on the tables, and in their spare time they could practice dancing until they're good enough so people will pay to see them."

It is the practical, businesslike approach to the whimsical notion that creates the strange marriage between monotonous reality and colorful fantasy. Illustrator Emily Arnold McCully accompanies the conversation with a line drawing of the man and woman seated across the table from each other, eating. She captures both whimsicality and practicality with the design and perspective of the scene. First of all, the image is drawn from directly above, as though the viewer is looking through the ceiling. We see the top of each character's head, and a design of variants on circles and squares. A round/oval rug sits at the base; above that is the square table, with oblong place mats, round dishes, glasses, and crock. The top of the chair legs, seen from above, are round ends of cylinders, and the circular hairdo of the woman balances the balding half-circle of the man's head. As a final touch, the dog's hindquarters with outstretched tail protrude from the back of the man's chair, placed so that, from above, they look almost like part of the man's body.

Hoban further complicates the dynamic layering of art and life when the customers for the restaurant arrive before the man has finished building it, and sit down to watch the construction. Thus the eighteen elephant waiters dancing on the tables are upstaged by the man building the restaurant: "Down in front!" everybody said to the elephants. "Get off the tables, you're blocking our view." "Nothing goes right for me," said the man. "I start out to have a twenty-elephant restaurant and I wind up being a one-man circus." The stark line drawings are interspersed with color illustrations that are especially striking in contrast. Though it is not the first of the color illustrations, the picture of the elephants lined up on the sidewalk waiting their turn to telephone in response to the advertisement emphatically brings the man's notion to life: one elephant wears a chef's hat, another a black beret, and a third sports a pale blue cap. The next three color pictures present the fantasy in action: in the first, the man is beginning to build the restaurant, the customers are seated at tables, and the enormous elephants are dancing on the rather small tables. The second in the series shows the man, still building, with the elephants, each with a small tray balanced on a forefoot, waiting on the customers, while the restaurant with pink, white, and blue awning and its sign set up in neon lights provides a circus air. The third illustration pictures a mature establishment with brick walls, counters, furniture, and appliances, with elephants running the show and keeping very busy: the bookkeeper with his eyeshade sits at the desk, the chef in his white hat stirs with a spoon held in his trunk, while the others are receiving lessons in dance from their instructor.

The restaurant becomes a great success, but the wobble that started the whole thing recurs repeatedly. When this happens, the couple and their team of elephants simply pack up the restaurant in an enormous truck and find a flat place to re-create the entire performance, from construction to dancing elephants waiting on tables. Finally the man and his wife accept the wobble as a feature of an acceptable existence: life and performance have become inextricably intertwined.

> "Maybe there aren't any places that'll stay flat," said the woman. "Maybe that's just how it is."
>
> "I think maybe you're right," said the man. "Sometimes it's a one-man circus and sometimes it's a twenty-elephant restaurant. And that's life."
>
> "Still," said the elephants, "it's not a bad life."
>
> "No," said the man, "it isn't."

Like *The Twenty-Elephant Restaurant,* Hoban's enchanting *The Marzipan Pig* expresses a mood of whimsy and playfulness, while featuring performance art as a central motif. In this book, the sweetness of the candy pig that makes its way through the food chain, from mouse to owl and beyond, is associated with a sense of loneness and loneliness, of wasted life, and longing for love and significance—the lack that Lacan continually identifies. It is this sense of longing that repeatedly leads to performance art in Hoban's work, but the focus of the performance in this book has shifted from the organized stage of the restaurant to an impromptu, informal performance in the street or on a windowsill and is characterized by an increased personal and emotional dimension.

The marzipan pig, a fleeting figure whose picture appears only on the cover and on the second page of the book, has a brief and poignant existence. Having fallen behind the sofa, he is missed by no one, but the emotions that he experiences flavor the book from start to finish. " 'There is,' he said, 'such sweetness in me!'. . . Day after day he waited as the months went by. 'I am growing hard,' he said, 'and bitter. What a waste of me!' " When he hears the mouse gnawing her way toward him he dreams of rescue and recognition, and composes the speech he intends to give when he finds himself at the center of a grand celebration surrounded by admirers.

The themes of sweetness, waste, melancholy, recognition, performance, and love are revealed in turn by each of the characters affected by the marzipan pig: the mouse who eats him, the owl who eats her, the bee who sips from the flower that grew from the owl's droppings, the hibiscus flower that the bee visits, and another mouse that is touched by the evanescent beauty of the flower. The "craving and . . . sadness" signified by the fading sweetness of the marzipan is expressed repeatedly in the drive of the characters to find love through performance. For example, the owl falls in love and sings and dances in the street, the bee performs his honey-dance on the windowsill for the hibiscus flower; and the mouse fashions a pink petal frock for herself from one of the flowers, thinking she can become a flower herself, and failing in that, goes dancing in the street. The mixture of dreams and reality in these performances offers vignettes of the splintered images of self, the ego fictions that make up personality.

Of the performances, one in particular stands out: that of the owl who falls in love with the taxi meter "violet-glowing in the dark." His dance on the pavement accompanies the taxi driver's trumpet practice, and, like his hooting voice, expresses both rage and desire. "What have I done, what have I done, what have I done to make you dark?" he sings to the meter, whose light is turned off because the taxi is stationary. His perverse misinterpretation of the situation readily exemplifies the "meconnaissance" or misrecognition that Lacan ascribes to the working of human desire. Because he is in love (the effect of consuming the mouse that has eaten the marzipan pig), the owl not only believes that the Albert Bridge has been lit up specially for him, but that the meter which has become the focus of his desire returns his feelings.

> "I love you so much!" said the owl to the meter. "How much do you love me?"
> "25p," said the meter.
> "Love me more," said the owl.
> "30p," said the meter.
> "More and more," said the owl.
> "35p," said the meter. "40, 45."

The black-and-white illustration of the owl in his dance characterizes him as a humorous, cartoonlike, rather scruffy bird, strutting awkwardly by the taxi and contrasts with his own exalted vision of himself and his passion. Later, when the mouse, rocketed into the air by the postman whose finger she has bitten, thumps into the owl's stomach, he once again reveals his inflated and inappropriate sense of his own import and the significance of his feelings. "'Love!' shouted the owl as he grabbed the branch and opened his eyes. 'Love has hit me like a thud in the stomach! Love, love, where are you?'"

The mouse's drive to performance is more aesthetic than that of the owl, and far more self-centered and self-directed. Rather than falling in love with a clock, as had the first mouse, or in love with a taxi meter, like the owl, the second mouse is captivated by an image of herself, and seeks to verify it in a mirror. In her initial desire to become a hibiscus flower, she seeks both a behavioral transformation and one of appearance. Besides her practice in method acting, "Sometimes when there was no one in the bedroom she would run out onto the carpet and strike hibiscus poses in front of the full-length glass," and her motivational study, "'The thing to do is, once you've bloomed, hold on. Just simply hold on and don't let go,'" she knows the transformative power of dress. "The mouse went to the sewing basket and got a needle and thread. She stripped the pinky-orange petals from the crumpled hibiscus flower and out of them she made herself a stylish little frock. 'Chic,' she said, turning round and round in front of the glass. 'Either one has it or one hasn't.'"

In both of these picture books, Hoban presents the performers as comical and appealing, their artistic expression directly related in *The Twenty-Elephant Restaurant* to their work and their lives in a very practical way, and in *The Marzipan Pig* as a direct consequence of their emotions and their essential being. In the three more complex and enigmatic works, *The Mouse and His Child* (1967), *Riddley Walker* (1980), and *The Trokeville Way* (1996), Hoban develops these performance themes with greater psychological, philosophical, and symbolic intricacy and depth.

While the Caws of Art Experimental Theater Group is the primary source of performance art in *The Mouse and His Child,* the sense of life as performance permeates the book from start to finish. Visual performance images are crucial from the tramp's first gaze through the shop window that catches the windup toys acting out their fated parts. Circus images are the first: the purple head-clothed elephant who decorously walks up and down, swinging her trunk and flapping her ears, and the tin seal who is spinning a red and yellow ball on her nose. Like other Hoban circus images they bring glamour, excitement, and a magnified sense of self or Lacanian self-perception as signified by the mirror-imaged tin seal whose "reflection in the glass counter top smiled up at her and spun its own red and yellow ball."[7] Others include the dancing toy Mouse and Mouse Child, the monkey who plays "La Golondrina" on a little violin, and a furry white rabbit who clashes tiny cymbals.

But these images are simply meconnaisance, mechanized performances that substitute for desire and the yearning for real experience. The monkey tires of playing "the same tune over and over on a cheap fiddle"; the furry white rabbit complains that his cymbals have no meaning; and the dancing mice rebel at "the futility of dancing in an endless circle" (9). Mechanized performance is not art, but does offer opportunity for the creativity of improvisation. Like the practical man in *The Twenty-Elephant Restaurant,* first the tramp, then Manny Rat, Muskrat, the Mouse Child, and finally the whole company repair, design, or fabricate mechanical constructs that shape performance to the desired end, whether it be a mouse-powered chopper to fell a tree, a capstan system to move the house, the reassembling of parts to re-create clockwork toys, or the creation of a self-winding mechanism that provides some degree of independence to the Mouse and the Mouse Child.

The notion of life as performance is also pursued in the recurrence of "The Last Visible Dog" that appears in a number of guises. The most striking of these is C. Serpentina's play performed by the Caws of Art, a performance that provides a dynamic focus for a number of the book's themes. When the audience reacts to the play with mayhem and carnage, the Mouse and his Child save the show by transforming their search for family and territory into stage business, and, segueing niftily into high melodrama, entice Manny Rat onto the stage and reveal him as the arch villain that he is. The performance is also a fulcrum for later developments, preparing the way for the Mouse Child's philosophical meditation, inspired first by the nestled images on the dog food can and later by his own image mirrored by the metal, on the subject of truth, being, and nothingness. The end result is his decisive move to self-determination and the eventual establishment of the "Last Visible Dog" hotel, which becomes the center of theater and community at the close of the book. Improvisation is again the key to matching dream, image, and desire with reality. The mouse in *The Marzipan Pig* pursues her dream by fashioning her frock from the fallen hibiscus flower, striking "hibiscus poses," and taking her "place as a flower on the end of [the stem]." Though she is not successful, nonetheless the attempt at self-actualization through art does lead her to greater self-knowledge and joy as expressed in a marzipan pig of her own to eat as well as a the drive to performance—a night out dancing in the streets. For the Mouse and the Mouse Child, the pursuit of their dream similarly leads to fulfillment, though, as is so often the case in Hoban's work, the final expression is somewhat different from what they originally imagined.

In *The Trokeville Way,* the spectrum of art again extends to include street performance, circus acts, music, and painting, though the painting is subdued into everyday life by its reduction into a jigsaw puzzle that provides some control over its power. Nick meets Moe Nagic, a former stage magician and the owner of the jigsaw puzzle painting, playing his concertina in the street. More than any of the other figures, Moe, trailing reminiscences of the world of entertainment, evokes its glitter, its compelling fantasy, its glamorous allure, and its tawdry meretriciousness. Haunted by a sense of failure in life and in love, Moe plays music "full of darkness" that evokes powerful emotion-laden images: the tune "Fear" makes Nick "see the shine of streetlamps on wet cobblestones and a figure hurrying down a dark alley and looking back over his shoulder."[8] (13) And for Nick the music named "Libertango" is "a spooky shadowy-sounding thing I had heard years ago at the circus during a trapeze act. A kind of darkness came into the light and I could see the bright spangled figures high up in the rigging of the tent, I could feel in my stomach the rush of danger when they let go and flew through the air. . . ." (6) At home the tune metamorphoses into a track on a CD played by Nick's father with lyrics picturing a haunting, frightening face.

The powerful jigsaw puzzle painting called "The Brudge" serves as a magical gateway to a psychic stage on which all of the significant figures in Nick's life act out their desires and those images of themselves that lie beneath the surface of their ordinary lives, pulsing with a still energy. The world of the puzzle-painting is both real and illusory, for it projects reflections of desires and dreams, truth and fantasy, recognition and misrecognition, what might have been, what is, and what will be. Not only does Nick embark on a sometimes real and sometimes symbolic playing out of his own adolescent wishes for love, for courage, and for self-knowledge, but he also finds his parents searching for their own truths and pursuing their own youthful and still unfulfilled dreams and desires.

Barbara Freedman's comment regarding the definition of the ego, already cited, is particularly relevant here: "unfolding progressions in psychic functioning set into play by the spatial lure of the other's image." In *The Trokeville Way,* Hoban offers a complex playing out of the dynamics of desire and image in interrelationships with the others with whom one interacts in the real world, and with the multiple images of self and others who exist within the psyche. Hoban further compounds the reflections and relationships by blurring the boundaries between reality and illusion, to present a portrait of life that, like real experience, sometimes communicates a sense of reproduction or facsimile in its imaginative disjuncture from bare existence.

There are a number of plays and puzzles in *The Trokeville Way.* The painting named "The Trokeville Way," originally named "The Old Brudge," features "an old stone bridge over a little river" (9). The word "brudge," Nick's lost love Zelda tells him, must be, through verbal legerdemain, "a bridge with a grudge." This wordplay not only shifts the reader's and later Nick's angle of perception from recognizably visual to symbolic, but ties into other literary and artistic bridges where danger and courage are significant: the bridge that Horatio and his comrades defend against the Tuscan army in Macaulay's "Horatius," which Nick studies in English class; or the trapeze, where one artiste becomes the human bridge for another as they transverse space.

It is Moe who expresses his fear and his experience of loss and failure in his concertina playing, his personal philosophy, and his aberrant use of words as keys to a deeper psychological understanding. While the painter of the picture first introduced the notion of bridge/brudge, Moe continues to develop this use of words: "Maybe when I first started with it I didn't want to call things by their right names," he tells Nick (18). So "puzzle" becomes "juzzle"; a "troke" is "partly a trick and partly a stroke"; the wood becomes "would," and the maze is called "mise"—the latter tied by Nick into Keats's "wild surmise—Silent, upon a peak in Darien" (29). When Nick steps into the juzzle through the magical pathway created by the gyroscope, entering "the world that lives in your head" (30), he is confronted by the image of the performer, "Moe Nagic on the brudge pulling nothing out of his hat" (40). The notion of magic and the magician's sleight of hand that confuses perception so that reality and fantasy merge, impossible to distinguish, pervades the book. This notion of perception as the key to reality, particularly in relationships with others, clearly relates to Lacan's sense of meconnaissance, of the self fooling the self by misperception and misapprehension.

Nick is Moe's spiritual heir, purchasing his dreams, fears, and experiences along with the juzzle and gyroscope for 2 pounds 42 pence and meeting, both in the juzzle world and the real one, the significant characters of Moe's story. While Moe as magician sets the tone of magic that is so easily lost from relationships and from life, it is his music that leaves the final impression. While he played concertina in the street for the last year of his life, remembering his failures and his loss of love, Nick ends *The Trokeville Way* by finding his courage in the juzzle world, using it in the real world to defeat the bully Harry Buncher who has tormented him, and then entering a love relationship expressed in a musical partnership with Felicity, who plays piano to his flute. While Moe busked in the street, Nick and Felicity bring the music home, and progress from Bach flute and harpsichord sonatas to "Faure and Hindemith and transcriptions from Debussy piano works. . . ." (117).

This discussion would be incomplete without some mention of Hoban's 1980 work *Riddley Walker,* which displays the dark side of performance in human expression. This enigmatic work, challenging to read because of the pervasive use of idiosyncratic spelling and corrupted language, has inspired controversy over its intended audience. While I defend the status of young adult literature for this work that focuses upon the coming of age of a twelve-year-old boy, I acknowledge the barrier to easy reading created by the re-creation of language, unlike *The Trokeville Way,* where just a few words are remade. However, familiarity with Riddleyspeak does uncover the aural clues and geographic distortions that make the action understandable. The use of language gives great poignancy to the sense of cultural loss and cultural deprivation that the book depicts, and reminds us of Lacan's belief, very relevant in this context, that language is a system of rules that substitutes for desire and attempts to negotiate it, becoming "not only a field of decorative tautologies, but also a life preserver surrounding the real of lack and loss." Though *The Marzipan Pig* was characterized by a sense of loss and loneliness, it was revealed with humor, in contrast to the dominant sense of what Riddley expresses as "that thing whats in us lorn and loan, and oansome"[9] (7).

While *The Trokeville Way* took us into a use of performance art that was sophisticated, colorful, and slick, *Riddley Walker* plunges us into a post-holocaust future where performance art is stripped back to rudimentary forms including stylization and ritualized repetition, the use of hand puppets as actors, and the pervasive dogma that strangles improvisation. In contrast to the inner drama of *The Trokeville Way,* the theater of the Eusa Men is a politico-theocratic presentation used to dramatize the social controls placed upon the populace by a power elite.

Just as the story and philosophy of Eusa is captured in the ritualized forms of the Eusa show and precise gobbledygook of the debased words whose meanings have long been lost, so the metaphor of rebellion and rebirth of hope is similarly expressed in the recovery of an old-new puppet show, the traditional Punch-and-Judy show. Although, in the mid-twentieth century at least, the Punch-and-Judy show has been regarded as theater for children, it is a strange choice, for the action of these hand puppets is characterized by threats and violence including wife beating, murder, and killing and eating the baby. The awe with which Riddley receives Goodparley's emotion-laden rendition of the Punch-and-Judy show, which he himself inherited, is a tragi-comic experience for the reader familiar with it.

Although very crude, the performances in *Riddley Walker* involve the audience in an impassioned way, for they are of highest significance in this primitive society where reality and myth are so strongly interwoven. Here image and reality walk hand in hand and cannot be disentangled. The puppet shows represent the last debased vestiges of art in a society that clings to the tattered remnants of a lost civilization. Like the words that Riddley uses, deformed and inadequate indicators of the history and achievements of the past, the puppet shows conserve and present distorted shadows of what has been lost.

Yet, while the reader is aware of the extent of the destruction and the crude poverty of life that survives, it is clear that Riddley perceives the discovery of the Punch-and-Judy puppets and his new life as showman as the opportunity for a real advance in civilization, as valuable and as powerful as the rediscovery of explosives that drives the plot.

Familiarizing himself with the puppets, he describes the way they take on a life of their own:

> You take a figger out of the bag nor it aint nothing only some colourt clof [colored cloth] with a paintit wood head and hans [hands]. Then you put it on. You put your head finger in the head you put your arm finger in the arms then that figger look roun [round] and takes noatis [notice] it has things to say. Which they wont all ways be things *youwd* think of saying. . . . (204)

His description of the creative surge that envelops him as he steps into the performer's role is described as an electric charge, a sense of power:

> You myt (might) talk about how youre going to show you myt think about it only on the nite there it is if its the 1st time or the 100th it aint never happent befor it aint nothing you know any thing about. You look out thru the weave of the back cloth and you see the torches shimmying and glimmering you hear a hummering and mummering from the crowd in front of you. There's a prickling all over your skin and you feal like therewl be sparkls coming off you in the dark" (204–205).

This new puppet show that is "jus to make peopl larf [laugh]. Give peopl a bit of fun," (140) is merged with the social and political traditions of the Eusa Show, with Riddley moving into the leadership role previously held by the religious/political elite. As performer, he becomes the source of wisdom and insight for the community, carrying a new understanding and philosophy of life and of the revealed "truths" of his time.

In these works of Hoban, performance art is employed to portray complex aspects of human life and experience involving a wide range of perception stretching from impromptu expression of emotion and desire, to deeply symbolic depictions of the dynamics of the psyche, of human interrelationships, of the individual and society, and of the self and the soul. They involve the exhibit of down-to-earth carpentry, the mechanics of production, the shaping of a persona through dress, the evocation of image and reminiscence through music, the magic of imagination, and legerdemain that tricks the eye but not the spirit. The performers themselves are sometimes simply caught up in creative aspects in their lives that express themselves in impromptu performance. But for others, performance is a studied art to which they have committed their lives. Magic in performance is often ephemeral and unsubstantial, and its glamour and excitement are frequently used to cover over danger, despair, loss, and longing. These performers live dangerous lives, for their performances lead them too close to the ultimate truths of existence; this knowledge brings the power with which wise men are burdened and which forces them too often to become outsiders, living on the edges of society.

It is clear that, for Hoban, even though many performances are at odds with or a denial of reality, and even though the magic may fade away leaving painful memories of ephemeral ecstasies, nonetheless the performance arts represent humankind's irrepressible spirit, the spirit of creativity, and the manifestation of the dreams that celebrate human imagination. Even if aspirations do not always lead to realization, their expression usually inspires enrichment, growth, and new insights. When the mouse in *The Marzipan Pig* fails in her attempt to transform nature into art, to become a hibiscus flower that blooms forever, she doesn't mope or "take off her hibiscus-petal frock" but is "seen at three o'clock in the morning dancing on the Embankment by the Albert Bridge."

NOTES

[1]The use of Lacan's concepts is limited to those relevant to this discussion and specifically mentioned in the text. Other aspects of his theory (e.g., his analysis of image/imaginary) are not intended to be considered in this context.

[2]Barbara Freedman, *Staging the Gaze: Postmodernism, Psychoanalysis and Shakespearean Comedy* (Ithaca and London: Cornell University Press, 1991), p. 31.

[3]Ibid., p. 32.

[4]Ellie Ragland-Sullivan, *Lacan and the Subject of Language* (New York & London: Routledge, 1991), p. 77.

[5]Ibid., p. 2.

[6]Ibid., p. 74.

[7]Russell Hoban, *The Mouse and His Child* (New York: Harper & Row, 1967), p. 2. All future references will be to this edition and will be included in the text.

[8]Russell Hoban, *The Trokeville Way* (New York: Knopf, 1996), p. 13. All future references will be to this edition and will be included in the text.

[9]Russell Hoban, *Riddley Walker* (New York: Summit Books, Simon & Schuster, 1980), p. 7. All future references will be to this edition and will be included in the text.

The hibiscus-frocked mouse, who doesn't get eaten by the owl, dances on the Albert Bridge. Illus. Quentin Blake.

Monsters, Machines, and the Place of Chocolate Cake
Hoban's Picture Books

JAMIE MADDEN

When Russell Hoban's books for children are considered, the discussion often centers around either his "Frances" series or *The Mouse and His Child,* possibly because of the charm and popularity of the former and the fascinating complexity of the latter. Frequently overlooked, despite their excellence, are Hoban's numerous other picture books. Since this volume celebrates both the length of Hoban's career and the abundance of his work, it seems appropriate to devote this essay to a broad array of these books. Like a sonnet or a fairy tale, a picture book is a highly economical form; how is an author who has stated that "man's lot is not . . . to be comfortable except in the active encounter with discomfort" to incorporate such thinking into a children's book of some twenty-five or thirty pages?[1]

To begin answering this question, I wish to look first at one of Hoban's most ambiguous (and amusing) picture books, *Monsters*. This is the story of John, who "liked to draw monsters."[2] In fact, the only things that John draws are monsters, and he doesn't draw the nice little monsters that we see in *Where the Wild Things Are* with wide eyes and childlike, oversized heads, with body parts drawn from recognizable animals. As delightfully drawn by Quentin Blake, John's monsters have grasping claws and nasty spiky bodies and horns sticking out of improbable places. They attack each other with weapons held in their arms (of which they usually have more than two), or mounted on their backs, or spurting from their stomachs, though some monsters have to settle for using their teeth or maybe breathing fire. So it isn't surprising that John's parents are concerned.

Hoban's depiction of John's fascination with monsters draws on two different ways of thinking about monsters. The first is attested to in critical literature such as Bruno Bettelheim's *The Uses of Enchantment,* which describes the monster as a figure that embodies the child's repressed fears, aggression, or guilt.[3] John's parents seem to view the monster drawings in this light, so that when John draws a spiky purple monster tail that fills an entire sheet of wrapping paper, they decide that this "drawing doesn't seem quite the same as John's other drawings. . . . It seems somehow more *serious* than the others" (italics original). And they react in a way that might be expected of worried parents in our age—they consult experts. Dr. Plunger duly prescribes medication and tells the parents "if the drawings continue let me see the next one." The purpose of the medication, then, is not to treat whatever "problems" John is supposed by his parents to have. Indeed, Dr. Plunger has not seen John at all. The purpose of the medication is precisely and solely to stop the drawings themselves. So Bettelheim would perhaps recognize the ending of *Monsters,* in which John's monster comes to life and presumably destroys Dr. Plunger, as a statement of the inevitable failure of repression, the falsity of believing that "the child would supposedly repress his unpleasant fantasies and have only pleasant ones."[4] But to interpret the book this way overlooks another possibility, a different way of interpreting John's monster.

For if human beings are ordinary, monsters are always and necessarily extraordinary. They are what exists outside normal experience, their "very existence is a rebuke to boundary and enclosure."[5] It is a commonplace among critics of children's literature that children are drawn to the power of the monster, which compensates for the child's own lack of power. But beyond this, monsters make manifest a sense of "the wonder and strangeness of the living world, full of freaks, beauty, dangers, mixtures and myths that might be true somewhere."[6] And this is, I think, the world that Hoban is trying to express through John's monster. In "Thoughts on a Shirtless Cyclist," Hoban muses that "maybe we think we don't need to know more about that nameless creative chaos, but we do, because in it we must find all real order."[7]

The reason we think we don't need to know more about that nameless creative chaos is, of course, fear. Whatever its aesthetic appeal, a world in which monsters are real, and there is no security, and, above all, we are required to act rather than be acted upon, to leap instead of looking, is a world that can send people to Dr. Plunger's office. Hoban addresses that fear and specifically links the figure of the monster to such a

Are the monsters John draws real? From *Monsters*. Illus. Quentin Blake.

philosophy in "Thoughts on Being and Writing," arguing that "we have to learn to feel for it, to go beyond our swimmer's fright . . . to touch it as a child, in a dark room, gets out of bed to touch the clothes trees that bulk monstrous in the dimness, magnetic with terror."[8] When viewed this way, *Monsters* becomes a book not about John's fears, but his parents'.

In fact, all of the language expressing anxiety comes from John's parents. They try to deal with their concerns directly with John, first by urging him to draw something besides monsters, "real animals like dogs and cats" and calling on the reality principle, asking if John has ever seen a monster "just walking around." His answer, "Not yet," doesn't help them. John completely refuses to participate in his parents' narrow, safe view of reality. Seeking reassurance, they approach Mr. Splodge, John's art teacher, who fails to validate their concern. In fact, he admires the tail, saying, "It almost jumps right off the paper at you, doesn't it." Of course, that is precisely what worries John's parents, who say that "John says the rest of it is coming" and "whatever's on the other end of it is going to be so very big." Mr. Splodge tries to relieve their minds by telling them that "boys are naturally a little monstrous." But this does not help; John's parents are not worried about John. They are worried about his monster.

In "Thoughts on Being and Writing," Hoban writes that "for security, we put our little single sensings together in one big consensus."[9] Their trip to Dr. Plunger is a retreat to such a consensus, supported by the authority of the doctor's title and white-coated uniform. But the consensus comes at a cost, which is portrayed iconographically. Whereas Mr. Splodge was shown to be of the same size as John's parents and is presented in his environment, Dr. Plunger looms over the mother and father in the picture. The pictures also do not portray his surroundings; Dr. Plunger is not a strongly individuated figure who exists in a certain place, but a powerful social force that is present, not in one place, but in all places. John's parents refuse the equality offered to them by Mr. Splodge—because it comes with risk. Dr. Plunger, with his greater power, offers a risk-free answer to their fears. Accordingly, he asks not about John's feelings, but about John's parents' feelings, and promises to do the one thing that they really want done. He can erase the monsters. The prescription written for John is actually a placebo for his parents.

One placebo that is commonly offered to readers of books with monsters, works of "fantasy," is the final closure of the magic world, usually either through the protagonist's return to the real world or through the disappearance (or exhaustion) of whatever magical object gave access to the magic world. Such closure has the effect of "officially resolving and fixing meanings (offering, in particular, the 'correct' interpretation of what precedes)."[10] *Monsters* refuses to offer this placebo. The book ends when John draws the complete monster at Dr. Plunger's request, following which his parents hear a tremendous noise "like two or three heavy metal rock bands all playing at once." John comes out of the office, hands casually in his pockets, smiling in modest satisfaction, as the door swings slowly open behind him to reveal the monster (and an abandoned notebook, presumably all that remains of Dr. Plunger). "Drawings?" John asks. "Who needs drawings?"

The ending seems abrupt, not because it is an illogical conclusion to the book, but because it runs counter to the reader's expectation that the magic world will be closed as the text closes. Instead, the ending of *Monsters* seems like a beginning because the monster now openly inhabits reality. The style of the picture here also reinforces the validity of the monster. John's pictures were clearly the drawing of a child (as imitated by Quentin Blake) scribbled in crayon and colored pencil and felt-tip marker. The monster as it appears on the final page is very different. Done in watercolors, it has the multiple eyes and jagged teeth and spiky body that John saw, but it is not identical with John's picture. The visual distinction between John's pictures and the monster as it finally appears reveals that this is not a monster created by John's imagination, but a real monster that John was willing to acknowledge.

The reader never knows how John's parents react to the monster, nor does Hoban show what John will do after meeting the monster. *The Rain Door,* however, offers a different perspective on a being closely related to the monster: the fearsome magical beast. The lion that brings thunder in *The Rain Door* is not an enemy to be destroyed, but the appropriate partner to the horse, Lightning, which brings the rainstorm. He is not, then, to be destroyed, which Harry at first does not understand. Instead, the hero-quest in this book requires that the lion remain alive and roaring, as the rag-and-bone man explains: "It's okay. Thunder after Lightning is as it should be. It's only when he thunders out of turn that he makes [the horse] nervous"[11] (n.p.).

The beast is an integral part of the group that will bring water to the parched and overheated day that is described on the book's first page, and which will be relieved, not by a gentle shower, but by the fierceness of a storm. Christine Wilkie suggests that *The Rain Door* "belongs to the genre of folk tales that attempts to explain natural phenomena."[12] But I think it is worth noting here that Harry's means of actually putting Thunder in his proper place is not magical. In fact, the text specifically declines a fairy-tale solution, for "Harry thought he might see a magic sword stuck in a rock or perhaps a magic ring lying about. But he didn't see any swords or rings." Instead, Harry hits on a plan that will seem familiar to most readers of Hoban's work. He builds a machine.

The usual literary attitude toward machinery is well described by Leo Marx in *The Machine in the Garden:* "by placing the machine in opposition to the tranquility and order located in the landscape, [the writer] makes it an emblem of the artificial, of the unfeeling utilitarian spirit, and of the fragmented, industrial style of life that allegedly follows from the premises of the empirical philosophy."[13] But this attitude is itself a historical product, the creation of Romantic notions of organic wholeness and codified in Carlyle's 1829 essay "Signs of the Times."[14] Other traditions, particularly the progressive spirit that dominated the early part of our century, present machinery in a more positive light, as an expression of human power in the face of overwhelming force from natural elements, such as the storm that Harry is working to release.

In fact, the mechanical dinosaur that Harry builds follows a pattern repeated through a number of Hoban texts. Harry "used bones and rags and iron and rope, he used wire and rusty bolts. He used gears and wheels and mainsprings from all the old clocks he could find. When the

The mechanical dinosaur Harry builds in *The Rain Door* is an impromptu creation. Illus. Quentin Blake.

dinosaur was all put together it had keys all over it for winding up the different parts of it." Harry's machine, for it is his machine, is an impromptu creation from the bits and pieces at hand (like so many of Hoban's scenes, this one takes place in a junkyard), and seems not so much a machine as an invention. Gears, another motif repeated through various Hoban writings, figure prominently in this creation, and I think it is worthwhile to consider the importance of gears themselves in a mechanical construction. Cecilia Tichi suggests that "under the aegis of this technology human beings intellectually understood the material world as dynamic, integrated assemblies of component parts . . . [which] could be reconceived in new relations to each other."[15] Clearly, Harry's pieced-together monster is such an assembly of parts, and building such a creature implies Harry's view of a dynamic world, capable of changing. The

gear itself is the mechanism that transforms energy from the keys that
Harry winds to the machine monster that he builds, and the gear-driven
construction is a means of magnifying Harry's energy to match the
lion's. The final product is far from perfect "because the different parts of
the dinosaur all ran down at different times and Harry had to keep jumping off to wind them up." The mechanical dinosaur expresses both
Harry's willingness to deal with physical reality—he works with the
materials at hand, flawed as they may be—and his willingness to deal
with the life beyond ordinary reality—he creates a monster. And then he
climbs atop it and drives it.

Hoban's first published book, and one of the two he himself illustrated, was *What Does It Do and How Does It Work?*, and his interest in
things mechanical has been noted by a number of critics. Alida Allison
writes that Hoban's "interest wasn't really in machines per se, but in the
idea of the mechanical, and its complement, the idea of breaking out of
perfunctory existence."[16] A close look at the illustrations for Hoban's
first book suggests how those two ideas are linked in his picture books.
First of all, the illustrations are remarkable for the sense of power and
life that they possess. I say "life" here not intending to say that Hoban's
pictures are faithful mimetic representations of machines. I say "life"
here in the sense that the monster and beast convey the break from "perfunctory existence." In fact, the machines are themselves much like monsters, with the appearance of gaping jaws or fierce claws, so huge that
they overwhelm both written text and the pages on which they are barely
contained, even though all the illustrations are on two-page spreads. The
heavy black outlines of the machines are surrounded by the sketchy lines
that usually indicate motion—these machines almost shake with immi-
nent movement.

The text, like the illustrations, emphasizes the power of the machines. But it also emphasizes the endless repetition of the machine's
motion. The power shovel drops one load, and "then back swings the
boom and the dipper digs in—digging the dirt and digging the rocks to
fill up the trucks again."[17] The tractor shovel shifts one bucket of gravel
and then "you lower the bucket, and scoop up the gravel for another
load." The last line of the book, describing the motor scraper, tells the
reader that "when the bowl is empty, you go back for more." No matter
how deep you dig among the rocks of this world, there will always be
more to move.

The chthonic nature of the machines is also suggestive in *What Does
It Do?*, for every single machine in this book is an earth-mover. There are

no cranes, no forklifts, no wrecking balls. The earth-movers, I believe, have special importance for Hoban, who writes in "Thoughts on Being and Writing" of a space that confronts the individual with both the loss of identity and the recognition of a world that is dangerous, not contained by the definitions and institutions of those who live on top of it. He describes this space as "far down, dim in green light through the ancient reeds and tasting of the primal salt."[18] It is the space that the mouse and his child face in the mud at the bottom of the pond. And it is, quite simply, the monster. The machines in *What Does It Do?*, like the mechanical dinosaur in *The Rain Door*, are human responses to the monster, are mechanisms for confronting the inexhaustible power of a universe that is not, as we so fondly imagine, human-centered.

In light of this understanding of *What Does It Do?*, the Walt Whitman quotation that begins the book takes on a different meaning. ". . . And there is no trade / Or employment / But the young man following it / May become a hero" is no longer a statement of the Puritan work ethic, as might be expected of a children's picture book with wholly didactic purposes. This picture book is not only a celebration of good honest labor, but also an expression of the hero task that Harry accomplishes in *The Rain Door* and John in *Monsters*, the task of "unearthing" monsters and bringing them to daylight. We should note, then, that although there is no pictured child in *What Does It Do?*, the text itself constantly addresses the child-reader, placing the child literally in the driver's seat of these machines.

> You back up, as the tree sways, then you push again and the engine roars as you open the throttle. The bullozer quivers and shakes as it pushes and the roots tear out with a ripping sound. . . . Then you lower the blade again and clear the roots away.

This kind of heroic child skirts close to the edges of the Romantic conception of childhood before the Victorians sugar-coated it. Hoban's child protagonists may not come trailing clouds of glory, but they do seem to occasionally ooze the primordial sludge of Life-with-a-capital-L, though Hoban's prose in these books never loses his lightness of touch or dips into mysticism. Still, he does seem to associate children with a kind of freedom that confers power. He describes how "with [King Richard's] return, Robin Hood's power is drained off into the power of lawful authority. The outlaw self is assimilated into the lawful self, the puissant youth becomes the waning man."[19]

In *How Tom Beat Captain Najork and His Hired Sportsmen,* Hoban pits the puissant youth, Tom, against the waning man, Captain Najork, and allows "Robin Hood" to stay in Sherwood Forest—even avoid marrying Maid Marian! In this book, as David Rees points out, "childhood innocence [is] pitted against adult incomprehension, repressed adults disliking nonconformity."[20] The book tells the story of Tom's battle to remain a child, and page after page shows him engaging in his favorite activity, fooling around. He transforms "sticks and stones and crumpled paper, . . . mewses and passages and dustbins, . . . bent nails and broken glass and holes in fences" into impromptu toys, using the materials at hand much as Harry does.[21] His maiden aunt, Miss Fidget Wonkham-Strong, whose iron hat, bustle, and tight collar would give away her character if her name didn't, objects, telling him that "too much playing is not good. . . . You had better stop it and do something useful." In a reading at San Diego State University, Hoban made his personal feelings about turning play into work quite clear: "Let's say someone turns a kid loose and the kid is walking along the beach picking up stones. You just know that some grown-up is going to come along and say, 'Isn't that nice, picking up stones. Now let's sort the stones into colors and let's put them in a box and let's write about sorting stones. Let's work with that.' . . . I just wish that that kid who picked up the stone could be left alone."[22] However, the main thrust of *How Tom Beat Captain Najork and His Hired Sportsmen,* of course, is not that play should be allowed despite being impractical, but that all of Tom's fooling around actually is useful, for it allows him to defeat Captain Najork, who is employed by Aunt Fidget Wonkham-Strong to teach Tom a lesson.

In fact, Aunt Fidget Wonkham-Strong makes an attempt to present Captain Najork as a kind of didactic monster, the monster who "stands as a warning against exploration of its uncertain demesnes."[23] But despite her threatening description of the captain, he turns out to be no monster at all, being "only six feet tall. His eyes were not like fire, his voice was not like thunder." Instead he is a man who has turned "fooling around" into a series of elaborate, competitive, highly constructed games. The bits and pieces with which Tom played have become structured into ridiculous pieces of equipment, as in the sneedball ramp stamped "Sneedball Mfg. Coy." But the very seriousness with which Captain Najork and his men attack the sports assures their failure, for they "poled too hard and shovelled too fast and tired themselves out. Tom just mucked about and fooled around, and when the tide came in he led the opposition 673 to 49."

In Captain Najork, the creative impulse has been tamed. Although the text shows repeatedly that the captain's sports have roots in the kind

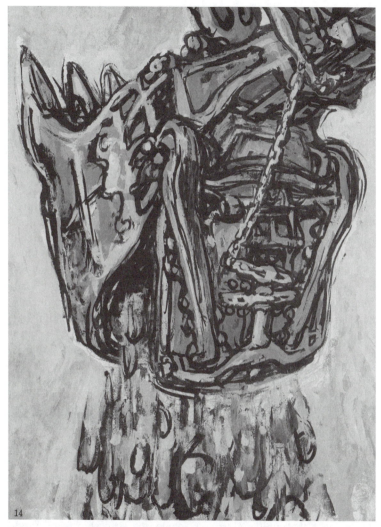

This early illustration by Russell Hoban from *What Does It Do and How Does It Work?* reveals his fascination with digging deeply. Illus. Russell Hoban.

of fooling around that Tom does, games played on ladders and in mud and with barrels, the captain has turned play into a species of work. His sportsmen are hired. He participates in the Sneedball Championship. This is play socialized and thereby weakened; Tom defeats Captain Najork handily.

But Tom's real enemy in this story is not Captain Najork. His enemies are two women, Aunt Fidget Wonkham-Strong, and the princess who does not appear in the book. The first of these two women wants to strip away his childhood; so would the second if she were allowed into the story. Just as marriage to Maid Marian domesticates Robin Hood, so too would the marriage to a princess that so often follows the protagonist's defeat of a powerful male. Instead, the defeated captain is given the maiden aunt as a bride, and Tom advertises for a new aunt. Bundlejoy Cosysweet, who "had a floppy hat with flowers on it [and] long, long hair," is the woman who combines the best of both worlds for Tom, allowing him both the mature power to determine his own actions and the ability to remain a free creative child. Unlike Tom's real and powerful aunt, Bundlejoy is a weak figure. In fact, her weakness is an important part of her appeal for Tom, who flatly tells her "no mutton and no cabbage-and-potato sog. . . . And I do lots of fooling around. Those are my conditions." She accepts them; clearly, if she had not, Tom would have looked for another new aunt. But because she is an "aunt" instead of a princess, Tom is not required to assume the sexual maturity that would follow marriage. So he abjures maturity in favor of the freedom of childhood—of course, he is only able to do so through the collaboration of an adult who abdicates her own powers of maturity.

A more positive solution to the question of how to keep "our outlaw strength alive and brother to our lawful vigour" is presented in the four books of *The Great Fruit Gum Robbery* series. The great fun of these books is the gap between the pictures and text. For instance, when the text of *They Came from Aargh!* reads, "all of them were alien, all of them were strange. Their ship was strange and alien, it had twelve legs," the matching picture shows three little boys in flower-pot or colander helmets, whose twelve-legged ship is made up of three chairs.[24] The three children, like Harry, have assembled a hodgepodge of stray items into a spaceship—the conspicuous difference being that their spaceship does not actually move, as Harry's mechanical dinosaur does. Worth noting at this point is that, unlike Harry's machine, the spaceship from Aargh! does not have any gears, even though it does have an old clock, from which Harry took the gears that drove his machine. This trip will remain wholly imaginary, and lacks the power of Harry's creative act; all of the books of this series are light and nonthreatening, without the danger of *The Rain Door* or, especially, *Monsters.*

Instead, the "monster" encounters are also patched together by the boys out of common household encounters. There is no attempt here to

Aunt Fidget Wonkham-Strong instructs an unimpressed Tom about the uselessness of too much playing. From *How Tom Beat Captain Najork and His Hired Sportsmen.* Illus. Quentin Blake.

persuade the reader that the "monsters" are real; in the first encounter, the boys cower in a corner, announcing that they are being approached by something "shocking and horrible," while at the far end of the picture, an orange, clawed foot is seen just peeping through an open doorway.

> "It's a shock horror," said Blob. "It has seven heads and five wings," said Blub. "It's flying in a circle," said Blob. "That's because it has three wings on one side and two on the other," said Blub. "It's an asymmetrical shock horror," said Blob. "We'd better bimble it before it bimbles us." "Let's try giving it some milk," said Blub.

On the next page, the asymmetrical shock horror is revealed to be a marmalade striped cat—not even black!

The other encounter with a "monster" is also comical, for the explorers meet a "mummosaurus," which turns out to be their mother, wearing an apron and house slippers. The mummosaurus has made a chocolate cake, but forbids access to it until the boys eat their cheese omelettes. She attacks the spaceship, tearing it apart, turning it back into kitchen chairs. The destruction of the boys' game recalls Aunt Fidget Wonkham-Strong, but this book is a little kinder to adults, and the mummosaurus agrees to a deal. "Eat your omelettes and your beans and French fries and then you can have your chocolate cake and after that you can put your spaceship back together." On the one hand, the mummosaurus does not object to the boys' "fooling around," and will allow it to recommence after the meal. On the other hand, she is firmly in control of the situation, as Tom's aunt never is, and so the boys do not rebel against her authority. The very lightness with which she wields power assures that she will not be challenged, and the boys of this book do not progress toward maturity as, for instance, John and Harry do. Of course, they are also not driven to defend a protracted childhood, as Tom is.

Instead, they accept moderate limits on their power, the deal being literally sweetened by chocolate cake. Their game remains clearly a fiction, but the mummosaurus respects that fiction, telling the explorers, who ask what planet this is, "We call it Earth. . . . What do you call it?" They call it Plovsnat because "in our language that means the place of chocolate cake." Adults and children in this book have worked out the compromise that they were not able to make in the others, and the children both gain and lose in the arrangement. The boys do not have the opportunity to realize their fantasy, remaining trapped in what is merely pretense, and therefore they never face the necessities and dangers that would stimulate the creative energy that drives the mechanical dinosaur. But neither do they have to learn to live with monsters. And, child or adult, there's nothing better than a chocolate cake made for you by someone who loves you.

NOTES

[1]Russell Hoban, "Thoughts on Being and Writing," *The Thorny Paradise: Writers on Writing for Children,* ed. Edward Blishen (Harmondsworth: Kestrel Books, 1975), p. 72.

[2]Russell Hoban, *Monsters* (New York: Scholastic, 1989), n.p. All future references will be to this edition.

[3]Bruno Bettelheim, *The Uses of Enchantment: The Meaning and Importance of Fairy Tales.* (New York: Vintage Press, 1989), p. 120.

[4]Ibid., p. 121.

[5]Jeffrey Jerome Cohen, "Monster Culture (Seven Theses)," *Monster Theory: Reading Culture,* ed. Jeffrey Jerome Cohen (Minneapolis: University of Minnesota Press, 1996), p. 7.

[6]Margaret Blount, *Animal Land: The Creatures of Children's Fiction* (New York: Avon, 1974), p. 97.

[7]Russell Hoban, "Thoughts on a Shirtless Cyclist, Robin Hood, Johann Sebastian Bach, and One or Two Other Things," *Children's Literature in Education* 4 (1971): 13.

[8]Hoban, "Thoughts on Being," p. 67.

[9]Ibid., p. 65.

[10]Sarah Gilead, "Magic Abjured: Closure in Children's Fantasy Fiction," *PMLA* 106 (1991): 278.

[11]Russell Hoban, *The Rain Door* (New York: Thomas Y. Crowell, 1986), n.p. All future references will be to this edition.

[12]Christine Wilkie, *Through the Narrow Gate: The Mythological Consciousness of Russell Hoban* (London: Associated University Presses, 1989), p. 94.

[13]Leo Marx, *The Machine in the Garden: Technology and the Pastoral Ideal in America* (New York: Oxford University Press, 1984), p. 18.

[14]Ibid., p. 179.

[15]Cecelia Tichi, *Shifting Gears: Technology, Literature, Culture in Modernist America* (Chapel Hill: University of North Carolina Press, 1987), p. xii.

[16]Alida Allison, "Living the Non-Mechanical Life: Russell Hoban's Metaphorical Wind-Up Toys," *Children's Literature in Education* 32 (1991): 189.

[17]Russell Hoban, *What Does It Do and How Does It Work?* (New York: Harper & Brothers, 1959). n.p. All future references will be to this edition.

[18]Hoban, "Thoughts on Being," p. 66.

[19]Hoban, "Thoughts on a Shirtless Cyclist," p. 9.

[20]David Rees, *Painted Desert, Green Shade: Essays on Contemporary Fiction for Children and Young Adults* (Boston: Horn Book, 1984), p. 144.

[21]Russell Hoban, *How Tom Beat Captain Najork and His Hired Sportsmen* (New York: Atheneum, 1974), n.p. All future references will be to this edition.

[22]Russell Hoban, "Russell Hoban Reads Russell Hoban: Children's Books San Diego State University, Oct. 18, 1990," ed. Alida Allison, *The Lion and the Unicorn* 15 (1991): 104.

[23]Cohen, "Monster Culture," p. 13.

[24]Russell Hoban, *They Came from Aargh!* (New York: Philomel Books, 1981), n.p. All future references will be to this edition.

BIBLIOGRAPHY

Allison, Alida. "Living the Non-Mechanical Life: Russell Hoban's Metaphorical Wind-Up Toys." *Children's Literature in Education* 22 (1991): 189–94.

Bettelheim, Bruno. *The Uses of Enchantment: The Meaning and Importance of Fairy Tales.* New York: Vintage Press, 1989.

Blount, Margaret. *Animal Land: The Creatures of of Children's Fiction.* New York: Avon, 1974.

Cohen, Jeffrey Jerome. "Monster Culture (Seven Theses)." *Monster Theory: Reading Culture.* Edited by Jeffery Jerome Cohen. Minneapolis: University of Minnesota Press, 1996, pp. 3–25.

Gilead, Sarah. "Magic Abjured: Closure in Children's Fantasy Fiction." *PMLA* 106 (1991): 277–92.

Hoban, Russell. *How Tom Beat Captain Najork and His Hired Sportsmen.* Illustrated by Quentin Blake. New York: Atheneum, 1974.

———. *Monsters.* Illustrated by Quentin Blake. New York: Scholastic, 1989.

———. *The Rain Door.* Illustrated by Quentin Blake. New York: Thomas Y. Crowell, 1986.

———. "Russell Hoban Reads Russell Hoban: Children's Books San Diego State University, Oct. 18, 1990." Edited by Alida Allison. *The Lion and the Unicorn* 15 (1991): 96–107.

———. *They Came from Aargh!* Illustrated by Colin McNaughton. New York: Philomel Books, 1981.

———. "Thoughts on Being and Writing." *The Thorny Paradise: Writers on Writing for Children.* Edited by Edward Blishen. Harmondsworth: Kestrel Books, 1975. 65–76.

———. "Thoughts on a Shirtless Cyclist, Robin Hood, Johann Sebastian Bach, and One or Two Other Things." *Children's Literature in Education* 4 (1971): 5–23.

———. *What Does It Do and How Does It Work?* Illustrated by Russell Hoban. New York: Harper & Brothers, 1959.

Marx, Leo. *The Machine in the Garden: Technology and the Pastoral Ideal in America.* New York: Oxford University Press, 1964.

Rees, David. *Painted Desert, Green Shade: Essays on Contemporary Fiction for Children and Young Adults.* Boston: Horn Book, 1984.

Tichi, Cecelia. *Shifting Gears: Technology, Literature, Culture in Modernist America.* Chapel Hill: University of North Carolina Press, 1987.

Wilkie, Christine. *Through the Narrow Gate: The Mythological Consciousness of Russell Hoban.* London: Associated University Presses, 1989.

An Epistemology for Frances

MARTIN TEITEL

"Can I wander with you?" asked Frances.[1]

Like physicians, philosophers should obey the injunction "Do no harm." The very idea of philosophizing about any children's book, much less the exquisitely self-contained Frances books of Russell Hoban, is fraught with danger. The following comments on one aspect of the philosophy of Frances are offered in a spirit of circumspection and reticence, hoping to avoid the classic pitfall of philosophical writing: dissection without revelation.

Children's books are more than vehicles for the entertainment of small children. They inform, and they transmit values: ideas and injunctions about what people should or should not do. A parent or teacher might take up a book looking for a "message"—a set of values—that will reflect values the adult wants to include in the child's education.

Values desired for a child's education might be assumed to arise from the adult's own values, which derive from culture, experience, and education. Most parents and teachers would consider themselves at least somewhat familiar with their own values and the values that they would like to see transmitted to children. Yet underneath assumptions about values lies a substrate that is too often ignored: epistemology.

The philosophical term "epistemology" comes from the Greek *episteme* ("knowledge") and *logos* ("knowledge").[2] This magnificent redundancy is usually summarized as meaning the theory of knowledge. What it really means in everyday life is found in the question "How do I know what I know?" The usual subject of exploration in epistemology covers the Big Three of classical philosophic inquiry:

- Belief
- Knowledge
- Truth

This list might seem to the casual observer to be obvious and perhaps even a further redundancy. Yet it is actually the case that epistemology varies significantly from time to time and from place to place. Knowing one's epistemological context is so crucial that a misstep can result in penalties ranging from embarrassment to incarceration. Yet, knowing one's epistemological orientation can be as difficult as knowing the look of one's own face without a mirror.

Epistemology is the foundation of all our knowledge—including our values. What we consider to constitute knowledge and what we don't frames our every thought. Our notions of belief and truth are so built into the mechanisms of our ways of thinking that we have trouble thinking about it. This is the great relativist difficulty in thinking about thinking: one can't easily examine one's mechanism for thinking without thinking, without employing that mechanism. In other words, it is difficult to stand outside of our own heads, our own epistemological universes, to see how our thinking frame might look to others.

Epistemology might seem like the kind of useless and obscure puzzling that delights philosophers. Yet in Western society—the kind of world we find described in the Frances books—the dominant epistemological frame is strictly and even ruthlessly enforced. The contemporary Western paradigm of knowing is based on the Cartesian, rationalist rules of science. Our ways of knowing are quite concrete, specific, and numerable. In our world, we rely on the evidence of our senses and on our rational thought. Intuition, nonlinear and nonrational thoughts and ideas, multiple contradictory truths, paradoxes, and knowledge of the numinous are not considered standard thinking in our schools, colleges, and universities.

Other cultures employ differing epistemologies and various approaches to epistemological dissent. Once during a visit to Laos, I was having my car fueled, and I noticed the attendant whispering to the hose sticking into my automobile. I discovered that she was wishing the fuel a good, safe journey. In Western culture, a conversation with a petroleum product could easily result in a diagnosis, perhaps medication, even incarceration. In Laos, the attendant could accommodate both the mechanistic notions of burning fuel to produce energy and motive power, and simultaneously the idea that inanimate objects—fluids—have spirits that one can relate to or converse with.

Western epistemology is characterized by rigidity. Alternative ways of knowing do not fit comfortably within the scientific paradigm, which often produces an impulse toward debunking or scoffing at what doesn't fit.

Along with rigidity goes narrowness. Once, visiting Mayan-descended Cakchiquel people in the highlands of Central America, I discovered that they did not know that they lived in a country called Guatemala, yet they knew what was Number One on the Hit Parade in Miami. They were quite sure that Noah had only recently sailed his ark near their mountains, which is how they explained the pottery shards in their cornfields. Yet these same people showed me how to rig up a sophisticated antenna and earthing system for my radio—obviously the source of their Miami pop music information.

The Cakchiquel people use an epistemology that welcomes several kinds of belief as legitimate; they are comfortable with numerous levels of truth, and various ways of knowing—from spirit divination, to praying in the local Catholic church, to reading the owner's manual.

We teach our children a narrower range of epistemological choices. Put most baldly, we suffer from a kind of epistemological impoverishment, often permitting only one kind of truth, and subordinating believing to knowing. Our values are based on this. We teach our young people that it is important to tell the truth, and we might denigrate those foreign people from Guatemala or Laos whom we suspect don't value *the* truth. We emphasize knowing the one right answer and acting on what one knows to be the case as preferable to going on a hunch or a guess. A child in a modern Western school who suggests asking spirits for guidance while making a decision or answering an exam question might be sent to the principal or the school nurse.

The distinction here is more than that of culturally based value systems, although that is part of it. Our children are immersed in a world that permits certain choices in thinking and disparages other ways of organizing cognition. Our young ones run the risk of growing up unable to appreciate some of the great cultural and intellectual legacies of humanity, unable to spring their minds free from the scientific epistemological box that we have put them in—the same one we live in.

A complete critique of Western ways of knowing more is then a bit beyond the scope of this chapter, much less necessary to an examination of the work of Russell Hoban. Perhaps the foregoing very brief sketch of epistemological issues will suffice so that we may return to Hoban's work.

The main thesis of this chapter is that in fact a significant aspect of Russell Hoban's value, power, and charm arises from his challenging of the dominant Western epistemological status quo. Hoban contests epistemological rigidity and narrowness. Through humor, example, even song, Hoban pushes the limits of our science-based epistemological box. In doing so he delights children and enchants their parents.

In many cultures, including our own, it is a sense of irony, a willingness to bend but not break the dominant paradigm of thinking that forms the basis for much of our humor. Thus does the jester tweak the king's nose—and live to tell the tale.

Hoban announces his sense of epistemological freedom in his unique novel *Riddley Walker.* For example, Lissener challenges Ridley's ways of knowing:

> In the dark beside me Lissener begun to cry.
> I said, 'Whatre you crying about?'
> He said, 'Im crying for what ben Im crying for whats going to be.'
> I said, 'Whats the use of that?'
> He said, 'Whats the use of not?'
> I said, 'May be it dont have to be.'
> He dint say nothing he jus let my words littl off and dwindl stopid in the air.[3]

In a few lines, utilitarianism, temporal orderliness, and rational argumentation are dismissed. *Riddley Walker* challenges a great deal of the conventional wisdom—from conventional spelling to conventional reason.

Similarly, although perhaps less blatantly, Russell Hoban bends the rules of Western knowing in his Frances books. In this series of children's classics, Hoban bases much of the sense of wisdom, and a good deal of the humor, on his pushing of the epistemological envelope. It might be instructive to look a bit further into this feature of the Frances books.

Frances is one of the most appealing characters in all of children's literature. Part of what makes her so is her straightforwardness, her matter-of-fact pronouncements. What Frances declarations can we find that discuss belief, knowledge, and truth?

One quickly discovers that Frances is not a scientist who permits only one kind of truth. Factual reporting is for her relative to emotional need. For example, in *Best Friends for Frances,* Frances rebuffs her little sister Gloria's request to play ball. Frances is in turn rebuffed by the boys she has gone to play with. She quickly returns to her sister, who says, "How did you play so fast that you are home so soon?" "It was a fast game,"[4] says Frances. Legions of parents do not slam the covers of the book together at this point, in objection to this obvious lie. Instead, they smile at the child on their lap, sharing the joke of the bending of the truth in the service of the ego, the sweet humor of the little epistemological warp.

Frances clearly considers her world to contain lots of room for varying truths. Quite a few of her departures from absolutism occur around food, for example, when she is questioned about eating eggs,[5] or when she eats much of the candy she bought for her sister's birthday and, with mouth full, denies it.[6] Hoban tells us, repeatedly, that truth is sometimes in the eye of the beholder, and that children's truths might be different from grownups'. And that it's okay if children don't always operate according to grownups' truths, even when they see them.

In our world of standard tests, Algebra II, and computer programs, what one believes is often subordinated to what one knows, or claims to know. Frances seems less under the sway of these priorities. The importance of getting all the facts right, she repeatedly tells us, is secondary to other considerations, such as how people feel or what it's all right not to know. Even Father, the person one might expect to be the fount of information, doesn't want to tell what he knows when other considerations intervene. When interrogated about where veal cutlets come from and why stringless beans are called string beans, he simply says, "We can talk about that another time."[7] And, of course, he never does.

All in all, Frances does not live in a world dominated by factual tests, managed by empiricism, and regulated by rationalism. In book after book, the young badger asserts herself according to how she feels: specifically, how she assesses the people around her. Frances's epistemological testing is based not so much on what she observes others doing, as on what she thinks or feels about them. Frances is less interested in reportorial accuracy, and more in seeing where and how the world reflects her inner state. This quality is seen frequently in the songs that Frances sings for us:

> *Sisters that are much too small*
> *To throw or catch or bat a ball*
> *Are really not much good at all,*
> Except for crying.[8]

Or, when Frances has run away from home to a spot under the dining room table, while she is eating her chocolate sandwich cookies she sings,

> *I am poor and hungry here, eating prunes and rice.*
> *Living all alone is not really very nice.*[9]

These songs are charming, amusing, and central to Hoban's story. What makes them so, partly, is Frances's epistemological independence, the tension between the rationalism of our cultural mainstream and her more subjective and relational theory of knowledge.

Perhaps Frances is only demonstrating for us the more self-centered epistemology of a child. Yet given the consistent delight of adults who encounter Frances, one can speculate that perhaps Frances is less a narcissistic infant, and more an articulator of the kinds of knowing that—liberated from the Western straitjacket of rationalism and empiricism—many of us would choose.

Frances is not the only person to challenge our conventional ways of knowing. What about Father and Mother? We look to parents to create the value set that children grow into, so Mother and Father are not only modeling and teaching for Frances, but for those of us who are parents reading to our little ones. What do Mother and Father teach us about belief, knowledge, and truth?

Frances's parents display two interesting strategies in teaching their daughter—and the rest of us—about parent-child epistemology. These two methods might be called the Creative Non Sequitur and the Parental Absolute.

What parent has not wished at some point that she or he had not responded to some question that only draws them into a hopeless, circular, or unanswerable debate? Yet many of us learn as children that questions have answers, and, underlying that, a kind of epistemology of sequence: first we have A, then B, and so on.

Not so with Mother and Father. In their way of organizing the world, some sequences are meant to be broken—or more correctly—ignored. When this happens, no one complains, Frances does not yell, "Hey, you didn't answer my question!" Rather, the scene shifts; we move on.

Mother is a real expert in moving along when it suits her. When Frances invents some spelling, we have the following exchange started by Frances:

> "Alice will not have h-r-n-d, and she will not have g-k-l-s. But we are singing together."
> "What are h-r-n-d and g-k-l-s?" asked Mother.
> "Cake and candy. I thought you could spell," said Frances.[10]

Now, many parents would subscribe to a way of organizing thought that dictates one way to spell words. Further, on a more epistemological level, most of us would say that spelling has a particular function in life, which is that certain sequences of symbols signify certain objects in the real world. Anyone deviating from this convention is running the risk, therefore, of failing to understand what the real world is and how we describe it. Epistemological instruction from mother to daughter is nothing if not an attempt to anchor the young one in reality. This is especially the case when the daughter herself suggests that the mother is incompetent, unable even to spell.

In Hoban's stories, Mother apparently suffers from no anxiety that her daughter is not firmly in reality. In fact, Mother settles the argument, evidently to everyone's satisfaction, by ignoring the opportunity to correct her daughter, choosing instead to leap over this argumentative issue and get to the core of what Frances is talking about. Mother says simply, "I am sure that Alice will have cake and candy on her birthday."[11]

What's the epistemological content here? The Reality and Truth of this exchange for Mother are not about spelling conventions or assuring her daughter that in fact she can spell, that it is Frances who cannot. Rather the truth of what Mother responds to is her daughter's feelings about her friends, her birthday, her favorite foods. Rationalism and the epistemology of correct or incorrect spelling give way to a mother's way of knowing about where her daughter is heading with her thinking and especially with her feelings. Note that Frances's feelings are not discussed. Instead, her mother gives Frances's feelings primacy—reality—above lesser truths about words and letters.

This is a powerful lesson in inventing epistemology, one that is derived from the inside, from a mother's feelings for her daughter, in place of an externally derived truth emanating from social convention. Hoban teaches us radical epistemology: that a parent can create reality for her child based on her intuition and her love.

Now we can see this apparent non sequitur for what it is, not an actual non sequitur, but a response to the deeper message of child to mother, mother to child.

Another example of this kind of apparent non sequitur arises when Frances has had it with her baby sister and decides to run away. "Well," Frances says:

> Things are not very good around here anymore. No clothes to wear.
> No raisins for the oatmeal.
> I think maybe I'll run away.[12]

Mother doesn't explain how being busy with the baby made her unable to buy more raisins, nor does she try to convince Frances that she is

In *Bedtime for Frances,* Frances's parents treat her bedtime stalling patiently.
Illus. Garth Williams.

unreasonable. Instead she simply tells Frances to finish her breakfast before the school bus arrives. Because Mother doesn't argue with the reality of Frances's situation as Frances is experiencing it, Frances can feel accepted. Her reality is not challenged, so she can move past this crisis by asking when supper will be, and pointing out that there is plenty of time to run away after that.

The other epistemological innovation in Hoban's stories, which could be called the Parental Absolute, arises around one of the maladies of modern life, relativism—what might be called the ascendancy of opinion. In liberal Western culture, people are careful to honor the opinions or values of others. Absolute opinions or values are suspect as fundamentalist or rigid. In some contrast to the rigidity of rationalism in our epistemology, matters of opinion or values are held to be utterly personal. This causes the kind of wishy-washy parenting in which parents are reluctant to affirm the reality of the rendering of opinions.

Not so with Father and Mother. When Frances discovers a tiger in her room, she is questioned with total seriousness by her parents: "Did he bite you?" asks Father, while Mother adds, " Did he scratch you?" When Frances replies "no,"

> "Then he is a friendly tiger," said Father.
> "He will not hurt you. Go back to sleep."[13]

There is no existential discussion of the reality of tigers, no pseudo-analysis of anxiety, no rationalist appeal based on a child stalling. Instead, as is common for Frances, there is an acceptance of her framing of her own life. Then there is an absolute pronouncement: the tiger is friendly. The world is safe.

This sureness, the lack of doubt, is characteristic of Mother and Father's anchoring of Frances in their moral universe. When Frances keeps arguing about not going to sleep, Father patiently explains that Frances needs to go to sleep because she needs to be fresh for school, which is her job as much as Father has his job that he too must be rested for. After going down this logical chain about jobs for some time, Frances volunteers that if she does not go to bed, perhaps she will get a spanking. Father has a one word reply: "Right."[14]

After a similar long exchange about all the things that might happen if Frances plays with Thelma, Mother says finally, ". . . when you play with Thelma you always get the worst of it."[15] No hesitations here, rather, a moral absolute: this is how it is—base your decisions on how it is with this person.

In a sense, what Hoban is doing with Mother and Father is putting our conventional epistemology on its head. The Western, rational rigidity is called into question, as if Hoban is saying, perhaps there are other, equally valid ways of knowing things. Yet the softer relativism of our values and opinions is made more certain, definite. In this way, Hoban says to us that in dealing with small children, our ways of knowing should be more like those of the children: conventional rationalism is subordinated to judgments based on feelings and needs, while judgments about values are firmer, giving a child a simpler but much more secure universe in which to live.

Perhaps Russell Hoban's children's books succeed because they challenge a bit of our conventional wisdom, our too-narrow and stuffy ways of knowing. In the end, Hoban's Frances delights us because this young badger girl is charming, earnest, and spunky—and she most likely has little need for philosophers to tell her how to think. And yet to that, perhaps Frances would reply:

How do you know what I'll like if you won't even try me?[16]

NOTES

[1]Russell Hoban, *Best Friends for Frances* (New York: Scholastic, 1994), p. 7.

[2]W.L. Reese, *Dictionary of Philosophy and Religion* (Atlantic Highlands, NJ: Humanities Press, 1991), p. 151.

[3]Russell Hoban, *Riddley Walker* (New York: Summit Books, 1980), p.108.

[4]Hoban, *Best Friends for Frances,* p. 112.

[5]Russell Hoban, *Bread and Jam for Frances* (New York: HarperCollins, 1993).

[6]Russell Hoban, *A Birthday for Frances* (HarperCollins, 1968).

[7]Hoban, *Bread and Jam for Frances,* p. 12.

[8]Hoban, *Best Friends for Frances,* p. 5.

[9]Russell Hoban, *A Baby Sister for Frances* (New York: HarperCollins, 1992), p. 18.

[10]Hoban, *A Birthday for Frances,* p. 6.

[11]Ibid.

[12]Hoban, *A Baby Sister for Frances,* p. 10.

[13]Hoban, *Bedtime for Frances,* n.p.

[14]Ibid., n.p.

[15]Hoban, *A Bargain for Frances,* pp. 7–12.

[16]Hoban, *Bread and Jam for Frances,* p. 28.

Questions of "What" and "Where," and Contexts of "Meaning" for *The Mouse and His Child* in the Late Twentieth Century

JOHN STEPHENS

Nearly thirty years after its first publication, I was using *The Mouse and His Child* as a set text for an undergraduate course in children's literature. The students were mostly around twenty years old, and the bulk of them were not literature majors. To my great chagrin, very few of them liked the book (though those who did were very enthusiastic about it), and when I sought to determine why this was so, it seemed to me that there were two broad reasons. On the one hand, the students were apt to become annoyed because they found too much in the book that was unrecognizable. Few of them had any concept of what a windup toy would be like, or of the principle of the spring that was tightened and then ran down, and so they neither recognized nor understood the figurative uses of the spring that recur in the text. Further, they experienced difficulties, similar to those that the Rustins had identified as problematic for child readers,[1] with the "diversity" of the narrative and its "range of cultural and social references." Thus they did not recognize the parodies of Beckett, or the tenets of existentialism, and tended to resent such things when they were pointed out. On the other hand, they did not know how to read the book in a more general way, and seemed puzzled by the genre. This problem of reading characteristically emerged as an inability to distinguish story and theme, but that inability in turn reflected two more basic problems of textual interpretation. One lies in the implicit claim of the text to pose simultaneously empirical and universal questions (as, for example, in the interlocked questions, what is the way out of the mud at the bottom of the pond? and, what is the basis of agency?); the second lies in a distinction, also perceived by the Rustins, between a narrative focused on "the child's internal world" (that is, another humanistic narrative dealing with the theme of subjectivity) and a narrative focused on "the qualities of the social world,"[1] and the propensity for recent theories of subjectivity to efface this distinction.

If we know both ourselves and the social and phenomenal elements of the world through intersubjective apprehension, then the separation of the "internal" world from the "social world" can be no more than a manner of speaking. To put this another way, citing a formulation by Leví-Strauss, "Being human signifies, for each of us, belonging to a class, a society, a country, a continent and a civilization."[2] The social ideologies children encounter and absorb in the home, the classroom, and in television programs inevitably involve an orientation toward class, society, country, continent, and civilization, though generally more nuanced toward identity as membership of a particular (national) community than toward the abstraction of "being human," and more palpably present in the circumstances of economics, ethnicity, and gender that map the social, political, and emotional worlds each of us, adult or child, inhabits. As Chantal Mouffe reminds us, however, a crucial element in the creation of identity as membership of a community is that it is constituted as thus by what is *other, outside,* or *excluded:*[3]

> Once we have understood that every identity is relational and that the affirmation of a difference is the precondition for the existence of any identity (i.e. the perception of something "other" than it which will constitute its "exterior"), then we can begin to understand why such a relationship may always become a terrain for antagonism—the "us/them" relationship will become one of "friend and enemy." This happens when the "other," who up until now has been considered simply as different, starts to be perceived as someone who is rejecting "my" identity and who is threatening "my" existence.[4]

The potential application of this stance on identity to the obsessive desire of Manny Rat to destroy the windup mice will be obvious, as also will be Mouffe's further argument that the foundation of democratic politics must be not an eradication of distinctions between "us" and "them," which is an impossibility, but the establishment of an "us" and "them" discrimination "in a way that is compatible with pluralist democracy."[5] Some other observations in Mouffe's article, "For a Politics of Nomadic Identity," have an illuminating bearing on how we might read the identity politics of *The Mouse and His Child,* and I will return to her arguments later.

When, early in *The Mouse and His Child*, the windup mouse child first comes to consciousness, he voices two questions—"Where are we?" and "What are we?"—which, as versions of the central question of being, have resonated throughout the second half of the twentieth century. Pointing to the key, always imbricated issues of place and identity that shape both story and theme, these questions inevitably are addressed by or underlie commentaries on the novel.[6] In the three decades since the novel's first publication, however, what we mean when we ask these questions in "real world" contexts has changed significantly, and this in turn can mean a large transformation in the intertextual relationships, in the widest sense of that term, within which *The Mouse and His Child* is read. For instance, theories of subjectivity, political bases for the identification of evil, and literary genres dealing with exile or with dystopias have all undergone major transformations since the late 1960s.

The effect of such transformation is clear in, for example, Valerie Krips's "Mistaken Identity" paper, which, pivoting on the premise that *The Mouse and His Child* interrogates the "fantasy" of subjectivity as a whole and unitary entity[7] and, reading the novel from the perspectives of theorists whose work postdates it (Lacan, Gallop, Riffaterre, Rose), describes a narrative that strives to resist "a too-simple reading of its representations." The novel's outcomes have now become contingent, and an ending that the Rustins referred to as "the ultimate attainment of safety and happiness"[8] is instead seen as ambiguous, lacking a sense of final closure. It is always arguable that such a re-reading, induced as it is by shifts in theoretical perspective, is merely another misreading of the text produced by setting aside the literary and cultural assumptions of the late 1960s and substituting instead a complex of assumptions that had emerged by the late 1980s. Many readers will not be persuaded that the novel's closing line ("'Be happy,' said the tramp.") is an unfulfilled promise of closure, that an argument based on the nuances of narratorial framing can override the strong, conventional signs of closure in the language that expresses the tramp's focalization of the scene: he "saw father and son with their family and friends about them. . . . He saw . . . the brightness of [the dolls' house's] lights against the night; he heard the singing and merriment inside; and he smiled and spoke. . . ." Such a scene at the beginning or an earlier point of a narrative is very likely to presage a reversal of fortune, as the novel's two previous descriptions of a party in the dolls' house testify. In each, however, Hoban has presented the scene as characterized by kinds of lack. In Chapter 1, when still in the toy shop, the doll house is a setting for social vacuity, its papier-mâché inhabitants uttering random phrases now separated from any referents. It is a moment of sharp satiric comment on the separation between information and understanding in a society with burgeoning mass communications. At the beginning of Chapter 8, the discourse through which Manny Rat's housewarming party is presented clearly evokes the gangster-story strand of the text, so that the "cream of rat society" is depicted pejoratively, as social dregs devoid of moral consciousness and incapable of intersubjective communication. As part of a structural pattern, then, the closing scene not only conforms with the expectation of a happy outcome in a quest narrative but also replaces those earlier scenes of social and moral lack with a scene of moral and social plenitude. In the context of family, friends, and laughter, the bright lights against the night sky are metonymic of that plenitude. Such a reading tends to confirm Lois Kuznets's optimistic interpretation of the closing line as "apparently offering a godlike blessing."[9] One might then ask why that possibility seems excluded, albeit implicitly, from Krips's range of interpretations—"a command or entreaty, a statement of fact or the invitation to another pilgrimage."[10] Is it the perspective from which the book is being read that excludes the most positive interpretation? Is it the modern incredulity toward the metanarrative that presages a happy ending for a quest story?

The mouse and his child begin their journey toward self-identity as intersubjective parts of a whole. Illus. Lillian Hoban.

At the risk of seeming tediously old-fashioned, this argument can be taken further, to claim that what *The Mouse and His Child* exhibits quintessentially is a particular *modernist* conception of subjectivity, but now with a strong emphasis placed on the dependence of selfhood on intersubjective relationships. E. Doyle McCarthy argues that modernism contains "a thoroughly social and historical idea of the human being—its experience, mental life, and its particular social identity as subject to change."[11] Hence against the nihilism of C. Serpentina, for example, the windups demonstrate what McCarthy refers to as "subjectivity as ingredient to action, serving as the source of the continual change human societies undergo." He continues, "Modernism brings with it a particular consciousness about self and society, one that not only demands social and political changes and renewals, but also renewals that only men and women themselves can bring about."[12] The possibilities of agency for the windups, however, are limited not only by the social embeddedness of all subjects but also by their status as pseudo-children, a limitation reiterated as a metonymy of lack at every point at which they need someone to rewind them or, more extremely, rebuild them. Hence, to return once more to the escape from the pond, the mouse child's insight that "there's nothing on the other side of nothing but us"[13] constitutes a primary understanding of "subjectivity as ingredient to action," but the sequence of events for which it is a catalyst necessarily involves others, whose actions, whether friendly or hostile ("us" or "them"), propel the windups further towards selfhood.

To read *The Mouse and His Child* at the end of the twentieth century, then, is to read dialogically. The book doesn't simply look different because "we" are different from its original audience, but it has its own capacity to read us, to expose our presuppositions about reality and textuality. What an analysis such as Krips's reflects is not just that the thematic questions "What are we?" and "Where are we?" mean something else if refracted through more contemporary theories of being, textuality, and culture, although that itself is an important factor in the aesthetics and politics of reception experiences, but also that the world itself and the nature of our consciousness of everyday life are now different in ways that shift the meanings. This is an obvious phenomenon, of course, and happens all the time with texts of the past. At the end of the twentieth century we experience an acute version of it because the rapid acceleration of change in our era highlights both dramatic innovations (the microchip revolution, for example) and intensifications of processes begun much further back (for example, the worldwide spread of individualism as "one of the constitutive doctrines of modern society,"[14] and because of the development of global communications that have the potential, at least, for making peoples more aware of what goes on beyond their own borders. Major changes in the state of the world itself and in ways of thinking about it thus produce different possible answers to the questions "Where are we?" and "What are we?" and these will in turn have a retrospective impact on the exploration of these questions in a book such as *The Mouse and His Child.*

The question "What are we?" in the context of the past thirty years implicates three intertwined processes: actual, material change; retrospective recognition *now* of the significance of social upheavals *then;* and the kind of transformation of the intellectual frames used for thinking about cultural life that left my students so puzzled by the now largely forgotten arguments of existentialism. The latter point is not confined only to philosophical issues, such as the shift toward a preference for thinking of the self as historicized rather than as universalized, but also involves perceptions of literary genre. I will here deal mainly with the first of these processes, considering the kinds of impact it might have on end-of-the-century receptions of *The Mouse and His Child,* but as the three are closely intertwined I will begin with some brief comments on the second and third.

The different ways we think about identity and subjectivity at the century's close are a consequence of all three processes of change, but how we read a book is more implicitly influenced by our assumptions about elements that are more or less everyday realities in the world of the 1990s, but which in the 1960s were incipient, unrecognized, or contested. Unjustly, perhaps, it is in these areas that my recalcitrant undergraduates showed least patience with *The Mouse and His Child.* They were especially critical of the traditional and limited roles assigned to female characters, and vehemently pointed out, as Kuznets has done,[15] that the female windups are not only denied self-winding (that is, agential subjectivity) but are denied any interest in self-winding.

There are several other areas where, incipience now having become assumption, there is a gap between the book's representations and 1990s assumptions. I mention a few interesting possibilities here. First, the belief that the concept of the nuclear family is central to social stability is now considerably diminished, so that what the mouse child desires is no longer a broadly recognized, functional metaphor for stability. Second, the effect of mass migration, whether produced by the demands of labor markets, displacement of peoples by war or economic pressures, or migration of (de-)colonized peoples to the metropolitan "center," was to produce, from the early 1970s, concepts of multiculturalism with specific local orientations. As I will suggest below, *The Mouse and His Child* promotes an ideology of interculturalism, but this is not (of course) inflected by subsequent multicultural theory. Third, conceptions of childhood have undergone considerable change, perhaps most notably as a consequence of the evolution of an independent youth culture between the 1950s and the present.[16] The metaphor of a child joined to his father's hands and having no independent source of movement, and only separated and endowed with independent motion when "restored" to the nuclear family, bespeaks a limited child agency at odds with the mouse child's driving determination. Conversely, though, more recent children's fiction recognizes that a child's agency is limited, and works within more restricted parameters.

Fourth, we now recognize that much going on in the arts and in society in the 1960s was an aspect of postmodernism. Hoban showed more readiness to exploit such phenomena in writings subsequent to *The Mouse and His Child,* and hence they may seem foregrounded by their absence from this book. Kuznets remarks that the novel "is not particularly poststructuralist,"[17] but that seems to me symptomatic of the kind of anachronistic expectation I am concerned with here (the originary moment for American poststructuralism, after all, was the 1966 "The Languages of Criticism and the Sciences of Man" conference held at Johns Hopkins University). As the pervasive allusions to existentialism suggest, the novel is engaged with some philosophical ideas of the previous generation still current in the 1960s, and reflections of (firstly) structuralism do not appear in Hoban's work until about a decade later. I suggested earlier that *The Mouse and His Child* exhibited a modernist conception of subjectivity, but the argument can go further to say that in retrospect it is a modernist *book*—ultimately humanistic in ideology, potentially pessimistic in outlook, and concerned with problems of alienation, individuality, and subjectivity (the question "Who am I?" is also posed by a character in Virginia Woolf's *The Waves*).

These modernist elements in the novel, especially the tinge of pessimism conveyed through setting and situation, may also invite a rereading refracted through a subsequent genre that Hoban himself brilliantly used in his adult novel *Riddley Walker.* The first publication of *The Mouse and His Child* slightly precedes the emergence within children's fantasy fiction, in England, of the genre of "post-disaster" fiction with which it shares several traits. But instead of being set in an imagined

future when the world we know has been reduced to primitive technological and social forms through some cataclysmic disaster brought about
by twentieth-century people, Hoban's novel is set on the periphery of the
contemporary world, revolving around the modern wasteland of the
dump. Like post-disaster fiction, it involves a quest and journey, and depicts a reconstitution of society out of the fragments of what has been destroyed. In retrospect, then, we might thematically and structurally
associate, if not assimilate, the novel to the post-disaster genre with its
characteristic function of articulating a warning about destructive ten-
dencies in human behavior and advocating other possible behaviors.

The term "postmodernism" refers both to social practice and a body
of theory and, as the latter, is an analytical frame that postdates *The
Mouse and His Child.* Krips has demonstrated how the application of
other recent frames shifts the meaning of the book, in a study that in itself illustrates the relatively recent transition in literary (and critical) the-
matics from an emphasis on the angst of alienation to what Habermas
has described as the "one basic aesthetic experience" that concerns
the contemporary creative arts, "the increasing decentration of subjectivity."[18] This may influence academic interpretation of the novel when en-
capsulated within various poststructuralisms, but more characteristically
influences the readings of my (largely untheorizing) undergraduates as
they experience it as social ideology. The common answer to the question "What are we?" is that we are "individuals," an answer that, Mc-
Carthy argues, "has undermined any effective sense that culture really
matters as far as real people are concerned."[19] Hobsbawm agrees, suggesting that in the later twentieth century the individual has triumphed
over society and "the threads which in the past had woven human beings
into social textures" have been broken.[20] If the "language of desired grat-
ification" has replaced judgment and values, "the old moral vocabulary
of rights and duties, mutual obligations, sin and virtue, sacrifice, con-
science, rewards and penalties,"[21] how can readers possibly make sense
of a book such as *The Mouse and His Child,* which presupposes that social cooperation hinges on those values? When the seal accepts the offer
of mouse father and child to form a family with them she does so in what
now seems like a renunciation of individualism: "Her past life came back
to her all in a rush. . . . On the whole it had not been a bad life, and yet it
seemed a long and weary time that she had been alone of her kind in the
wide world."[22] As the slightly heightened, slightly archaic turn of phrase
here underscores, the experience of exile with its yearning to fashion
identity through intersubjective relationships grounded in community

and place (see further below) throws out a challenge to the cult of ultra-individualism.

These questions lead to my principle concern here, that is, with how global change affects the questions "What are we? and "Where are we?" There have been substantial changes in the past half century to how the world is politically structured and organized, and these changes are having an enormous impact on how ideas of nation and identity are formed, and, in turn, on how people respond to those ideas. Mouffe points to the ending of the Communist hegemony in eastern Europe as strongly symptomatic. For forty-five years, while the camps of the two superpowers, the United States and the Soviet Union, confronted one another in the "Cold War," the meaning of Western democracy was grounded on the differences between the two systems of governance.[23] The Rustins' contrast between the dump, "a fascist world of tyranny and sadism . . . a parody of industrial organization, in which Manny Rat exploits his mechanical ingenuity to enslave the windups and casts them aside when they are no longer productive," and its other, a society where characters care for each other,[24] is intertextually underpinned by an implicit evocation of cold war rhetoric.[25] And, of course, Hoban began work on the novel shortly after the Cuban missile crisis (1962) and completed it during the early years of the Vietnam War (1965–1975), so it would not be surprising if conventional hero ("us") and villain ("them") rhetoric influenced the formation of character and situation.

Mouffe argues that the identity of democracy has now been destabilized by the loss of its evil, monolithic opposite, and instead of a new and peaceful world order emerging—rather like the world of positive and peaceful coexistence envisaged at the close of *The Mouse and His Child*—identity is now being defined against "an internal enemy represented by immigrants, particularly those who differentiate themselves by their ethnic origin or religion."[26] Part of the allegorical thrust of *The Mouse and His Child* is to instantiate the ideal whereby throughout its history the United States has conceived of itself as plural, a society that welcomed peoples from all over the world and gave them the chance to prosper. The refusal of the mouse and his child at the end of the novel to teach "a success course" gestures fairly directly toward this ideology of selfhood in an ultimately benevolent and open society: "The whole secret of the thing, they insisted, was simply and at all costs to move steadily ahead."[27] Hence the extended family inhabiting "The Last Visible Dog" represents a range of "ethnicities"—the core, nuclear family of windups (two mice, an elephant, and a seal); and the four "uncles" (frog, rat, kingfisher, and bittern). Their community outreach program, so to speak, depicts a kind of microcosmic United States, ranging from the homeliness of the "Fashion Forum and Homemaker's Clinic"[28] to the global policeman functions of the frog's "Committee for the Surveillance of Territories and the Resolution of Inter-Field Enmities" (the war in Vietnam had not yet become a military, political, and moral quagmire, and the invasions of Grenada [1983] and Panama [1989] lay far in the future). Thus, while there is much to be said for the Rustins' proposition that "the trajectory of the windup mice . . . suggests a story of European immigrants to America,"[29] or that the story subtly conforms with a rags-to-riches metanarrative (with the hard-won wealth being spiritual rather than material), a perspective from the end of the century might regard much of the ideological underpinning as something not so readily to be taken for granted. The image of a small-town, ethnically and culturally integrated community looks more than a little shaky in relation, for example, to the subsequent theories of multiculturalism: the novel still depicts culture as controlled and mediated by a social elite, albeit a homey and benign one, though of course it would have been somewhat ahead of its time if it had envisaged the "profound restructuring and reconceptualization of the power relations between cultural communities"[30] at the core of multicultural theories.

Other aspects of global politics that have significant bearing on the meanings of *The Mouse and His Child* at century's close are, first, the end of the era of colonialism (which approximately coincides with the book's first publication) and with it the appearance of postcolonial literatures and an extensive body of theory dealing with both the experience and the literature, and, second, the huge waves of forced exile and migration that have blighted our era. The key issue here is the complex of selfhood, place ("territory"), and displacement played out in the windups' quest, an issue that the novel generally treats perceptively, although within the limitations of its situation within the modernist literature of exile. Edward Said, pondering on the paradox that exile has been transformed "into a potent, even enriching, motif of modern culture,"[31] protests that the scale of human displacement and mass immigration in the twentieth century negates the positive, humanistic deployment of this motif, and that "the views of exile in literature and, moreover, in religion obscure what is truly horrendous: that exile is irremediably secular and unbearably historical; that it is produced by human beings for other human beings; and that . . . it has torn millions of people from the nourishment of tradition, family and geography."[32] Since the Second World War, which displaced millions of people in Europe, fifteen million refugees were created by the decolonization of India, five million by the Korean War, and well over a million by the establishment of Israel.[33] As I write, a calculated program of "ethnic cleansing" is emptying Kosovo of its ethnic Albanians. At century's end it becomes more difficult to accept an analogy between exile and Adam and Eve's "fortunate fall" and its consequent process of development and growth,[34] though it is perhaps inevitable that children's fiction, with its deep preoccupation with subjectivity, will continue down this track. Nevertheless, we can look back and see that the tradition of the literature of exile has drawn Hoban into what Said refers to as the "modest refuge provided by subjectivity."[35] In focusing his tale of exile on the experiences of the windup mice, displaced first from the toy shop—representing a place, a community, and a heritage to which they innately belong—and then from their first place of exile, because the mouse child already feels a sense of loss and nostalgia for his original home (that is, a sense of exile), Hoban plays out the motif of loss and gain experienced in the search for identity.

In the next stage of their exile, their brief enslavement by Manny Rat, the windups are placed in the same position as colonial subjects. This construction pivots on their essential difference: as windups, they are not the "real thing" but function as other, and inferior, to that of which they are simulacra, and hence can be subjected to domination. The fact of "windupness" thus functions in the place of skin color as a key signifier of cultural and racial difference. This point is spelled out late in the novel, when Manny Rat, his long persecution of the windups approaching its end, finally realizes that "They were not unlike him . . . almost they were tin caricatures of himself,"[36] though their quasi-fur (the moss that covers them) is green. Manny then goes on to consider the irony of the role reversal that they have experienced, but the moment of recognition has also incorporated an explanation. In articulating the windups' similarity as caricature, he draws attention to their otherness and discloses the grounding motive of his long-maintained determination to destroy them, that is, their refusal to be a racialized, subordinated other. And one process that moves toward effacement of difference, their growth of "fur," reinscribes difference as color.

"We are born into relationships that are always based in a *place*. This form of primary and 'placeable' bonding is of quite fundamental human and natural importance," wrote Madan Sarup.[37] The mouse child's innate desire to be part of a nuclear family, to live in *that* doll house with two parents and a sister, is his response to his sense of dislocation and, as the focus of his "struggle of being against non-being," constitutes what Anthony Giddens calls "ontological reference points" created "as an integral aspect of 'going on' in the contexts of day-to-day life."[38] The relationship of identity to family and place gains sharper definition in the discussion with the shrews about the semantics of *territory:*[39]

> "A territory is your place," said the drummer boy. "It's where everything smells right. It's where you know the runways and the hideouts, night or day. It's what you fought for, or what your father fought for, and you feel all safe and strong there. It's the place where, when you fight, you win."
>
> "That's *your* territory," said the fifer. "Somebody else's territory is something else again. That's where you feel all sick and scared and want to run away, and that's where the other side mostly wins."
>
> The father walked in silence as a wave of shame swept over him. *What chance has anybody got without a territory!* he repeated to himself and he knew the little shrew was right.[40]

This is a key moment in the novel's unfolding teleology. Unlike the shrews, who for putatively economic reasons are at war with neighbors of the same species (that is, they are "ethnically identical"), the windups are projected into a war of liberation against an imperialistic oppressor. The justness of their cause is affirmed in various ways which preclude any suggestions that they might not have an inalienable right to the dolls' house: it is their "native" home, both because it is the site where they first came to consciousness and met the elephant and the seal (that is, it is their site of "placeable" bonding), and because it is a simulacrum of a house just as they are simulacra of animals; these arguments in turn invoke the cultural presupposition that each of us has, or should have, his or her proper place, a home; and finally, Manny Rat has both "preempted" the territory,[41] by misapplying the "law" of *terra nullius,* and has then made bad use of it (painting it black; employing "press gangs" and the slave labor of windups to renovate it). Some aspects of this argument are quite tricky, however. The historical argument can be readily adduced to justify wars of liberation, as often in the case of colonized countries, but has also been used to efface centuries of history (as in the case of Israel) or to fabricate history (as in the colonization of Tibet, East Timor, or Irian Jaya). The argument that a territory is being misgoverned and its people oppressed may seem to carry moral weight, but historically has masked other motives. It is crucial, then, that end-of-century readers of *The Mouse and His Child* recognize that the windups are first positioned as colonial subjects and then depicted as a displaced people seeking to (re-)constitute identity by a return to their site of "placeable" bonding. The novel offers sufficient cues for such a reading. It also tempers the comprehensiveness of the windups' ultimate victory, as the inflicting of "a defeat so crushing that every rat . . . will live in abject terror of us and leave us masters of that house . . . our territory"[42] is followed first by an uneasy détente with Manny Rat and finally by a community of culture and customs (though the unaddressed dark side of the victory is that the rest of the dump's rat population has now in turn been driven into exile). Despite various elements of unease in the outcome, the loose threads that might unravel it, the form does come close to anticipating what Mouffe describes as identity as a permanent process of hybridization and nomadization, and attachment to place is grounded not in "the exclusive type of ethnic nationalism" but in "a kind of 'civic' nationalism, upholding pluralism and democratic values," in which desire is for "multiplication and pluralization of allegiances and loyalties."[43]

So, then, what does *The Mouse and His Child* mean for readers at the close of the century? I have argued that a concentration on the question(s) of being, "Where are we?" and "What are we?", not only remains a vital way into the text but also enables readers to think dialogically about what these questions mean and have meant. I argue that a productive way to read the novel is to take on board the various ways social, political, and intellectual life over the past three decades, having changed ways of being and seeing, have inevitably changed the range of answers that might come to those questions. Hence we might read the novel historically, not in the sense of trying to determine the possible horizon of meaning at the end of the 1960s, but in the sense of how its themes and concerns remain embedded in the history of our era. Its insights and assumptions will no doubt seem uneven, according to how their significance in culture has been subsequently judged, but the dialogue might remind readers that not all change is progress, and reading a novel such as this might promote greater self-awareness and self-reflectiveness in deriving the answers for *now* to those central questions: What are we? . . . Where are we?

> It is only when we acknowledge that any identity is always relational and that it is defined in terms of difference that we are able to ask the crucial question: how can we fight the tendency towards exclusion?[44]

If we retain faith, as I do, in the power of literature to become part of our intersubjective creation of identity, then we can regard *The Mouse and His Child* with a great deal of optimism.

NOTES

[1]Margaret and Michael Rustin, *Narratives of Love and Loss* (London and New York: Verso, 1987), p. 183.

[2]Claude Leví-Strauss, *Tristes Tropiques,* (New York: Viking Penguin, 1992), p. 393.

[3]That self-consciousness is produced by apprehensions of what is exterior to the self, or by a consciousness of our own *otherness* in a world of others, enters discourses about subjectivity in a substantial way in the writing of George Herbert Mead (but goes back at least to Kant). See E. Doyle McCarthy, *Knowledge as Culture,* Chapter 4.

[4]Chantal Mouffe, "For a Politics of Nomadic Identity," in George Robertson et al. (eds.), *Travellers' Tales: Narratives of Home and Displacement* (London and New York: Routledge, 1994), pp. 106–07.

[5]Ibid., p. 108.

[6]For example, Rustin & Rustin, 1987; DeLuca, 1988; Krips, 1993; Kuznets, 1994.

[7]Valerie Krips, "Mistaken Identity: Russell Hoban's *The Mouse and His Child,*" *Children's Literature* 21 (1993): 97.

[8]Rustin and Rustin, p. 194.

[9]Lois Rostow Kuznets, *When Toys Come Alive* (New Haven and London: Yale University Press, 1994), p. 175.

[10]Krips, p. 98.

[11]E. Doyle McCarthy, *Knowledge as Culture: The New Sociology of Knowledge* (London and New York: Routledge, 1996, p. 74.

[12]Ibid.

[13]Russell Hoban, *The Mouse and His Child* (London and Boston: Faber and Faber, 1969), p. 126.

[14]John W. Meyer, "Myths of Socialization and Personality," in Thomas C. Heller et al. (eds.), *Reconstructing Individualism: Autonomy, Individuality, and the Self in Western Thought* (Stanford: Stanford University Press, 1986).

[15]Kuznets, p. 178.

[16]Eric Hobsbawm, *Age of Extremes: The Short Twentieth Century 1914–1991* (London: Michael Joseph, 1994), pp. 324–34.

[17]Kuznets, p. 176.

[18]Jürgen Habermas, *Moral Consciousness and Communicative Action.* Transl. Christian Lenhardt and Shierry Weber Nicholsen (Cambridge: Polity Press, 1990), p. 17.

[19]McCarthy, p. 81.

[20]Hobsbawm, *Age,* p. 334; and see his extensive discussion pp. 334–43.

[21]Ibid., p. 338.

[22]Hoban, *Mouse,* pp. 147–48.

[23]Mouffe, p. 105.

[24]Rustins, *Narratives,* p. 192.

[25]This is not to deny, however, that Manny signifies polysemously. Thus one

might also argue that his operations in the dump illustrate the dark side of capitalism (see Kuznets, p. 176), as indicated by the "mobster" schema evoked through protection rackets, bank robbery, and brutal murders. It would be productive to examine this aspect of *The Mouse and His Child* in comparison with such pretexts as George Orwell's *Animal Farm* and Bertold Brecht's plays *The Threepenny Opera* and *The Resistible Rise of Arturo Ui*.

[26]Mouffe, p. 106.

[27] Rustins, p. 195.

[28]As Kuznets remarks, p. 178, "obviously not a consciousness-raising group."

[29]Rustin and Rusin, pp. 186–87.

[30]Robert Stam and Ella Shohat, "Contested Histories: Eurocentrism, Multiculturalism, and the Media," in David Theo Goldberg (ed.), *Multiculturalism: A Critical Reader* (Oxford and Cambridge, Mass.: Blackwell, 1994), p. 299.

[31]Edward Said, "Reflections on Exile," in Russell Ferguson et al. (eds.), *Out There: Marginalization and Contemporary Culture* (New York: The New Museum of Contemporary Art, 1990), p. 357.

[32]Ibid., p. 358.

[33]Hobsbawm, p. 51.

[34]Joanne Lynn, "Threadbare Utopia: Hoban's Modern Pastoral," *Children's Literature Association Quarterly* 11, 1 (1986): 19–24.

[35]Said, p. 359.

[36]Hoban, p. 180.

[37]Madan Sarup, "Home and Identity," in George Robertson et al. (eds.), *Travellers' Tales: Narratives of Home and Displacement* (London and New York: Routledge, 1994), p. 97.

[38]Anthony Giddens. *Modernity and Self-Identity: Self and Society in the Late Modern Age* (Stanford: Stanford University Press, 1991), p. 48.

[39]Ibid., p. 58.

[40]Hoban, p. 58.

[41]Ibid., p. 145.

[42]Ibid., p. 148.

[43]Mouffe, pp. 110–11.

[44]Ibid., p. 109.

BIBLIOGRAPHY

Allison, Alida. "Living the Non-Mechanical Life: Russell Hoban's Metaphorical Wind-Up Toys." *Children's Literature in Education* 22 (1991) 3: 189–94.

Baumeister, Roy F. *Identity: Cultural Change and the Struggle for Self.* Oxford and New York: Oxford University Press, 1986.

De Luca, Geraldine. " 'A Condition of Complete Simplicity': The Toy as Child in *The Mouse and His Child.*" *Children's Literature in Education* 19 (1988): 211–21.

Giddens, Anthony. *Modernity and Self-Identity: Self and Society in the Late Modern Age.* Stanford: Stanford University Press, 1991.

Habermas, Jürgen. *Moral Consciousness and Communicative Action.* Transl. Christian Lenhardt and Shierry Weber Nicholsen. Cambridge: Polity Press, 1990.

Hoban, Russell. *The Mouse and His Child.* London and Boston: Faber and Faber, 1969.

Hobsbawm, Eric. *Age of Extremes: The Short Twentieth Century 1914–1991.* London: Michael Joseph, 1994.

Krips, Valerie. "Mistaken Identity: Russell Hoban's *Mouse and His Child.*" *Children's Literature* 21 (1993): 92–100.

Kuznets, Lois Rostow. *When Toys Come Alive.* New Haven and London: Yale University Press, 1994.

McCarthy, E. Doyle. *Knowledge as Culture: The New Sociology of Knowledge.* London and New York: Routledge, 1996.

Meyer, John W. "Myths of Socialization and Personality," in Thomas C. Heller et al. (eds.), *Reconstructing Individualism: Autonomy, Individuality, and the Self in Western Thought.* Stanford: Stanford University Press, 1986.

Mouffe, Chantal. "For a Politics of Nomadic Identity," in George Robertson et al. (eds.), *Travellers' Tales: Narratives of Home and Displacement.* London and New York: Routledge, 1994.

Rustin, Margaret, and Rustin, Michael. *Narratives of Love and Loss.* London and New York: Verso, 1987.

Said, Edward. "Reflections on Exile," in Russell Ferguson et al. (eds.), *Out There: Marginalization and Contemporary Culture.* New York: The New Museum of Contemporary Art, 1990.

Sarup, Madan. "Home and Identity," in George Robertson et al. (eds.), *Travellers' Tales: Narratives of Home and Displacement.* London and New York: Routledge, 1994.

Stam, Robert, and Shohat, Ella. "Contested Histories: Eurocentrism, Multiculturalism, and the Media," in David Theo Goldberg (ed.), *Multiculturalism: A Critical Reader.* Oxford and Cambridge, Mass.: Blackwell, 1994.

Toward Linearity
A Narrative Reading of
The Mouse and His Child

MARIA NIKOLAJEVA

The conventional way of investigating children's fiction is to divide it into "genres" or kinds: fantasy, adventure, family story, school story, animal story, toy story, and so on. Unless treated within a separate category of toy stories, *The Mouse and His Child* will most likely fall within the fantasy genre.[1] It has also been treated as an "animal fantasy."[2] Toy stories, as well as animal stories, are most often presented as genres specific for children's fiction, and indeed there are not many adult books with these motifs. Obviously, the Romantic belief in the child's unity with nature has contributed to the vast number of animal stories for children, while the nostalgic idealization of play accounts for the abundance of toys. In her study of toy stories, *When Toys Come Alive*, Lois Kuznets suggests several purposes that animated toys can serve in a children's narrative.[3] Anthropomorphic animals, whether they are indeed described as real animals or toys, represent children, while the stories often have the same narrative structure as regular adventure or family stories. "Giving . . . animals human qualities is to put them out of reach of inevitable fear, pain and death which is their natural lot. But the device also . . . makes humans small, giving them animal qualities and cutting them off from human miseries and frustrations, sexual pangs, jealousy, bitterness or revenge, so that these minute societies have the best of both worlds."[4] The common denominator is the innocent childhood.

Unlike John Stephens, who proclaims the distinction between fantasy and realism "the single most important generic distinction in children's fiction,"[5] I do not make such a distinction, instead treating all children's fiction as essentially "mythic" or at least non-mimetic. My

59

point of departure is the concept of literature as a symbolic depiction of a maturation process (initiation, rite of passage) rather than a strictly mimetic reflection of a concrete "reality." In looking at *The Mouse and His Child,* I am interested in the degree of accomplishment of initiation, grading from primary harmony (Arcadia, Paradise, Utopia, idyll) through different stages of departure toward either a successful or a failed mission, from childhood to adulthood.[6]

The view of children's fiction as a depiction of the maturation process is by no means a revolutionary idea; however, it can be used for different purposes. John Stephens remarks: "Arguably the most pervasive theme in children's fiction is the transition within the individual from infantile solipsism to maturing social awareness."[7] I am not specifically interested in ideology in the way Stephens presents it in his book, even though I am well aware, as he maintains, that all literary texts, and particularly children's texts, are ideologically manipulated. Instead, I will look at the narrative perspective and, through it, a possible authorial position and control.

The concept of childhood and innocence is often used to distinguish between children's fiction and adult fiction. Humphrey Carpenter suggests: "Adult fiction sets out to portray and explain the world as it really is; books for children present it as it should be."[8] This seems very doubtful to me. Neither category—children's or adult fiction—is a homogeneous group of texts. *The Mouse and His Child,* with its ambiguity and explicit violence, obviously does not portray the world "as it should be," but rather "as it really is," at least from an adult point of view. We cannot, however, completely ignore the way in which the concept of childhood is reflected in *The Mouse and His Child,* whether we regard the novel as written specifically for children or as the kind of literature that uses the child as an image and a symbol, notably the symbol of purity and innocence. It is a commonplace to point out that before Romanticism, children were hardly believed to be different from adults, and certainly not thought to be better than adults.[9] Anglo-Saxon criticism tends to focus on Blake and Wordsworth as sources of the new concept of childhood emerging in the early nineteenth century. The most essential issue is that childhood in the Romantic tradition is equal to idyll, while growing up is equal to loss of Paradise. However, the idea of the child as innocent continues to influence children's fiction long after mainstream literature has abandoned the Romantic views. Traditional children's fiction creates and preserves what may be called a pastoral convention. As Alison Lurie remarks: "It is assumed that the world of childhood is simpler and more natural than that of adults, and that children, though they may have faults, are essentially good or at least capable of becoming so."[10] As a consequence, children's fiction maintains a myth of a happy and innocent childhood, apparently based on adult writers' nostalgic memories and bitter insights about the impossibility of returning to the childhood idyll. This myth has little to do with the real status of child and childhood, and indeed Hoban's novel successfully subverts this myth. Yet the very texts that Lurie calls subversive ("sacred texts of childhood, whose authors had not forgotten what it was like to be a child"[11]) are examples of the most conservative children's fiction, aimed at preserving the young readers' illusion that childhood is a happy, secure, and, not least, an eternal state. It is from this point of departure I would like to take a closer view of *The Mouse and His Child.*

The cornerstone of my examination is the notion of linear and nonlinear time, originating from the works of the Romanian-born mythologist Mircea Eliade, especially his concept of sacred or cyclical time, *kairos,* as opposed to the measurable, linear time, *chronos.*[12] It is quite essential to my reading of Hoban's text that contemporary Western children's fiction is written from a philosophical viewpoint based on linear time, which has a beginning and an end, and recognizes every event in history as unique. The changes from circular to linear narrative in the novel appear in a new light against this background. An adult writer, like Hoban, who describes childhood as a cyclical, mythic state is apparently reconstructing the archaic form of time, perhaps subconsciously associating children with this form.

The insight about the linearity of time invokes the problems of growing up, aging and death. Since mythic time, *kairos,* is reversible, death in myth is transitory. The myth of the returning god, the most universal myth in all cultures, presupposes that death is always followed by resurrection. In children's fiction, the idea of the everlasting time is often expressed by the so-called iterative frequency: telling once about an event that has taken place several times or is taking place regularly.[13] The iterative is opposed to singulative, the most common narrative frequency in literature, when we assume that the described events take place only once. This idea is directly connected to the notion of *kairos* and *chronos,* as well as to pagan versus Judeo-Christian tradition.[14] The cyclical, repetitive character of events is the very essence of traditional children's fiction, which often has a purpose, conscious or subconscious, to create an illusion of a neverending paradise, for instance, the very last sentence of *The House at Pooh Corner:* "in that enchanted place on the top of the

Forest a little boy and his Bear will always be playing." The circular character of narrative time in archaic thought has been reflected in children's novels because the Arcadian time of individual childhood is similar to the mythical time of the childhood of humanity.

Viewing *The Mouse and His Child* as a description of a rite of passage, I am compelled to decide at which stage of initiation the characters are depicted and also in what direction the author is taking them. What may be called Utopian or prelapsarian children's fiction creates a myth of childhood by describing it as a myth of the Golden Age. The text most often associated with Arcadia (or Utopia, or pastoral) in the English-language children's fiction is Kenneth Grahame's *The Wind in the Willows*. According to some critics, it is based on "the tension between a longing for travel and 'nostalgia' (homesickness),"[15] while Lois Kuznets argues that the notion of nostalgia has a negative tone, whereas what we encounter in *The Wind in the Willows* is a positive sense of affection for a particular place, the love of home. Kuznets prefers to call this feeling "topophilia," and the setting *locus amoenus,* the felicitous space.[16] Most children's stories portraying all-toy societies will qualify as pastorals, especially doll house stories, such as Rumer Godden's *The Dolls' House* or Helen Clare's *Five Dolls in a House,* the doll house being a powerful, but ambivalent symbol of both security and imprisonment. Paradoxically, one of the most famous toy stories, *Winnie-the-Pooh,* treated by many critics as Arcadian,[17] also points clearly toward the drama of leaving home and the childhood idyll.[18]

While *The Mouse and His Child* has been treated as a pastoral narrative,[19] most of the features described in critical works as being typical of Utopian, Arcadian, or pastoral works[20] are conspicuously omitted from this novel, such as: a general sense of harmony and innocence; absence of the repressive aspects of civilization such as money, labor, law, or government; and most essential, absence of death and sexuality.

On the other hand, at least two indispensable pastoral aspects are undoubtedly prominent in *The Mouse and His Child.* The first is the rural setting, autonomous from the rest of the world, suggesting the character's closeness to nature; as Lois Kuznets expresses this, "Pastoral literature traditionally demonstrates the human need for the healing power of the simple, rural, or rustic, life by contrasting that life with the complex, urban, or urbane one."[21] The second is a special significance of home. However, if the tension of *The Wind in the Willows* is between the urge to explore the world and the need for the security of home, in *The Mouse and His Child* the long and painful journey is not brought about by curiosity, but is the result of persecution, "lack" in Vladimir Propp's fairy-tale terminology,[22] "split" in Jungian psychoanalytical terminology;[23] that is, something is imposed on the character and apprehended as tragic and traumatic. Yet, in structural as well as in psychoanalytical models, the journey is imperative if the character is to progress toward maturity. As Juliet Dusinberre points out: "The child unhampered by parents has become a commonplace of twentieth-century children's books."[24] The mythic, non-mimetic approach to literature makes adults superfluous. In her pastoral reading of *The Mouse and His Child,* Joanne Lynn confirms this view: "As the shepherd of traditional pastoral is removed by occupation from participation in urban life, so the child is barred by age, thus making him a natural agent for the modern writer who casts his evaluation of contemporary life in the form of fantasy for children."[25]

The more profound meaning of home, as of a pastoral setting at large, must be seen in the notion of the sacred place in archaic thought—the center of the universe.[26] Home in idyllic fiction is the foremost security. Home is where the protagonists belong and where they return to after any exploration of the outside world. "When home is a privileged place, . . . when home is where we ought, on the whole, to stay—we are probably dealing with a story for children. When home is the chief place from which we escape, either to grow up or . . . to remain innocent, then we are involved in a story for adolescents or adults."[27] The ambiguity of home in *The Mouse and His Child* prompts me to view the novel not only, and not primarily, as a pastoral, but rather as a quest, that is, a linear narrative that describes the breaking away from Utopia and innocence. Lois Kuznets mentions that time in *The Mouse and His Child* is measured in seasonal changes, which I regard as a typical feature of Arcadia, but she also mentions the linearity of a quest narrative.[28] This first stage of initiation offers the child a possibility to investigate the world in the form of play, a temporary departure from idyll and *kairos,* a short disruption of harmony. It can be described in Bakhtinian terms of carnival,[29] where the lowest in societal hierarchy—in the medieval carnival a fool, in children's books a child—is allowed to change places with the highest: a king, or an adult, and to become strong, rich, and brave, to perform heroic deeds, to have power. However, the very idea of carnival presupposes a temporal limitation. The child, who has been allowed to leave the security of home and experience breathtaking adventures, is taken back, and the established order is restored. This is what we sometimes call a happy ending, on the whole a dubious notion.[30] The time pattern of *The Mouse and His Child* interpreted as a carnivalesque text goes from *kairos* to *chronos* and back to *kairos,* the protagonists are brought back into the cyclical state, and no further progress toward adulthood is allowed.

The next step in initiation takes the character out of circularity and makes the process irreversible. Seemingly, this is what happens in *The Mouse and His Child,* where two main goals are successfully achieved: linear instead of circular movement, and self-winding. In terms of both structural and psychoanalytical approaches, we are dealing with accomplished initiation: in Vladimir Propp's model, the character has reached the enthronement (in his own castle high up over the rest of the world!), in a Jungian model, the reunion of the conscious and the unconscious, the achievement of the Self. However, a closer look of the novel reveals considerable contradictions.

The Mouse and His Child starts with a perfect image of childhood, a doll house, "splendid," "large and expensive," (2)[31] a felicitous space, a self-sufficient world existing wholly in the cyclical time:

> The dolls never set foot outside it. They had no need to; everything they could possibly want was there. . . . *Interminable*-weekend-guest dolls lay in all the guest room beds, sporting dolls played billiards in the billiard room, and a scholar doll in the library *never ceased* perusal of the book he held. . . . In the dining room, beneath a glittering chandelier, a party of lady and gentleman dolls sat *perpetually* around a table. . . . It was the elephant's *constant* delight to watch that tea party through the window. (4f; my emphasis).

The very idea of a windup toy is repetition, predestination, things going on forever. Another aspect is absence of change and free will. But the mouse child is at once anxious about linearity:

> "What happens when they buy you?" he asked her.
> "That, of course, is outside of my experience," said the elephant, "but I should think that one simply *goes out* into the world and does whatever one does. One dances or balances a ball, as the case may be."
> The doll house was bright and warm; the teapot gleamed upon the dazzling cloth. "I don't want to *go out* into the world," he said. (6; my emphasis)

The elephant has apparently been around for a while (why, we may ask? Her own self-righteous explanation—"I'm part of the establishment . . . this is my house,"—is not quite satisfactory), so she knows about Christmas and its rituals. Therefore she is displeased: "it is expected of this young mouse that he go out into the world with this father and dance in circles" (6). This statement contains a contradiction. Going out is linear, dancing in circles by definition circular; this contradiction sets up the whole movement of the book.

Moreover, looking at the preceding metafictional frame of the story, featuring the tramp, we notice that the circular-linear binarity is already there: "for a moment the man and the dog were the only two creatures on the street *not moving in a fixed direction*" (3; my emphasis). The tramp, dancing, is re-creating the circularity of childhood, while the Christmas shoppers, representing adulthood, are moving purposefully and consciously. The contrast child-adult is set in relation to circular-linear. The subsequent pages intensify, but also reverse the contraposition:

> The windup toys were not presents for the children; the grown-ups brought them down from the attic *every year* with the Christmas ornaments, and *every year* after Christmas they were packed away again. (8f; my emphasis)

The arcadian, static perfection of the toy shop scene in Chapter One is soon to be disrupted. Illus. Lillian Hoban.

This passage, more than any other, accentuates the adults' nostalgia. It is no coincidence that the novel starts at Christmas, the time of year when most adults get nostalgic. But for the toys, representing children, eternity does not seem attractive:

> The monkey complained of being made to play the *same* tune *over and over* on a cheap fiddle; the bird complained of having to peck at a bare floor; the rabbit complained that there was no meaning in his cymbals. And soon the mouse and his child complained of the futility of dancing in an *endless* circle that led nowhere. (9; my emphasis)

The regularity of the two mice dancing in circles is reminiscent of the wonderful mechanical toys in E. T. A. Hoffmann's *The Nutcracker:* after a while, the children ask their godfather to make the figures in the windup castle do something else, for instance, go out from another door, and when this proves impossible, they get bored. This is a perfect metaphor of the *adults'* idea of what children might enjoy—far from the real perception.

Thus if the mice were to dance Christmas after Christmas until the end of the world, there would be no story, no change, no growth. "So it was that four Christmases came and went, until there came a fifth Christmas that was different from the others" (9). This is a step away from circularity as well as from the iterative. There is a doll house among the new toys, a small one, but it reminds the mouse child of his lost dream, and he cries, breaking the rules and performing a singulative action. The expulsion from paradise follows immediately. The cat, disturbed by the sound of his crying, jumps on a table, knocks over a heavy vase, and the toy is smashed and thrown away. As always in children's fiction, this is an ambivalent episode: tragic, but necessary. All the further events of the novel are stations on the toys' linear (or rather pseudo-linear, as I will show) journey. Joanne Lynn, reading the novel as a pastoral, observes: "Each subsequent escape is toward a more pastoral scene—or so it seems."[32] Indeed, the pastoral elements of the novel are more than dubious.

The tramp, who throughout the novel acts a *deus ex machina* toward the toys, repairs them, but they cannot dance anymore; they go straight, the father pushing the child backward in front of him. This is of course physically a linear progress, but only a token one for the psychological dimension of the story. The mice cannot go further than one winding-up takes them, yet they like walking better than dancing in circles. When the fortune-telling frog tells the mice: "You have broken the circle . . . and a *straight line* of great force emerges. Follow it" (28; my emphasis), the author seems to be telling us that linearity is preferable. The idea is reinforced repeatedly in the text: "There is no going back," said the father; "we cannot dance in circles anymore" (34).

At the same time, the idea of circularity continues to be central. The mice watch the circle of nature: weasels eat shrews, the owl eats the weasels, and carries away Frog. Muskrat makes the mice more or less walk in a circle again, in his crazy endeavor to fell a tree. The enterprise can take a long time:

> *Day after day* the Muskrat and the mouse and his child worked at the tree. . . . While Muskrat's project trudged ahead, the life of the pond *went on as always.* . . . Above the mouse and his child *waxed and waned* the icy moon, and bright Sirius *kept* his track across the sky while they trod theirs below. (88f; my emphasis)

This is a temporary return to circularity and iterative. The unique feature of this novel is that its linear, measurable time, *chronos,* can be infinitely long, because the toys, unlike child protagonists, do not grow up, do not have to eat and are not in a hurry. Therefore, story time takes many years, which is normally impossible in a children's book. But it emphasizes the sense of *kairos,* the eternal mythical time.

Further wisdom is preached by Serpentina the turtle:

> This mud being like other mud, we may assume that other mud is like this mud, which is to say that one place is all places and all places are one. Thus by staying here we are at the same time everywhere, and there is obviously no place to go. Winding, therefore, is futile. (102)

Serpentina translates mythic time into mythic space. Amplified by the idea of infinity, expressed by the famous can of Bonzo Dog Food, this is a perfect philosophy of mythic existence.

The world the toys have come to is as far away as possible from childhood paradise: dump, commercialism, violence (Manny kills the donkey who is too feeble to work), crime (bank-robbing), hard work and exploitation, frauds (the fortune-teller), war (between shrews), incomprehensible art forms, pure-thought philosophy—definitely the world of adults.

The novel is also very much about eating and being eaten up—amazing, given the fact that the main characters do not eat at all and cannot be eaten, or, as the hawk remarks, they are not part of the balance of nature (119). Many critics have observed (and objected to) the violence in the animal world, especially the episode with shrews, weasels, and owl. However, all these violent deaths do not affect the toys, just as "adult" deaths in children's fiction most often do not affect child protagonists, but are rather a necessary part of the narrative, the extreme case of "absence" in Propp's sequence of functions. The mouse child is not frightened by being carried away by the hawk, since he knows that the predator will soon discover that they are inedible. Being inedible (as well as not having to eat) is a tragedy much worse than not being self-winding, although this aspect is deliberately circumvented by the author. Toys are not part of the circle of life and can never be. In a totally toy (idyllic, pastoral) world, it would not matter; but since there is a constant juxtaposition between nature and culture, flesh and tin, we cannot wholly neglect this aspect. In her study of toy stories, *When Toys Come Alive,* Lois Kuznets is especially preoccupied with the transformation of a toy into a living being and the sexual implication of this transformation, notably in *The Nutcracker, Pinocchio,* and *The Velveteen Rabbit.* Unlike the characters of these stories, the toy mice have no objective of becoming alive. They are inanimate (literally: lacking soul!) objects and so they remain, even though the father says: "We aren't toys any more. . . . Toys are to be played with, and we aren't" (131).

Let us consider this absence of transformation. According to Mircea Eliade, there are three major components in archaic man's initiation: the sacred, death, and sexuality.[33] If we assume that the state of cyclical time, as childhood is described, introduces the protagonist to the sacred, then the following stages of initiation must involve death and procreation, two most essential aspects of human existence. As soon as children's fiction departs from the innocent, idyllic state, the initiation into these two mysteries becomes inevitable. Alison Lurie remarks: "Of the three principal preoccupations of adult fiction—sex, money, and death—the first is absent from the classic children's literature and the other two either absent or much muted."[34] In Hoban's novel, commercialism, death, and sexuality become manifest, and death even pervasive. Lurie continues: "Although there are some interesting exceptions, even the most subversive of contemporary children's books usually follow these conventions. They portray an ideal world of perfectible beings, free of the necessity for survival and reproduction: not only a pastoral, but a paradisal universe—for without sex and death, humans may become as angels."[35] I see this statement as an example of the most dangerous fallacy in evaluation of children's fiction: viewing it as a homogeneous, static corpus of texts. What Lurie names cautiously as "some interesting exceptions" is indeed a vast number of texts, which in some way or other take a radical departure from the cyclical time, in many cases, such as *The Mouse and His Child,* bringing children's fiction to its antithesis. A number of the world's best children's novels are focused on the child's intuitive reluctance to grow up and take the first step toward initiation: *Peter Pan, The Little Prince, Pippi Longstocking,* the *Moomin* books, and many more. Most probably, these books reflect the adult writers' traumatic memories of growing up. Therefore the writers allow their characters to solve this problem in different manners; Peter Pan by moving to a place where he does not have to grow up; Pippi by taking a magical pill; Moomintroll's childish dependence on his mamma is suspended in later sequels, where the everlasting summer idyll is slowly supplanted by autumn and change. The discovery of inevitable growth is among the most traumatic in a child's life, maybe after the baby's discovery that it does not constitute a whole with its mother. Changes and the necessity to take the first step toward initiation, toward adulthood, are a natural central theme of all children's fiction, but this theme acquires a distinctive tone in *The Mouse and His Child.*

The notion of death is closely connected with sexuality. The characters in Arcadian children's fiction, whether they are humans or animals, are depicted at the pre-pubescent stage, the stage of innocence, where their sexual identity has not yet been discovered. Moreover, they are forever conserved in this stage and have neither wish nor possibility of evolving. Therefore, there is no growing up, no maturation, no aging, and subsequently no death. In *The Wind in the Willows,* the author omits "all aspects of the heroic life that might cause strife and pain and eventually death."[36] Similarly, the characters "will never have their Arcadia destroyed by the passion or treachery of love."[37] The perfect balance of the world has the function of eliminating desire.

In *The Mouse and His Child,* desire—spiritual as well as sexual— and pain constitute the primary motive power. However, since Hoban's protagonists are toys, and he chooses not to let them have the goal of coming alive, he introduces a special form of death for them, which they go through, as ritual prescribes, three times. Since death, for toys, unlike all other deaths in the story, is reversible, they are reborn, like the returning gods, described in one of Eliade's major works. In her most illuminating essay, Valerie Krips notes that after each destruction and resurrection, the mouse and his child reemerge with new qualities: first they go straight instead of dancing in circles, after the second remaking they are separated from each other, and finally they are made self-winding, or so it seems. Krips maintains in her Lacanian reading that they acquire a new identity each time, which she views as a problem, since the identity that the mouse child has discovered in his reflection in the tin can— going through the "mirror stage"—is no longer there.[38] For me the question is less relevant since the toys always remain essentially what they are. Therefore they seek their paradise in the company of other toys, and in the constrained world of the doll house.

The novel invites a Jungian interpretation with its many symbols and images, descents and reemergence, the Dante-like wandering through the circles of Inferno, Manny Rat as the dark Shadow, the seal as Anima, the three uncles as the Wise Old Men, the guides, the helpers, the three clever adults, without whose assistance initiation is not possible. Ironically, but quite consistent with the Jungian model, escaping from Manny Rat the mice get farther away from the elephant, one of the objects of their quest. The Shadow has to be met face to face, which also happens in the end. The most problematic aspect is that according to Jung and his disciples, the final goal of the process of individuation is to become whole, while the two mice are instead separated. Does this mean that individuation has failed?

For a Jungian critic, the essential question is who is going through individuation. What is the implication of a father and child stuck together? Lois Kuznets views the mouse child as the protagonist since it is a children's story,[39] which for me is a circular argument. Actually, the title itself emphasizes the adult rather than the child. Instead, I would suggest the notion of a collective hero. Significantly, collective protagonists are a typical feature of Arcadian children's novels, whether these portray animals, toys, or human beings (*The Wind in the Willows, Winnie-the-Pooh,* and *Little Women,* respectively), while they rarely appear in adult fiction, outside the purely experimental prose. There may be several reasons for this. Collective protagonists supply an object of identification to the readers of both genders and of different ages. Collective characters may be used to represent more palpably different aspects of human nature: for instance, one child (or animal or toy representing a child) in a group may be presented as greedy and selfish, another as carefree and irresponsible, and so on, which we see clearly in the three examples mentioned earlier. Basically, a collective protagonist in children's fiction is an artistic device used for pedagogical purposes.

In *The Mouse and His Child* we meet a collective protagonist in an unusual combination of child and adult. Further, the focalizing pattern of the narrative suggests the notion of intersubjectivity, an interplay and dialogue between two individual and widely diverse subjects. What do the mice represent? Does the child bring back childhood to the adult—a motif observed by many critics of Arcadian fiction, for instance, in *The Secret Garden* or *Anne of Green Gables*?

During the journey, the father is looking forward, while the son is looking backward, although logically it should be the other way around. Apparently, the mouse child does not wish to grow up and become independent, but on the contrary seeks to go back to the security of his early childhood, symbolized by the doll house. His faith in this paradise is unshakable:

> He had never been so happy, had never felt so lucky. He had never doubted that he would make his dream come true, and all the remaining difficulties shrank before him now—the doll house and the seal would certainly be found, the territory won, and he should have his mama. (95)

The father, forced to look forward, is much more skeptical about the future: "Our motor is in me. He fills the empty space inside himself with foolish dreams that cannot possibly come true" (35). The father is repeatedly prepared to give up. When the child suggests looking for the elephant, the seal, and the doll house, the father's immediate reaction is: "the whole idea of such a quest is impossible" (34). By contrast, the child never loses hope. But it is not hope for future, but hope to return to the mythic past, which the father, an adult, does not believe in. His statement above, which at first reading will be most certainly apprehended as the impossibility to find the concrete objects of the quest—the elephant, the seal, and the doll house—may be equally interpreted as the impossibility to recover the childhood idyll, a temporal rather than spatial quest.

Interestingly enough, the little we are allowed to share of the elephant's point of view reveals a striking similarity with the mouse child's dreams:

> How she had suffered! She who had thought herself a lady of property, secure in her high place—she had been sold like any common toy . . . she had endured what toys endure. She had been smeared with jam and worried by the dog, she had been sat upon, and she had been dropped. She had been made to pull wagons, had been shot at by toy cannons, and had been left out in the rain until her works had rusted fast and she was thrown away. Still she endured, and deep within her tin there

blazed a spirit that would not be quenched. Though the heavens should fall, she knew that justice one day would be done. (29f)

Reading this passage intersubjectively, we may notice that the female and the child's perception of events are equally circular and archaic, full of hope and resilience, in sharp contrast with the male (as well as adult) linear, irreversible view, leading to complete defeatism. Much in accordance with Jacques Lacan's or Julia Kristeva's ideas, the little child is longing for a symbiosis with his mother, while he is physically— and forcibly—attached to his father. Obviously, the child is still genderless, although the personal pronoun "he" is used about him; and he is not yet mature enough, and will never be, within the story, to acknowledge his gender identity.

However, when the father sees the seal, the elephant, and the house, after his second rebirth, he is prepared to fight for his territory. In a way, the father wholly takes over the child's role as protagonist (much like Colin's father at the end of *The Secret Garden*), because now he also wants to retreat into the mythical world of childhood. Paradoxically, this wish is combined with a clear erotic desire:

> The elephant was shabby and pathetic; her looks were gone, departed with the ear, the eye, the purple headcloth and her plush. The father saw all that, and yet saw nothing of it; some brightness in her, some temper finer than the newest tin, some steadfast beauty smote and dazzled him. He wished that he might shelter and protect her. . . . He fell in love. (95f)

The erotic subtext of the novel is obvious, especially in the rivalry between the mouse father and Manny Rat, and in the elephant's open aversion for Manny, who has, we might say, raped her. Through the father, initiation into sexuality is performed, thus completing the three stages of initiation in Eliade's model. However, the intersubjective construction of the protagonist allows the author to subdue the sexual undertones by shifting the focus to the child and his need of a mother, rather than the father's need of a sexual partner. The two aspects of desire are well-balanced in the story: "'Are you my mama?' asked the child. He had no idea what a mama might be, but he knew at once that he needed one badly" (7). But the father says, hearing about the child's dreams: "I cannot imagine myself being cozy with that elephant" (34).

After the reunion, the idea of self-winding—linearity—is suddenly overshadowed by the idea of home, security, peace, idyll, circularity. The notion of home is reinforced by the notion of territory that the toy mice learn from the war of the shrews (45). The recovery of the doll house is the foremost symbol of the restoration of paradise: "The house was *firmly* nailed to the platform" (156; my emphasis); "/ . . . / phoenixlike, the place seemed reborn of itself" (157). However, the author hurries to admit that the restoration is only partial:

> The doll house would never again be what it once had been; its stateli-
> ness and beauty were long gone, but something new and different
> emerged from the concerned efforts of the little family. (157)

The end of the novel depicts a final acceptance of a paradise sub-stantially inferior to the initial dream. The setting is still the dump. The house and its inhabitants are worn out and shabby. The flow of time is ir-reversible. Joanne Lynn maintains that Hoban pictures a sort of compro-mise of Utopia, "accepting the limitations of human nature," yet a "place in which human society rises above the junkheap of technological civi-lization and creates from however disparate material and human capaci-ties a world that glows with possibilities of the worth of human existence."[40] In terms of social or even psychological values, it may be true. In terms of restoring archaic, mythic time, the ending shows the fu-tility of every attempt to re-create Utopia.

Manny Rat makes the mice self-winding, which turns out only to mean going on forever without change: "self-windingly and inter-minably walking" (167). This may be seen as Manny's last attempt at re-venge. On the other hand, reforming Manny is also the final reconstruction of Eden to an adult, where Manny's function duplicates the mouse father. Since Manny is harmless—symbolically castrated—this doubling reflects the asexual nature of the father's union with the elephant, perfectly in concordance with the idea of restored innocence.

When the winding stops, the mice only feel relieved. The last pages of the novel bring back the iterative, stretching into the eternal future: an-nual drama festival, yearly Deep Thought Symposium, and the recurrent flow of guests at the hotel: "They could stop here *every year*," said the child, "flying north and flying south" (174; my emphasis). The eternal time is emphasized over and over again: "Your fortune has been made," said Frog, "and needs no more telling" (181). That is, the toys have no future, they are dead. The mouse child will forever be a child. Paradise is regained. The child creates this paradise according to his childish visions, even though they challenge common sense: his father marries the elephant, the seal becomes his sister. This is also communal rather than individual happiness, involving both animals and toys, which is a dubious message from the author. A very important question remains unanswered at the closure of the book: what happens to the animals, the kind uncles, who, being mortal, cannot possibly become part of this eternity? Are they disposed of when no longer needed? Apparently, the little child's vision cannot reach that far. The marriage oath of the mouse father and the elephant is an excellent illustration of the toy perspective: "Winding and unwinding . . . whole or broken, bright or rusty, until the end of your tin" (153).

The mouse child's dream of paradise is expressed by the iterative at the beginning: "will you sing to me *all the time*? And can we all *stay* here together and live in the beautiful house where the party *is on* and not go out into the world?" (7; my emphasis). The elephant explains that it is impossible. In the end, they seem to have achieved the impossible, but it is an illusion. There is no regular happy ending to the story, no reward for suffering, no punishment for the villains. It is more like the story of the Steadfast Tin Soldier, who, after a long time of trials, is united with his beloved ballerina in death.

The tramp's farewell to the toys: "Be happy" must be viewed as the narrator's comment. Is the essential component of the fairy-tale formula "happy ever after," with all its implications, truncated? As Lois Kuznets remarks, "Be happy" makes no promises about the future. Kuznets goes on: "And this relatively happy ending acknowledges the necessity of endless remaking, virtual recycling of the world to meet human desires. Hoban uses his toy narrative to mirror and exploit the uncertainties of human life."[41] I would add—adult life.

This brings me finally to the discussion of the adult position and the authorial control in the novel. The transformation of cyclical patterns into linear ones necessarily involves a change in narrative discourse. While an archaic narrative presupposes a single subject in unity with the world, in *The Mouse and His Child* this unity is disturbed, resulting, as already shown, in intersubjectivity and polyphony (multivoicedness), and making the narrator highly unreliable. As Linda Hutcheon remarks, contemporary literature "refuses the omniscience and omnipresence of the third person and engages instead in a dialogue between a narrative voice . . . and a projected reader."[42] This narrative mode creates, as well as reflects, a chaotic, postlapsarian view of the world in *The Mouse and His Child,* as opposed to the ordered, structured universe of the archaic mind, as manifested in traditional (pastoral) children's fiction.

As already hinted, the tramp may be interpreted as a personification of a covert narrator. Not only does he appear in crucial situations, repairing the toy mice and setting them off on their journey, but his appearance in the beginning and the end of the novel suggests a narrative frame (emphasized by the two almost identical vignettes of his face), in which the toys' quest is the product of the tramp's imagination. In the beginning, after dancing in circles in the street, "The tramp stopped with empty arms upraised" (3). In this clearly metafictional scene, he is imitating the mouse father, holding the child in his upraised arms; however, the "child" is not there. The child—as well as the story—is still to be created. Is the adult author projecting his nostalgic feelings about his own childhood onto the presumptive narrator? However, the ending is rather a disillusioned adult's rational contemplation of his own inevitable fate. We can see the first scene as a flashback in the frame and the ending as its actual time; or the other way around, the beginning as "now" and the ending as a pessimistic vision. In any case, we are dealing with an adult perception, and "Be happy," echoing the earlier "Be tramps," is a self-ironic comment.

The Mouse and His Child is written, like all children's fiction, whatever the authors themselves may say, by an adult for young readers. Consequently the notion of childhood and the ideas about growing, procreation, and death that we meet in the novel reflect an adult's views, which may or may not correspond to the real status of children and childhood in society. The central concept of many children's books, including *The Mouse and His Child,* seems to be that childhood is something irretrievably lost for adults, and this lost Arcadia can be restored only in fiction. With this premise, children's fiction is not, as it is commonly defined, literature addressed to children, but a sort of storytelling therapy for frustrated adults. The central theme in children's fiction may be seen as the irreversibility of time and the high price any individual who defies it must pay. In adult fiction, *The Picture of Dorian Gray* takes up the same theme.

Humphrey Carpenter maintains in his study that the Golden Age of children's literature is over with World War I,[43] by which he probably means the waning dominance of Arcadian-type books. *The Mouse and His Child,* appearing in 1967, reflects the persistent tendency to depict childhood as Arcadia, the tendency in which children's novels try to preserve children in the state of innocence and thus present childhood as a neverending paradise. "Be happy" is the message.

Among the many critics who interrogate the essence of children's literature, Jacqueline Rose has observed that "writing for children can contribute to prolonging or preserving—not only for the child but also for us—values which are constantly on the verge of collapse. The child, therefore, is innocent and can restore that innocence to us."[44] Rose's statement echoes Fred Inglis: "The best children's books reawaken our innocence."[45] Kimberley Reynolds speaks of childhood as adult fantasy.[46] The mythical, imaginary child of children's fiction "restores" the adult to a more natural state. Is this the true purpose of children's fiction? And is this what Hoban is doing in *The Mouse and His Child*?

Perry Nodelman states in an essay entitled "Progressive Utopia, or How to Grow Up without Growing Up" that while the assumption that children think, see, and feel differently helps us adults to assess children, it creates problems, in that it separates us from our past selves and makes children into strangers. Childhood becomes "agonizingly enticing *to us*" and "forces *us* into a fruitless nostalgia."[47] Nodelman maintains, however, that in the so-called novels of Progressive Utopia, we can experience childhood again: "It is the secret desire of grownups to be children again that makes these novels appealing to them. . . . a central concern of children's literature, no matter where or when it was written—how to grow up, as one inevitably must, without losing the virtues and delights of childhood."[48]

While Nodelman speaks of Progressive Utopia, I cannot but call it, on the contrary, regressive or even conservative. A child who does not grow up is conserved in his or her childhood, while an adult who goes back to the innocence of childhood is undoubtedly regressing, mentally and morally. If children's fiction has as its main function the fulfillment of adults' secret desires, why do we, as scholars, hypocritically call it "children's fiction"? On the other hand, if children's fiction is indeed intended for children, mustn't we, as mediators, acknowledge it as a powerful socialization tool used to make children believe that they are happier than adults? Aren't we then lying to them instead of to each other?

The fact that *The Mouse and His Child* is treated so radically differently by different scholars reveals the vague generic status of the novel. According to Joanne Lynn, most critics find the novel "disturbing."[49] She also notes that most critics give up when it comes to a close reading and decoding the message of the novel. While texts that are purely idyllic or purely carnivalesque, that is, either preserving children in a state of innocence or bringing them successfully back to it, are treated in critical studies unproblematically as "children's fiction," many texts showing a deviation from these patterns or interrogating them are immediately labeled as "in actual fact not books for children," including *The Mouse and His Child.*

As always when speaking of children's fiction we are dealing with double set of codes. Unlike adult fiction, in children's fiction we have double narratees and double implied readers. An adult writer evoking an adult co-reader's nostalgia is merely one aspect. Hopefully, the child reader is targeted as well, although in a different manner. With my approach, the essential difference is the stage of initiation described in the text. In *The Mouse and His Child,* despite the seemingly linear progress, the linear development rounds back into the circular pattern, at the same time accentuating that the initial Utopia can never be restored.

NOTES

[1]See, e.g., studies so diverse in the year of publication, purpose, and structure as Margery Fisher, *Intent upon Reading. A Critical Appraisal of Modern Fiction for Children* (Leicester: Brockhampton, 1964) and Perry Nodelman, *The Pleasures of Children's Literature* (New York: Longman, 1992).

[2]For example, Margaret J. Blount, *Animal Land. The Creatures of Children's Fiction* (New York: Morrow, 1974).

[3]Lois Kuznets, *When Toys Come Alive. Narratives of Animation, Metamorphosis and Development* (New Haven: Yale University Press, 1994), p. 2. The metaphorical interpretation of the toys in *The Mouse and His Child* is also discussed in Alida Allison, "Living the Non-Mechanical Life: Russell Hoban's Metaphorical Wind-Up Toys," *Children's Literature in Education* 22 (1991) 3: 189–94; Geraldine DeLuca, "'A Condition of Complete Simplicity': The Toy as Child in *The Mouse and His Child,*" *Children's Literature in Education* 19 (1988) 4: 211–21.

[4]Blount, p. 131f.

[5]John Stephens, *Language and Ideology in Children's Fiction* (London: Longman, 1992), p. 7.

[6]For a more detailed presentation of this notion see Maria Nikolajeva, "Literature as a Rite of Passage: A New Look at Genres," *Compar(a)ison* 2 (1995): 117–29.

[7]Stephens, p. 3.

[8]Humphrey Carpenter, *Secret Gardens. The Golden Age of Children's Literature* (London: Unwin Hyman, 1985), p. 1.

[9]See, e.g., Peter Coveney, *The Image of Childhood. The Individual and Society: A Study of the Theme in English Literature* (Harmondsworth: Penguin, 1967), pp. 52–90.

[10]Alison Lurie, *Don't Tell the Grownups. Subversive Children's Literature* (Boston: Little, Brown, 1990), p. xiii.

[11]Lurie, p. x.

[12]See Mircea Eliade, *The Myth of the Eternal Return* (London: Rutledge & Kegan Paul, 1955). For Eliade, myth describes events taking place in *kairos,* the primordeal time, and profane acts have meaning only as long as they deliberately repeat earlier sacred acts. The word *kairos* is used in the famous passage on time in Ecclesiastes 3:1–8. One of the few studies of children's fiction that makes use of the notion of *kairos* is Sarah M. Smedman, "Springs of Hope: Recovery of Primordeal Time in "Mythic" Novels for Young Readers," *Children's Literature* 16 (1988): 91–107.

[13]For a detailed discussion on the essence and implications of the iterative frequency see Gérard Genette, *Narrative Discourse. An Essay in Method* (Ithaca, NY: Cornell University Press, 1980), pp. 113–27. Notably, Genette maintains that the iterative is unusual in literature, and perhaps even unique for Marcel Proust, while it is indeed a most common temporal device in children's fiction.

[14]In archaic languages, there are often special grammatical categories to express the iterative nature of events, approximately "have always been doing." Modern languages, lacking the need to express the mode, have lost this grammatical category; they have retained the iterative meaning partially in some modalities, such as the English "he used to" or "he would," which, however, are firmly fixed in the past, while the iterative includes the present or, in fact, eliminates the actual, chronological sequence of time. Lexical indications of the iterative in modern languages are, for instance, "always," "sometimes," "often," "occasionally," "every day," etc. Often the iterative is implied rather than expressed directly.

[15]Tony Watkins, "Making a Break for the Real England: The River-Bankers Revisited," *Children's Literature Association Quarterly* 9 (1984) 1: 34.

[16]Lois Kuznets, "Toad Hall Revisited," *Children's Literature* 7 (1978): 115–28. Kuznets refers to Gaston Bachilard's study *The Poetics of Space;* the notion of *locus amoenus* comes originally from Ernst Robert Curtius's classical work *Europäische Literatur und lateinische Mittelalter.*

[17]Carpenter; Lurie; Peter Hunt, "Winnie-the-Pooh and Domestic Fantasy," in *Stories and Society. Children's Literature in Its Social Context,* ed. Dennis Butts (London: Macmillan, 1992), pp. 112–24; Kuznets 1994.

[18]cf. Roger Sale, *Fairy Tales and After* (Cambridge: Cambridge University Press, 1978), suggesting that the *Pooh* books "are essentially about the fact that Christopher Robin is too old to play with toy bears" (17).

[19]See, e.g., Joanne Lynn, "Threadbare Utopia: Hoban's Modern Pastoral," *Children's Literature Association Quarterly* 11 (1986) 1: 19–24.

[20]For example, Sale; Fred Inglis, *The Promise of Happiness. The Value and Meaning in Children's Fiction* (Cambridge: Cambridge University Press, 1981); Roderick McGillis, "Utopian Hopes: Criticism Beyond Itself," *Children's Liter-*

ature Association Quarterly 9 (1984–85) 4: 184–86; Carpenter; Peter Hunt, *The Wind in the Willows: A Fragmented Arcadia* (New York: Twayne, 1994).

[21]Lois Kuznets, "The Fresh-Air Kids, or Some Contemporary Versions of Pastoral," *Children's Literature* 11 (1983): 156–68.

[22]Vladimir Propp, *Morphology of the Folktale* (Austin: University of Texas Press, 1968).

[23]See, e.g., Marie-Louise von Franz, "The Process of Individuation," in ed. C. G. Jung, *Man and His Symbols* (London: Aldus, 1964), pp. 160–229.

[24]Juliet Dusinberre, *Alice to the Lighthouse. Children's Books and Radical Experiments in Art* (London: Macmillan, 1987): 90.

[25]Lynn, p. 20.

[26]cf. Eliade, p. 12ff.

[27]Christopher Clausen, "Home and Away in Children's Fiction," *Children's Literature* 10 (1982): 143.

[28]Kuznets, 1994, p. 176.

[29]Mikhail Bakhtin, *Rabelais and His World* (Cambridge, MA: MIT Press, 1968).

[30]cf. Walter Pape, "Happy Endings in a World of Misery: A Literary Convention between Social Constraints and Utopia in Children's and Adult Literature," *Poetics Today* 13 (1992) 1: 179–96.

[31]Page references are from Russell Hoban, *The Mouse and His Child* (New York: Harper, 1967).

[32]Lynn, p. 21.

[33]Mircea Eliade, *The Sacred and the Profane* (New York: Harper & Row, 1961).

[34]Lurie, p. xiv.

[35]Lurie, p. xivf.

[36]Geraldine Poss, "An Epic in Arcadia: The Pastoral World of *The Wind in the Willows*," *Children's Literature* 4 (1975): 83.

[37]Poss, p. 85.

[38]Valerie Krips, "Mistaken Identity: Russell Hoban's *The Mouse and His Child*," *Children's Literature* 21 (1993): 92–100.

[39]Kuznets, 1994, p. 171.

[40]Lynn, p. 23.

[41]Kuznets, 1994, p. 176.

[42]Linda Hutcheon, *A Poetics of Postmodernism. History, Theory, Fiction* (New York: Routledge, 1988), p. 10.

[43]Carpenter, p. 210.

[44]Jacqueline Rose, *The Case of Peter Pan, or The Impossibility of Children's Fiction* (London: Macmillan, 1984), p. 44.

[45]Inglis, p. 8.

[46]Kimberley Reynolds, *Children's Literature in the 1890s and the 1990s* (Plymouth: Northcote House, 1994), pp. 17–27.

[47]Perry Nodelman, "Progressive Utopia, or How to Grow Up without Growing Up." In *Proceedings of the 6th Annual Conference of ChLA,* ed. Priscilla A. Ord (Villanova, PA: Villanova University Press, 1980):153; my emphasis.

[48]Nodelman, p. 154.

[49]Lynn, p. 19. To the critics mentioned by Lynn and to those I have already discussed in my essay I can add, e.g., Joan Bowers, "The Fantasy World of Russell Hoban," *Children's Literature* 8 (1980): 80–96; Margaret and Michael Rustin, *Narratives of Love and Loss: Studies in Modern Children's Fiction* (London: Verso, 1987).

BIBLIOGRAPHY

Hunt, Peter. *The Wind in the Willows: A Fragmented Arcadia.* New York: Twayne, 1994.

———. "Winnie-the-Pooh and Domestic Fantasy," in *Stories and Society. Children's Literature in Its Social Context,* edited by Dennis Butts. London: Macmillan, 1992. 112–24.

Hutcheon, Linda. *A Poetics of Postmodernism. History, Theory, Fiction.* New York: Routledge, 1988.

Inglis, Fred. *The Promise of Happiness. The Value and Meaning in Children's Fiction.* Cambridge: Cambridge University Press, 1981.

Krips, Valerie. "Mistaken Identity: Russell Hoban's *The Mouse and His Child. Children's Literature* 21 (1993): 92–100.

Kuznets, Lois. "The Fresh-Air Kids, or Some Contemporary Versions of Pastoral." *Children's Literature* 11 (1983): 156–68.

———. "Toad Hall Revisited." *Children's Literature* 7 (1978): 115–28.

———. *When Toys Come Alive. Narratives of Animation, Metamorphosis and Development.* New Haven: Yale University Press, 1994.

Lurie, Alison. *Don't Tell the Grownups. Subversive Children's Literature.* Boston: Little, Brown, 1990.

Lynn, Joanne. "Threadbare Utopia: Hoban's Modern Pastoral." *Children's Literature Association Quarterly* 11 (1986) 1: 19–24.

McGillis, Roderick. "Utopian Hopes: Criticism Beyond Itself." *Children's Literature Association Quarterly* 9 (1984–85) 4: 184–86.

Nikolajeva, Maria. "Literature as a Rite of Passage: A New Look at Genres." *Compar(a)ison* 2 (1995): 117–129.

Nodelman, Perry. *The Pleasures of Children's Literature.* New York: Longman, 1992.

———. "Progressive Utopia, or How to Grow Up without Growing Up." In *Proceedings of the 6th Annual Conference of ChLA,* edited by Priscilla A. Ord. Villanova, PA: Villanova University Press, 1980. pp. 146–54.

Pape, Walter. "Happy Endings in a World of Misery: A Literary Convention between Social Constraints and Utopia in Children's and Adult Literature." *Poetics Today* 13 (1992) 1: 179–96.

Poss, Geraldine. "An Epic in Arcadia: The Pastoral World of *The Wind in the Willows.*" *Children's Literature* 4 (1975): 80–90.

Propp, Vladimir. *Morphology of the Folktale.* Austin: University of Texas Press, 1968.

Reynolds, Kimberley. *Children's Literature in the 1890s and the 1990s.* Plymouth: Northcote House, 1994.

Rose, Jacqueline. *The Case of Peter Pan, or The Impossibility of Children's Fiction.* London: Macmillan, 1984.

Rustin, Margaret, and Rustin, Michael. *Narratives of Love and Loss. Studies in Modern Children's Fiction.* London: Verso, 1987.

Sale, Roger. *Fairy Tales and After.* Cambridge: Cambridge University Press, 1978.

Smedman, M. Sarah. "Springs of Hope: Recovery of Primordeal Time in "Mythic" Novels for Young Readers." *Children's Literature* 16 (1988): 91–107.

Stephens, John. *Language and Ideology in Children's Fiction.* London: Longman, 1992.

Watkins, Tony. "Making a Break for the Real England: The River-Bankers Revisited." *Children's Literature Association Quarterly* 9 (1984) 1: 34–35.

Spring and Fall to a Young (Mouse) Child

A Blakean Reading of *The Mouse and His Child*

JAMES ADDISON

Although a number of recent critics have posited theories to account for the unsettling nature of Hoban's riddling 1967 text, none has seemed entirely satisfactory. For one thing, the readings advanced by Valerie Krips, for example, in "Mistaken Identity: Russell Hoban's *The Mouse and His Child*," and by Geraldine DeLuca, in "'A Condition of Complete Simplicity': The Toy as Child in *The Mouse and His Child*," concern themselves with how the novel "subverts the traditional idealistic themes in children's literature," seeing childhood not as an idyllic time, but as "a time of development,"[1] and with how the intrepid mechanical pair persist through the "dog-eat-dogness" of an unrelenting Darwinian universe.

Similarly, other recent treatments of the novel, such as those by Christine Wilkie (*Through the Narrow Gate: The Mythological Consciousness of Russell Hoban*), point out that, although the mouse and his child more closely resemble "antiheroes, insofar as the mouse is traditionally the victim and eternally vulnerable," nevertheless, they are also heroic and "their quest is conceived in heroic terms."[2] Almost all of the recent criticism of the novel has underscored the difficult, quizzical nature of the mouse father and child's existential dilemma and examined something of the milieu into which such a puzzling work best fits, yet few, if any, of these have provided anything approaching a systematic, thoroughgoing critical reading of the text as a whole.

In her article "Threadbare Utopia: Hoban's Modern Pastoral," Joanne Lynn makes an important point, echoed in Lois Kuznets's *When Toys Come Alive,* about the most critical moment in the novel—the fall from the doll house world and the world of Christmas ornament display into the dark world of dust bins and trash heaps. She observes that the windup pair's expulsion is "analogous to Adam and Eve's 'fortunate fall,' in that it permits development and growth beyond Eden."[3] And it is just this point that needs to be closely examined, the point at which the mouse child and his father, mechanical figures, discarded toys, are forced to leave their immaculate, hermetically sealed world, and venture forth, as vagabonds, transients, vagrants, putting one foot in front of the other.

In order to successfully account for this "fortunate fall," and to do justice to the movement of the windups as they move from the idyllic but vapid doll house world into the nightmare landscape, to finally return, through many ups and downs, to the now-restored, redeemed doll house, an overall interpretative scheme is required. Although several have been suggested by commentators, most noticeably Lynn and Kuznets, as well as DeLuca and Lenz, none has argued for the systematic Blakean reading that seems to most capably and persuasively explain the windups' elliptical journey and the book's problematic, unsettling conclusion. Such an interpretation can make sense of what has hitherto not made sense and give form and meaning to parts of the novel that have defied earlier interpretive gambits. Read in terms of Blake's artist-centered philosophy, much of the book unravels itself, and many of its mysteries clarify themselves, clicking into intelligible and almost inevitable place.

Although *Songs of Innocence and of Experience* remains the best known and most approachable of Blake's writings, and although much of a Blakean interpretation can be made from just these *Songs,* any full, systematic reading needs to include the later Prophetic works as well. This is because Blake only arrived at some of his most important ideas concerning the bard figure in these later, more difficult and demanding works. From the *Songs,* we get what Blake calls the "contrary states of the human soul"—that is, innocence and experience. Yet, in terms of Blake's philosophy, this is only an intermediate step. The oppositeness or contrariness of the two opposed "states" must be resolved in a third, completive or synthetic "state," one that he arrived at only with the writing of the incomplete *The Four Zoas* and with such prophetic books as *Milton* and *Jerusalem.*

Briefly summarized, Blake believed that there are three states of the human soul: innocence, "unconscious selfhood"; experience, its opposite or contrary, "the state of being lost"; and "organiz'd innocence," a "higher innocence beyond."[4] In his later works, he came to believe that only in "organiz'd innocence" or what Margaret Rudd, in her book *Organiz'd Innocence,* calls "reorganized innocence" is there true "liberty and freedom."[5] As Blake says, in a note written on a page of *The Four Zoas:*

"Unorganiz'd Innocence: An Impossibility. Innocence dwells with Wisdom, but never with Ignorance." And so it does, but it is a recast, redeemed sort of innocence, one transformed and resurrected, as it were, from its spending a "dark night of the soul" in the world of experience.

In Blake's "Preface" to *Milton,* the shortest of his major prophetic works, he describes his intent in these words, now set in an Anglican hymn:

> *And did those feet in ancient time.*
> *Walk upon England's mountains green:*
> *And was the holy Lamb of God,*
> *On England's pleasant pastures seen!*
>
> *And did the Countenance Divine,*
> *Shine forth upon our clouded hills?*
> *And was Jerusalem builded here,*
> *Among these dark Satanic Mills?*
>
> *Bring me my Bow of burning gold:*
> *Bring me my Arrows of desire:*
> *Bring me my Spear: O clouds unfold!*
> *Bring me my Chariot of fire!*
>
> *I will not cease from Mental fight,*
> *Nor shall my Sword sleep in my hand:*
> *Till we have built Jerusalem,*
> *In England's green & pleasant Land.*[6]

If looked at in these terms, Hoban's intent, like Blake's and Milton's, is clear and unambiguous, despite the enigmatic, indeterminate surface that the book presents. He wants to posit the redeemed thing within the fallen, nightmarish thingness that the world has erected—the restored doll house and reconstituted mouse family within the wasteland of broken toys and what Lois Kuznets calls the "predatory world of exploitation, violence, and . . . nonstop-talking."[7] Ironically, the ideal readers of *The Mouse and His Child,* despite what reviewers and critics have said, might well be Blake scholars, or at least those readers who know Blake's three-part scheme.

In these terms, the mouse father and his child's peripatetic, but largely oval, journey is most fully explained and made sense of. Despite others' interpretations of the text, and perhaps because of them, this Blakean reading seems to come closest to full explication, to a careful unraveling of the many mysteries that the book has presented since its publication. In order to trace the windup pair's journey toward their dual goal of self-windingness and family wholeness, a brief reiteration of the steps they go through is perhaps necessary.

As mechanical windups, the mouse father and his child begin "life" as Christmas toys for children. Their initial home is a pristine doll house, set in a toy shop window. In this "original" state, the pair are, in Blake's terms, "innocent," unfallen. In fact, as DeLuca notes, the pair "have no names; they are simply the thing itself." Here, the pair "have no existence to speak of."[8] At this stage, they are largely unknowing, thoughtless, bound by clockwork. Hoban describes their condition this way:

> When the saleslady wound the key in the mouse father's back he danced in a circle, swinging his little son off the counter and down again while the children laughed and reached out to touch them. Around and around they danced gravely, and more and more slowly as the spring unwound, until the mouse father came to a stop holding the child high in his upraised arms.[9]

One Christmas, when the old store clock strikes midnight, the windup pair gain consciousness; they come alive, through one of the clockwork rules. As in such comparable toy story beginnings as *The Velveteen Rabbit* and "The Steadfast Tin Soldier," cited by Kuznets in her book, the awakened pair ask the usual, expected questions of what she calls "awakening consciousness": "Where are we? And then *"What* are we, Papa?"[10] Although the mouse father doesn't know the answers, the answers, such as they are, come from the plush clockwork elephant, herself a part of the toy shop establishment, and a snobbish voice of realism:

> "What astonishing ignorance!" said the clockwork elephant."But of course you're new. I've been here such a long time that I'd forgotten how it was. Now, then," she said, "this place is a toyshop, and you are toy mice. People are going to come and buy you for children, because it's almost a time called Christmas."[11]

Their pair's "half-life," as Kuznets calls it,[12] continues with the child wondering about things, again quite innocently:

> The mouse child was still thinking of what the elephant had said before. "What happens when they buy you?" he asked her. "That, of course, is outside my experience," said the elephant, "but I should

think that one simply goes out into the world and does whatever one does. One dances or balances a ball, as the case may be."[13]

Hoban is careful to establish the toy shop world at Christmas and especially the pristine doll house as being perfect and unchanging, even if artificial and unreal. And he contrasts it sharply with its contrary, the fallen world of experience, the dark wasteland just outside the door in the cold and the snow. Like Blake, Hoban is concerned with the concept of contrariness and takes pains to ensure that such an awareness is not lost upon the reader. He describes the world outside, where the tramp, the single human character in the novel, makes his way through the streets, a hobo, a vagrant, a bricoleur, handy at repairs:

> The child remembered the bitter wind that had blown in through the door, and the great staring face of the tramp at the window with the gray winter sky behind him. Now that sky was a silent darkness beyond the street lamp and the white flakes falling. The doll house was bright and warm; the teapot gleamed upon the dazzling cloth. "I don't want to go out into the world," he said.[14]

According to one of the "clockwork laws," there's to be "No talking before midnight and after dawn, and no crying on the job."[15] Despite the rules, the mouse child begins to cry. He is fretful and not easily consoled, having glimpsed what is within and what is without. He is afraid of what lies outside what he knows, and yet he feels he is empty, with something missing:

> "Are you my mama?" asked the child. He had no idea what a mama might be, but he knew at once that he needed one badly. . . ."Will you be my mama," said the child, "and will you sing to me all the time? And we can all stay here together and live in the beautiful house where the party is and not go out into the world?"[16]

In Blake's philosophy, innocence is seen as "unconscious selfhood."[17] In Hoban's doll house situation, the windup pair exist almost unconsciously, too, seemingly suspended in a splendid, but somehow empty, hermetically sealed world. It is a world without change or oppositeness, a place where there is no movement or growth, since "without Contraries is no progression."[18] It takes a fall for the mouse father and child to change their situation. It is, among other things, a fall into consciousness; the fall is "fortunate."

Their "fall" is at least dual. The first slip occurs when the pair are sold as Christmas ornaments, interestingly, not as toys for children to play with, but as something for adults to wind up and display and admire. They remain this way, boxed up except for a few days at Christmas; the phase lasts four years. Each Christmas the pair are wound by the adults, they dance briefly, and they are put away, boxed up. Nothing changes. Further down, though, something already has:

> Around and around the mouse child danced, rising and falling as his father swung him up and down, while the little tea party in the window circled past him. How far away that other doll house seemed now! How far away that other tea party with its elegant ladies and gentlemen, and the elephant he had wanted for a mama! The mouse child was on the job and he knew it, but he began to cry.[19]

There has been a shift in consciousness, in awareness. The mouse father and child are becoming more "alive," but are not yet fully. They are at an in-between stage, an awkward "half-life" state. Writing about this "transient" condition in terms of Blake's three states of the human soul, Gleckner notes that "Innocence has been established, experience has been alluded to; now, despite the earthly mother's greatest efforts, experience is close upon the child, and in it lies the key to a higher consciousness beyond."[20] It is intriguing that Hoban, seemingly aware of the peculiar nature of this "transient" condition, has the elephant, whom the mouse child wanted for a "mama," snobbishly refuse the request, dismissing them (the mouse and his child) as "the transient element."[21]

As the fifth Christmas of their "half-life" rolls around, the mouse father and child are once again taken out, but now, in violation of the "clockwork laws," the mouse child cries, startling the family cat. As a consequence of this instance of breaking the rules, the "cat knocks over a vase that crushes the mouse and his child flat, making them fit only for the trash bin."[22] Here is their second "fall" and the key one, because at the moment they are broken and "thrown into the garbage . . . they really begin to 'live.' "[23] Discarded, banged up, they are cast away as useless, but here, on the ash heap, in the dump, the tin figures are picked up by the tramp, redeemed from their cast-down state, mended, and set on their picaresque path. An outcast himself, the tramp refashions the tin as best he can, "succeeding in making the father lurch 'straight ahead with a rolling stride, pushing the child backward before him.' No longer dancers in a circle, the mouse and his child, placed on the road and wound up, will obey, in so far as possible, the tramp's admonition to 'be tramps.' "[24]

As the prophetic frog intones in one of his cryptic utterances, "You have broken the circle . . . and a straight line of great force emerges. Follow it."[25] Intriguingly, though, although the mouse and child lurch ahead in something of a straight line, their journey, seen in overall terms, resembles an oval, an ellipse. As DeLuca notes, "And when the mouse and his child finally recover their family and the doll house, it is at the dump again, where, as T. S. Eliot puts it, 'the end of all our exploring / Will be to arrive where we started / And know the place for the first time.' "[26] As a quest narrative, the windups' tale is a journey toward self-windingness or independence, the secret of everlasting life. But before they can achieve such ends, before they are raised up, they must be cast down, must descend into the valley of the shadow—the dark world of experience, Blake's second, medial state.

Commenting on the necessity of change and the inevitability of the "fall" in Blake's scheme of things, Gleckner writes "Man must pass out of innocence; there is no real choice if imagination and the higher innocence are to be reached. Vaguely similar to a "fortunate fall," the Blakean fall from innocence to experience is necessary so that each of us, through a last judgment, may live eternally."[27] The fall into this bleak nighttown of Manny Rat and his gangster henchmen is horrifyingly real. Here Hoban describes a nightmare landscape where pestilence is rampant, garbage fires burn, and windups, like the mouse father and child, are impressed into work gangs, becoming "foragers for Manny Rat," itself assuming the quality of a haunting refrain.[28] So bleak is the landscape, so dark is the world in which the tin figures find themselves, one critic describes it as follows: "Its dystopic setting, amid not only feral nature but the garbage of a technological universe controlled by the paternalistic and capitalistic Manny, undercuts any complacency about permanence and security in the society created here or elsewhere in the universe."[29] And two others, writing together, conclude in *Narratives of Love and Loss* that "the dump is reminiscent at this point of a Nazi slave labor camp."[30] Hoban's descriptions of Manny and his fellow vermin in action are revealing. Here is an oft-cited instance of his doctrine of expedience. It occurs soon after the windups arrive in this pestilential, infernal region. Ralphie, one of Manny's henchmen, reports that a one-eyed, three-legged donkey is "slacking," not pulling his weight in their dump economy. Apparently, he can't work because his spring is broken. Hoban describes the scene this way:

"It's nothing," said the frightened donkey as he heard Manny Rat approaching his blind side. "I've got plenty of work left in me. I was just feeling a little low—you know how it is."

"You're not well," said Manny Rat. "I can see that easily. What you need is a long rest." He picked up a heavy rock, lifted it high, and brought it down on the donkey's back, splitting him open like a walnut. "Put his works in the spare-parts can," said Manny Rat to Ralphie.[31]

A bit earlier, Hoban paints the Dantean gloom of the nightmare world itself, the world Manny Rat rules over. It is dark and forbidding, lit intermittently by flickering tongues of flame, like gas jets pulsing in a noisy, greasy blackness. In such a world, hope and any future seem unattainable—and any thoughts of survival seem dim and far away.

Now the pair are near the low point, the nadir, of their existence, and their precipitous descent into the foul-smelling, pestilential den of iniquity is close to the way Blake describes his second state of the human soul: the world of experience. "London," a poem included in *Songs of Experience,* provides a glimpse. Here is the second stanza:

> *In every cry of every Man,*
> *In every Infants cry of fear,*
> *In every voice: in every ban,*
> *The mind-forg'd manacles I hear.*[32]

Similarly, in "The Chimney Sweeper," another poem from *Songs of Experience,* there is this related description:

> *A little black thing among the snow,*
> *Crying weep! weep, in notes of woe!*
> *Where are thy father & mother? say?"*
> *They are both gone up to the church to pray.*[33]

This is the Blakean world of experience, the world of the Tyger's "fearful symmetry," and the fallen world of chaotic delusion. It is a labyrinth in which man wanders aimlessly, existing, not truly living, because this is the world in which he finds himself when his knowledge is sensory, not imaginative. It is the fallen world because it is the world man "creates and perceives because he himself is fallen."[34]

Of this stage, the fall into the gaping, darkling abyss, Margaret Rudd, in her 1973 book *Organiz'd Innocence: The Story of Blake's Prophetic Books,* makes the following observation:

> Still more important, we are shown the way out of this nightmare world, not through being told to let go completely on the analyst's couch, but in an example of human courage and valiantly maintained love that seems to triumph like the dawn after seemingly endless night. It is a way out that worked in Blake's own experience and one, he claims, that is a universal remedy for a necessary and universal illness.[35]

Examined in terms of their largely elliptical journey, the windup mouse father and child begin life in a sheltered, if unreal, existence. In the "splendid doll house" in the magical toy shop the pair are mindless, instinctive, comfortable, and both innocent and childlike in the Blakean sense. Here the pair always dance in a perfect circle, when wound by someone, and have no real experience with anything outside themselves or their hermetically sealed, carefully inscribed world—like the measured and dissected world of Blake's Urizen. From this original condition, they are bought one Christmas, quickly thrust into the attic, brought down as mere ornaments, not toys for children, boxed up again, and finally, after getting smashed, thrown on the rubbish heap. Outcast, the pair are found by another outcast, the tramp, partially put back together, and set down near the railroad tracks to make their way in the world. Their internal mechanisms altered by the tramp's attempted repair, the mouse father and child feel for the first time a true sense of almost childlike wonder:

> How strange it is to walk straight ahead! he [the father] said.
> "I walked backward," said the child, "but I liked it better than dancing in a circle. What shall we do now?"
> "Who knows?" said the father. "There seems to be a good deal more to the world than the Christmas tree and the attic and the trash can. Anything at all might happen, I suppose."[36]

So life begins.

Their descent continues. The pair have their fortunes told by a prophetic frog, are involved in a bank holdup, and flee with the frog into the pine woods. In commenting on their necessary fall, their "fortunate fall," Hoban uses the wise bullfrog as his mouthpiece:

> "So it begins," said Frog. "For good or ill, you have come out into the world, and the world has taken notice."
> "A long, hard road," said the father to Frog. "That was what you saw ahead for us, was it not?"

"All roads, whether long or short, are hard," said Frog. "Come, you have begun your journey, and all else necessarily follows from that act. Be of good cheer. The sun is bright. The sky is blue. The world lies before you."[37]

The windup pair's largely elliptical journey resumes, as they witness a territorial war between bloodthirsty shrews and weasels, intent on maintaining lines and limits and margins, again, much like Blake's Urizen. In this eerily Darwinian contest, there are no winners, really. There is just the food pyramid or food chain, sorting itself out with a frightening inevitability. Next, the pair join the Crows' Caws of Art Experimental Theatre and join in with the animal troupe in what Kuznets calls "a Beckett-like play."[38] Here, again, Hoban underscores his point about the necessity of the tin toys' fall. While the windups want only to explain their predicament, the birds who run the Caws of Art see only acting potential. "Let's see what you can do," says the crow:

> The mouse and his child walked across the snow until they bumped into a twig and fell down. They lay there, the father's legs moving slowly back and forth while the company watched in silence. . . . "Can you help us?" asked the father. "We must keep moving on; we cannot stop here."
> "Pathos," said Crow. "Real pathos."
> "They've definitely got something," said Mrs. Crow, as she helped the mouse and his child to their feet. "The patter about the seal and the elephant needs working up, but the walk is good *and the fall is terrific.*"[39]

From this point, they fly with a parrot to an engineer-like Muskrat, who works with them on self-windingness and who thinks philosophically yet pragmatically in Xs, Ys, and Zs. They become part of a woodchopping mechanism, again of oval or elliptical movement; are shot out into a pond; sink to the bottom and get stuck in the mud with a Miss Mudd, a dragon fly in its larval stage, at the instant of metamorphosis; and encounter the deep-thinking C. Serpentina, a snapping turtle of great wisdom and profundity. They rise rapidly to the surface, are snatched up by a hungry hawk, are flown back over the dump from where their state of experience began, and, at last, unceremoniously fall from a great height, their parts scattering, they "saw and heard no more."[40]

After all these ups and downs, their peripatetic wanderings, their close encounters and hair-breadth escapes, finally the mouse father and

After the fall: The oracular frog, the mouse, and his child are caught up in the shrew's war. Illus. Lillian Hoban.

child are once again close to where they began. They have, in fact, lived out the prediction foretold for them nearly a year earlier by the oracular frog: "Low in the dark of summer, high in the winter light; a painful spring, a shattering fall, a scattering regathered. The enemy you flee at the beginning awaits you at the end."[41] About this same journey in Blake's writings, especially in his Prophetic Books, Laura James, in her study, concludes:

> Though man may have seemed to be wandering a hopeless journey, all is not lost. The path is curved; there comes a point at which the direction is once more homeward. . . . Blake's genius was dedicated to one end, a portrayal of mankind's slow journey over the Via Dolorosa which leads from sense to soul. That journey is not a brief, straight path linking the major events of birth and death. Rather it is an immense curve track for one-way traffic only. . . . Between the beginning and the ending lie the tangled convolutions of its wanderings through time-

space. . . . Restriction of vision leads it [the soul] into bypaths and dead-end streets. It loses its sense of direction. There is need for constant retracing of steps. . . . So the soul whirls through the great circle of destiny, and fiercely revolving wheel of nature, repeatedly, before it discovers the channel which, by transforming the circle into a spiral, permits it to start back to its ultimate goal.[42]

Near the end of the windups' harrowing experiences, the tin pair, now split apart, battered and rusted, but having achieved what DeLuca calls "a kind of unique, almost mysterious status in the world as 'in their long exposure to the weather, moss had rooted in the crevices of their tin, and . . . covered them like soft green fur,"[43] "attain a kind of luminosity."[44] It is perhaps both ironic and perfectly suitable that the pair's breakup, caused by their "shattering fall," should allow what Kuznets calls "the final testing and opportunity to be reborn with a new independence and identity, even before they become self-winding."[45] No longer toys, they have broken from the circle to discover, amid the filth and pestilence of the smoldering dump, the long-lost doll house from the toy shop. Hoban describes the moment of rediscovery this way, investing it with a sense of wonder: "Look, Papa!" said the child as the frog moved the tin seal to where the father and son could see her. "The elephant, the seal, and the house. It wasn't impossible! We've found them all!"[46]

Broken, patched together, moss-covered, with ill-fitting halves, the mouse and his child resemble the dilapidated doll house, once immaculate and "splendid," now forever changed. Both house and windup pair have been through Blake's world of experience, the world of rust and decay, but also of growth and change. In coming to such a place again, seemingly for the first time, the transformed pair now celebrate a marriage "and [have] the self-winding postponed until the elephant and seal have persuaded everybody to make the house into what they want it to be, not a carbon copy of its original bourgeois comfort, but a gaily painted, if battered survivor, resembling its toy inhabitants whose wounds have healed but whose scars remain."[47] A kind of paradise regained, the newly rediscovered, redeemed house and the newly reconstituted family have been the long-sought goals of the pair since the beginning of their meandering. It seems eminently suitable that the pair at last find proximate self-windingness here, amid the ruins and the restorations. Like Blake's children, a little boy lost and the little girl lost, like the chimney sweeper, the discarded, dumped-on pair have survived, have, in fact, "transcend[ed] their former existence."[48]

And, like themselves, the doll house has been significantly altered by its history in the world of experience. In Blake's scheme of things, the mouse father and child are poised to enter the third stage, the third state of the human soul: organiz'd innocence. Commenting on this aspect of Blake's philosophy, Rudd writes "Breakdown is simply a stage in every man's journey from innocence through the necessary anguish caused by experience, to that 'reorganized innocence' which is liberty and freedom."[49] And so, at the book's end, Hoban has his mouse father and child gain for the first time, really, their liberty and freedom. Although they don't attain complete self-windingness, even with the reformed Manny's practical genius applied to the task, they do achieve proximate self-windingness. And that is enough. In Gleckner's words, written about Blake's lost boys and girls, "they have been lost and now they are found." The pair have completed the basic Blakean pattern. They have gone through the three states from innocence, through experience, "the state of being lost," to arrive, finally, at journey's end, at "organiz'd innocence," the "higher innocence beyond."[50]

Having come, then, to this now restored, newly electrified doll house, so markedly distinct from the pristine one in that far-away Christmas window, the windups, incomplete for the whole of their journey up to now, complete themselves. The father marries the elephant, and the child takes the seal as sister. And, unlike in the dark night of experience, the pair now, in this paradise-regained state, that of "organiz'd innocence," find themselves surrounded by loyal friends and redeemed former enemies. They even have friends, like Uncle Frog, to wind them: "Well," said Frog, "I don't suppose anyone ever is completely self-winding. That's what friends are for."[51]

Of the fallen house, now itself redeemed and restored, Hoban writes the following, giving it plenty of space so that the changes are not lost on the reader:

> The house's character had changed much with the fire that had wrecked it and the several stages of reconstruction that renewed it; phoenixlike, the place seemed reborn itself. . . . The doll house would never again be what it once had been; its stateliness and beauty were long gone, but something new and different emerged from the concerted efforts of the little family.[52]

"Phoenixlike," risen from the ashes, the doll house, like the windups themselves, is again innocent, but it is an innocence tempered by trial and pain and loss. It is they themselves they have found through their long, hard search. After all, as they discovered when stuck in the mud at the bottom of C. Serpentina's pond, "there's nothing on the other side of nothing but us."[53] A motley family, a variegated ensemble, a traveling troupe, the mouse father and his child, and their new wife/mother and daughter/sister and the four adopted uncles, including the redeemed Manny Rat, have risen out of what Geraldine DeLuca calls:

> The dog-eat-dog world, [and] have moved from tragedy to comedy. . . .
> Beneficence has the upper hand. The book closes with the same picture
> of the face of the tramp, looking into the window of the repaired doll
> house, now a hotel welcoming "migrants yes," transcending the idea of
> territoriality and property that define the animal world and to a great
> degree our own. It is once again Christmas, and now we understand it
> more fully.[54]

Possessed of a deepened innocence, one tempered by experience, the tin toys have returned, via an ellipse, to the same place they began, but now both the place and they themselves are vastly different. To repeat the close of Eliot's "Little Gidding":

> *We shall not cease from exploration*
> *And the end of all our exploring*
> *Will be to arrive where we started*
> *And know the place for the first time.*[55]

All in all it has been a remarkable journey, a quest narrative that nicely traces Blake's three stages or states of the human soul. It is as Alfred Kazin notes, writing in his "Introduction" to *The Portable Blake:*

> Experience is the "contrary" of innocence, not its negation. Contraries
> are phases of the doubleness of all existence in the mind of man; they
> reflect the unalterable condition of the human struggle. As hell can be
> married to heaven, the body seen by the soul, so experience lifts inno-
> cence into a higher synthesis based on vision.[56]

For mouse father and mouse child, as for human children, lost and found, on the sooty streets of London, all is well that ends well. Stability and order, and innocence and love have returned. All has been redeemed by the mouse child's innocence, tenacity, and infectious, transforming vision. The tramp's final admonition "Be happy" falls like a benediction.

NOTES

[1]Valerie Krips, "Mistaken Identity: Russell Hoban's *The Mouse and His Child.*" *Children's Literature* 21 (1993): 97. Also, Geraldine DeLuca. "A Condition of Complete Simplicity: The Toy as Child in *The Mouse and His Child.*" *Children's Literature in Education,* 19, no. 4 (1988): 211–21.

[2]Christine Wilkie, *Through the Narrow Gate: The Mythological Consciousness of Russell Hoban* (Rutherford, NJ: Fairleigh Dickinson University Press, 1989), p. 28.

[3]Joanne Lynn, "Threadbare Utopia: Hoban's Modern Pastoral." *Children's Literature Association Quarterly* 11 (1986): 19–23. Also, Lois Rostow Kuznets. *When Toys Come Alive: Narratives of Animation, Metamorphosis, and Development* (New Haven: Yale University Press, 1994), p. 27.

[4]Robert Gleckner F., *The Piper & the Bard: A Study of William Blake* (Detroit: Wayne State University Press, 1959), pp.102 and 114.

[5]Margaret Rudd, *Organiz'd Innocence: The Story of Blake's Prophetic Books* (London: Routledge & Kegan Paul, 1956; Rpt. Westport, CT: Greenwood Press, 1973), p. 93.

[6]William Blake. *The Poetry and Prose of William Blake.* ed. David Erdman (Garden City, New York: Doubleday, 1970), pp. 94–95.

[7]Kuznets, p. 172.

[8]De Luca, p. 213.

[9]Russell Hoban, *The Mouse and His Child* (New York: Dell, 1990), p. 2.

[10]Ibid., p. 171.

[11]Ibid., p. 4.

[12]Kuznets, p. 171.

[13]Hoban, p. 6.

[14]Ibid.

[15]Ibid., p. 7.

[16]Ibid.

[17]Gleckner, p. 45.

[18]William Blake, *The Marriage of Heaven and Hell.*

[19]Hoban, p. 10.

[20]Gleckner, p. 114.

[21]Hoban, p. 8.

[22]Kuznets, p. 171.

[23]De Luca, p. 213.

[24]Hoban, pp. 11–12.

[25]Ibid., p. 28.

[26]T.S. Eliot, *The Complete Poems and Plays: 1909–1950* (New York: Harcourt, Brace & World, 1971), p. 215.

[27]Gleckner, p. 48.

[28]Hoban, p. 16.

[29]Kuznets, p. 176.

[30]Margaret and Michael Rustin, *Narratives of Love and Loss: Studies in Modern Children's Fiction* (London: Verso, 1987), p. 261, n. 10.

[31]Hoban, p. 20.

[32]Blake, *Poetry and Prose,* p. 27.

[33]Ibid., p. 22.

[34]Perkins, p. 57.

[35]Rudd, p. 19.

[36]Hoban, p. 14.

[37]Ibid., p. 36.

[38]Kuznets, p. 173.

[39]Hoban, p. 57 (italics mine).

[40]Ibid., p. 119.

[41]Ibid., p. 28.

[42]Laura DeWitt James, *William Blake and the Tree of Life* (Berkeley, CA: Shambala Press, 1971), pp. 11–14.

[43]De Luca, p. 213.

[44]Ibid., p. 215.

[45]Kuznets, p. 174.

[46]Hoban, p. 130.

[47]Kuznets, p. 175.

[48]De Luca, p. 221.

[49]Rudd, p. 19.

[50]Gleckner, pp. 102 and 114.

[51]Hoban pp. 180–81.

[52]Ibid., p. 157.

[53]Ibid., p. 111.

[54]De Luca, p. 215.

[55]Eliot, p. 145.

[56]Kazin, ed. *The Portable Blake* (New York: Viking Press, 1946), pp. 41–42.

BIBLIOGRAPHY

Blake, William. *The Poetry and Prose of William Blake.* ed. David Erdman. Garden City, NY: Doubleday, 1970.

DeLuca, Geraldine. "A Condition of Complete Simplicity: The Toy as Child in *The Mouse and His Child.*" *Children's Literature in Education,* 19, no. 4 (1988): 211–21.

Gleckner, Robert F. *The Piper & the Bard: A Study of William Blake.* Detroit: Wayne State University Press, 1959.

Hoban, Russell. "Thoughts on a shirtless cyclist, Robin Hood, Johann Sebastian Bach, and one or two other things." *Children's Literature in Education* 4 (March 1971): 5–22.

Inglis, Fred. *The Promise of Happiness: Value and Meaning in Children's Fiction.* Cambridge: Cambridge University Press, 1981.

Kuznets, Lois Rostow. *When Toys Come Alive: Narratives of Animation, Meta-morphosis, and Development.* New Haven: Yale University Press, 1994.

Lynn, Joanne. "Threadbare Utopia: Hoban's Modern Pastoral." *Children's Liter-ature Association Quarterly* 11 (1986): 19–23.

Rudd, Margaret. *Organiz'd Innocence: The Story of Blake's Prophetic Books.* London: Routledge & Kegan Paul, 1956; Rpt. Westport, CT: Greenwood Press, 1973.

Wilkie, Christine. *Through the Narrow Gate: The Mythological Consciousness of Russell Hoban.* Rutherford, NJ: Fairleigh Dickinson University Press, 1989.

Mice-en-Scene
A Comparative Study of the Novel and the Animated Feature Film
The Mouse and His Child

JAMES CARTER

A BRIEF INTRODUCTION TO HOBAN ON FILM

It would be fair to say that compared with their source novels, the film adaptations of Russell Hoban's texts—to borrow from Muskrat in *The Mouse and His Child*—have caused relatively few "ripples on the pond." Admittedly, the cartoon movie of *The Mouse and His Child* (1977) was decorated with two awards on release in the United States, but now, over twenty years later, the film has disappeared without trace.

The same year, 1977, also saw the release of Jim Henson's endearing "Muppet" version of Russell and Lillian Hoban's *Emmet Otter's Jug Band Christmas*. The adult novel *Turtle Diary* (1985) was the third of Hoban's books to be adapted to film. With a screenplay by Harold Pinter, the film starred Ben Kingsley as the directionless bookseller William G., alongside Glenda Jackson as the children's author with writer's block, Neara H. The film ignored the book's metaphysical elements and did little but realize the plot—the story of a middle-aged duo in existential crisis that gain a spiritual reawakening by stealing turtles from London Zoo and releasing them into the Atlantic. At the time of the film's release, Hoban remarked: "In the Caribbean, when they catch sea turtles they turn them over on their backs and they scoop the turtle out of the shell. And that's what they've done to my book."[1] And in an interview Hoban commented :

> The people who make films have enough sensitivity to respond to
> what's in a book, but they lack the artistic intelligence to make the
> translation into film. They are not able to sieze on what is the essence

of the book. For example, with *Turtle Diary,* I think of it as my Haiku
book, because the Haiku poems have to do with nicely observed detail
always—at a time of day, at a time of year, and whether it's the sound
of the frog jumping into the old pond, or going out to watch the cherry
blossoms, or moon-viewing, or views of Fuji, or whatever—but all that
was lost. All of the detail that really was the solid foundation for the
story—nobody bothered with.[2]

And what could have followed next was the film of *Riddley Walker:*

With *Riddley Walker,* I was just a damn fool at the time, I had an offer
of a very handsome—at the time—figure for buying the rights outright
with my having nothing to say whatever about how the film was made.
And at that time, my career in terms of public attention was at its highest point, and I had no idea that I'd have less bargaining power in the
future. [In self-parodying voice:] "I don't think these people are up to
making the kind of film I want." [laughs:] Hoity-toity! And, it never
happened. And then, some years later, I said to my agent "Find out if
that offer is still alive, please." And he enquired, and it was, but then
came what is known on the stock exchange as Black Wednesday, and
the people who would've put up the funding for the film found that
they could no longer do so, and that was that—so *Riddley Walker* is
still unfilmed.[3]

Hoban's own general sentiment as regards film adaptations of novels
is perhaps best summed up in the following remarks: "The history of film
is full of films that took something from a book and left the rest
behind. . . . more and more, as with Kieslowski, I think the best films are
written as films."[4]

Throughout its history, *The Mouse and His Child* has stimulated debate over its true readership, whereas the feature film, as this piece will
argue, has a more clearly defined notion of the audience that it wishes to
attract. After a general preamble, this piece will concurrently explore the
novel and the film in terms of Narrative, Themes, and Style: Implied
Reader and Audience.

The Mouse and His Child was first published in America in 1967.
The book was published in Britain two years later to great critical acclaim. The proposed sequel, *The Return of Manny Rat*—which Hoban
read from at the Exeter Children's Literature conference in 1970—long
unpublished, appears in *The Russell Hoban Omnibus.*[5]

This, Hoban's first novel, proved to be a pivotal text for the author. His earliest published works—which include the highly acclaimed *Frances* picture books and *Charlie the Tramp*—only obliquely hinted at some of the author's preoccupations that were later to reemerge in *The Mouse and His Child* (as well as the subsequent adult novels, children's texts, and essays), and revealed nothing of the richness of language he was capable of, as well as the depth and range of ideas that he would address. To categorize Hoban's texts post- and including *The Mouse and His Child* would be a fruitless and impossible task, as they defy any generic expectations, even according to chronological readership. Hoban himself has admitted that he does not believe in publishers' marketing categories, and that "books in nameless categories are needed—books for children and adults together, books that can stand in the middle of an existential nowhere and find reference points."[6]

Viewed holistically, Hoban's individual works could be construed as single fragments of one master thesis, as various ideas permeate, underpin, and interweave throughout his works from *The Mouse and His Child* onward. On a subtextual level, there is often little distinction between his works published for adult or child readers, as themes are common to both, for example:

- Filmic realism: *Turtle Diary, Monster Film*
- The interconnectedness of phenomena: *The Marzipan Pig, The Mouse and His Child, The Lion of Boaz-Jachin and Jachin-Boaz*
- Mythological iconography: *The Lion of Boaz-Jachin and Jachin-Boaz, The Court of the Winged Serpent*
- Primal consciousness: *Riddley Walker, Turtle Diary, The Mouse and His Child*
- Figurative journeys: *The Trokeville Way, La Corona and the Tin Frog, Riddley Walker*
- Father/son bonding: *The Lion of Boaz-Jachin and Jachin-Boaz, The Mouse and His Child*

Hoban believes that "everything comes from the same place, some can be put in a smaller form and some can be put in a bigger form, and some can be contained within a child's frame of reference, and some not."[7]

The movie of the novel had an alleged budget of $1,600,000 and was retitled *The Extraordinary Adventures of the Mouse and His Child.* The film was produced and animated in Hollywood by Murakami-Wolf

Productions. Walt de Faria, the movie's producer, bought up the film rights for the novel soon after it was published, though due to availability of animators and the raising of capital, the film took some years to reach fruition. Directed by Fred Wolf and Charles Swenson, with a soundtrack by Roger Kellaway, lyrics by Gene Lees, and a screenplay by Carol Mon Pere, the movie was drawn by thirty animation artists, and the voice-over artists included Peter Ustinov (Manny Rat), Andy Devine (Frog), Alan Barzman (the mouse), and Marcy Swenson (the child).

Released in the United States on June 22, 1976, the film was given the Ruby Slipper Award for "Best Feature Film" and an Award of Excellence from the Film Advisory Board. In Britain, the film was released for cinema in November 1976; the video of the film was released in the late 1980s and was deleted, due to poor sales, in 1995.

From here, to distinguish between the film and the novel, the film will be referred to as *The Extraordinary Adventures.* In addition, two other analogous novels—in terms of thematic content and episodic narrative structures—will be referred to throughout this piece: Antoine de Saint-Exupery's *The Little Prince* and Kenneth Grahame's *The Wind in the Willows.*

NARRATIVE

On one level, Hoban's polysemous, multilayered novel is an anthropomorphic fable of good overcoming evil. On another, the novel tells of the perennial quests for home, for identity, and for meaning in the chaos of existence. *The Mouse and His Child* is an intriguing, and in many respects, an original work, because of its idiosyncratic symbolism, its quirky characterization, its bathetic tones and wry humor, and also its unusual blend of satire, allegory, and metaphysics. Although a fantasy, the text has what Graham Hough would describe as "the reality of a myth," a universality that transcends space and time: "Myths are after all fundamental to the psychic life: no demonstration of what is merely personal or fashionable fantasy can do so, except for a limited time and class."[8]

The Mouse and His Child is a *bildungsroman,* a rite of passage for its two central characters—two interlinking clockwork mice, a father and son. The cast further includes Manny Rat—a Machiavellian, autocratic antihero; Frog—a mystical soothsayer; a human tramp—an outsider figure; Muskrat—a pure physicist; C. Serpentina—a philosopher/playwright; and two other wind-up toys—a seal and an elephant. And akin to the book's themes and symbolic motifs (the dog symbols and circular imagery), these characters occur and resurface at specific junctures. They, with the exception of the tramp, are personified beings; the toy/ animal facade is rendered only at surface level, for their thoughts, actions, discourses, and behavioral patterns are intrinsically human.

The narrative of the book is contained solely within the printed text, with Lillian Hoban's illustrations and map of the milieu serving to embellish the novel with graphic representations of the characters and specific events; her pen-and-ink illustrations of the mouse and child are based upon the very clockwork toy that originally inspired the story.

Brian Macfarlane's definition of narrative, "a series of events, causally linked, involving a continuing set of characters which influence

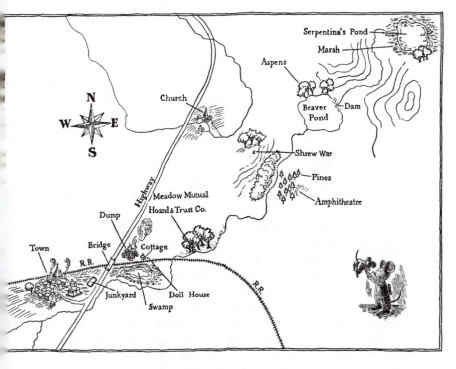

The journey of the mouse and his child is circular; at the end, they return to the doll house. Illus. Lillian Hoban.

and are influenced by the course of events" is especially relevant to *The Mouse and His Child*.[9] As the wholly linear narrative, punctuated by the changing seasons, can be compared to a domino effect, in which one action, with the mouse and child as the principal catalyst, leads inexorably to another, amid a great chain of events. And of the many phrases that recur throughout the book, the one that reflects most directly upon the narrative is "ever-widening circles." For, despite the linearity of the work, the narrative mapping is wholly cyclical, concluding and culminating where it originally began—at Christmas, at the doll house and with the tramp figure. And this phrase not only refers metaphorically to the circular motion of the mouse and child's dance, but also implies that one single action—in this case, the crying of the child beneath the Christmas tree—can have numerous ramifications. Furthermore, the circle is a significant motif for Hoban, a symbol that appears in a number of his texts—including the wheel in *The Lion of Boaz-Jachin and Jachin-Boaz,* the gyroscope in *The Trokeville Way,* and the circular flight formation of the birds in the poem "Circles of Storks" from the recent collection *The Last of the Wallendas.*

Hoban's novel is reasonably discursive, and particularly so in the final four chapters during the battle for and reacquisition of the doll house. Yet the animation retains a greater singularity of focus, and at any one time there are only two events that are juxtaposed as parallel sequences; one of many examples of this is the opening sequence in which the tramp is walking through the town at the same time that the toy shop is being shown.

The major events of *The Mouse and His Child* can be broken down into their chapter compartments and expressed in terms of the principal characters that the protagonists encounter within the various geographical milieux:

The cyclical pattern of the narrative is reinforced in the movie in two ways. One is through the use of non-diegetic music; the song "Tell Me My Name" is played during the two frame sections of the diegesis—the opening and closing credit sequences. The other is in the film's graphic symbolism, which accentuates the circular imagery. The film's very first image is that of the waxing moon in a starry sky; during the performance of *The Last Visible Dog,* the full moon is centrally framed between the two circular Bonzo tins; and, the penultimate frame is a suspended close-up of the circular "Migrant's Yes" sign for the doll house, which was previously an oval shape in Lillian Hoban's illustration.

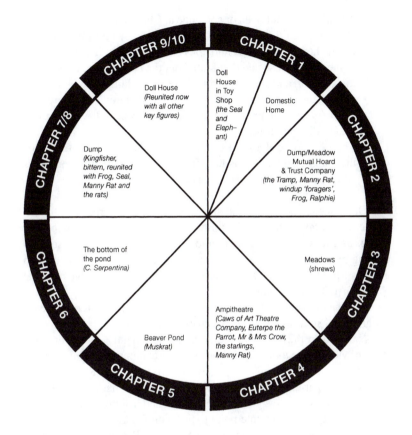

Though often greatly reduced in detail and length, much of the narrative of Hoban's novel remains intact overall in the film; this is unusual, for, as screenwriter and novelist William Boyd has estimated, on average some 60 percent of a source novel is usually discarded at the screenplay stage.[10] And being a highly episodic text, one that contains a series of interconnected events, there is much material for an adapter to utilize—and the majority of these episodes have been transferred to the animation. But in the process of contracting 173 pages of text into 83 minutes of film, some significant alterations have been made. For example:

- The film does not open or conclude at Christmastime.
- No longer do the mouse and child get sold or go to live in a domestic home; when the child cries in the toy shop (instead of at the home), the mouse and child fall from the counter, are broken and disposed of, and are taken from there to the dump.
- It is Manny Rat who breaks the mouse and child; Muskrat repairs them (instead of Frog) and allows them to be self-winding (instead of Manny Rat).
- The doll house does not become an academic center; the refurbishment of the house is not represented, and the film concludes when the father and the elephant are married.

Other scenes have been much abridged. The territorial war, for example, which takes up all of the third chapter, is given much less prominence, and now the mouse and child only observe the shrew soldiers passing by. Some incidental characters have also been eliminated, such as Miss Mudd, Iggy, Muskrat's firefly students, and the rabbit from the Caws of Art Theatre Company.

The major events of the film can also be represented in terms of their geographical settings and principal characters:

Narrated in third person, the novel predominantly adopts the dual point of view of the mouse and child. There are minor focal shifts that do not include the mouse and child and often involve Manny Rat; these sections serve to parallel Manny Rat's plight and predicament against that of the protagonists', to give greater background and insight to his character, and they function as a counterpoint to the central narrative. This method is similarly adopted by the film, in which Manny Rat (whose title for the film becomes "Emmanuel Wolfington Rat III") frequently talks directly to "camera" in pseudo-dramatic monologues.

Of the protagonists, it is the child who is generally the most proactive in the novel, and it is he who is responsible for their premature departure from the domestic home by breaking the "rules of clockwork." In addition, it is the child's own personal need to reunite with his "family" in the doll house that generates much of the narrative drive. Despite this, the narrative is still from the dual perspective of these two characters. The narrative of the film, however, is much closer to the child's viewpoint and, in effect, the film becomes the child's own story. It achieves this by:

- Giving more dialogue to the child.
- Showing more events from his direct point of view.

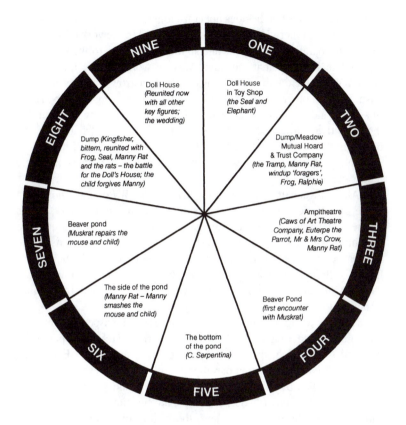

- And most importantly, by adopting an implied, quasi–first person narration within its non-diegetic soundtrack during the movie's opening and closing sequences. The latter is in the form of a song—"Tell Me My Name"—which is performed by the child. And by featuring instrumental versions of this song throughout the film, the child's perspective is again reinforced.

THEMES

Thematically, *The Mouse and His Child* is a cornucopia. And as a result, one could say that Crow's rhetorical statement "What doesn't it mean?," with reference to the play *The Last Visible Dog*, reflects upon the novel itself. Although critics favor the term "allegory" when discussing this text, Hoban claims that he does not consciously create in such terms. But deliberately or otherwise, the intricately layered framework of the narrative invites parallels to be made and significances to be formed.

Hoban has said that the novel was "a world-picture that was an attempt to see the thingness of things in a very narrow compass, a microcosm,"[11] or in other words, it is Hoban's way of viewing the very nature of society and existence in miniature. It is therefore not by accident that the adjective "little" occurs twenty times in the first chapter of the book, as the narrative is literally Hoban's own "Much-in-Little"—his distillation of the modern world into a diminutive, anthropomorphic landscape.

Akin to Kenneth Grahame's *The Wind in the Willows,* the novel is a satire of the social structures of postindustrial Western society; it sets up the proletarian rats in direct opposition to the bourgeois windups, and the dump-as-urban-ghetto in contrast to the doll-house-as-establishment. The hawk says that the mouse and child are not "part of the balance of nature"—though in sociological terms, their involvement is crucial, because as outsiders, they upturn the "balance," the status quo, from totalitarianism to a bourgeois-led democracy.

Hoban's worldview-in-micro encompasses other aspects of the contemporary world, ranging from the arts to warfare. Hoban lampoons the modernist "theater of the absurd" movement in the overtly Beckettian *The Last Visible Dog.* Further parodies include a take on esoteric pedagogies (personified by Muskrat), the introspection and self-indulgence of existential philosophy (C. Serpentina), sham mysticism (Frog), the sensationalism of the media (Bluejay), the futility of territorial wars (the shrews), bourgeois values (the elephant), and above all, the absurdities and atrocities of adulthood.

For some critics the text has implicit Semitic resonances. Christine Wilkie describes the central protagonists as "houseless vagrants, a placeless people in search of their homeland, the Jew in search of Jerusalem."[12] Ann Thwaite remarks that the novel is "*The Wind in the Willows* of this post-Buchenwald generation."[13] So to extend this Jewish analogy, the tramp would be the omniscient deity, Manny Rat the fascist persecutor, and his windup foragers the enforced occupants of his concentration camp; and thus the fight for the doll house may be seen not as a class war, but as an interracial struggle for the Holy Land. However, this proposed Semitic connection strongly contradicts with specific elements in the text. Manny Rat, for instance, possesses the Jewish first name "Emmanuel." And there is the novel's allusion to Shakespeare's *The Merchant of Venice;* during the performance of *The Last Visible Dog,* Manny

Rat says that he has "come to collect a debt long overdue," and he is referred to as "Banker Ratsneak"—a parodic sobriquet for Shylock, the Jewish money-lender.

With Saint-Exupery's *The Little Prince,* Hoban's novel shares the theme of the human condition, and specifically that of childhood—of children's cognitive, emotional, and spiritual development; the fact that the mouse and child are anonymous and are not given any form of epithet renders their situation universal. The novel indicates that life is comprised of a series of developmental stages, a series of rebirths; such ideas are depicted symbolically—when the mouse and child are twice broken and repaired, and with the dragonfly larva undergoing her metamorphosis. The book tells of the manner in which children assimilate and question the values of the complex world they find themselves in. The child appropriates the concepts that he encounters, vis-à-vis territorial warfare, existentialism, robbery, murder, and also Muskrat's "Much-in-Little" to make meaning of his predicament. The child comments, "Nobody can get us out of here but us. That gives us Why. Now we have to figure out the Hows and Whats." Thus the child is not separated from his father until his education is complete, and he himself is whole.

Though the child's search for absolute meaning is unfulfilled, he sees that there is "nothing" but himself beyond the infinity of dogs that he counts, only himself, his own subjective beliefs and the power to make of his life what he will. The mouse and child enter consciousness as a tabula rasa with no prior knowledge, free from social, moral, and cultural conditioning. Yet they are born with language, and the child, as the Rustins argue, has an "innate knowledge" of the concept of family, that "there must be a mother and sister for him."[14] Beyond their search for meaning, their rite of passage is a physical and spiritual quest for identity:

> "What are we, papa?"
> "I don't know. We must wait and see."

Self-empowerment:

> "We want to be self-winding, so we can wind ourselves up."

And belonging:

> "We can have a family and be cosy. . . . I want the elephant to be my mama and I want the seal to be my sister and I want to live in the beautiful house."

As the child says, they are no longer toys to be played with once they leave the domestic home; their identity is in flux—they are whatever others desire them to be: foragers, actors, or reluctant participants in the schemes of others—a clockwork machine to be exploited. Only Frog, the first "Uncle" of many, values them for something more.

In another sense, the mouse and child are identified by what they lack. They do not introduce themselves to others so much in terms of what they are, but what they need: autonomy and a family and a home. In addition, they are identified by what they are not. Until the conclusion, their counterpart Manny Rat embodies everything that is antithetical to them. He is powerful, despotic, corrupt, and vain; he rules his own territory, they are homeless; he is proactive, and they, without the assistance from others, can only be reactive; he is the pursuer, and they are the hunted. Finally, ironically but perhaps appropriately, he possesses the fundamental skill that is required for them to become "self-winding"—technological mastery.

It is paradoxical that the mouse and child do not achieve independence, their "self-winding," until they have finally acquired the family that they have gathered along the way around them—the community of "Uncles," as well as the elephant and the seal. Though once the father has married, he finds that he is not "wound up any more" (182), and begins to realize that commitment is more important than independence. And he has fought for a form of freedom that he was previously unaware of—the freedom of choice. And though the child accommodates and practices the ideologies of the shrew drummer boy—"A territory is your place. . . . It's the place where, when you fight, you win"—territory for the child becomes something of a spiritual rather than a geographical or political concept—a place that is connected with notions of family, community, and belonging.

C. Serpentina's statement "the child is the father to the mouse"—a deliberate misquote of Wordsworth—can signify that, like Saint-Exupery's pilot and prince, the mouse and the child are two halves or two manifestations of the same personality. Within the series of binary oppositions in the text, the mouse and child counterbalance each other as the negative and positive polarities of one psyche; the father's main priority is independence, the child's, commitment. Where the father is pessimistic, the child—embodying the sentiment of the "YOU WILL SUCCEED" lucky charm—is optimistic:

"Why not give up the struggle?" he sighed. "I can hold on no longer."

"Don't say that, Papa!" cried the child. "I've got you! You won't fall!"

"We had our hopes, and they are gone," said the father listlessly.

As Saint-Exupery's prince educates the pilot and reminds him of his former, more primal self, the child is the one who teaches his dogmatic father and the self-obsessed inhabitants of this micro-world the values of commitment. As Geraldine DeLuca believes: "The hopeful part of this particular fable is that some adults are awakened by the presence of the child from whatever cynical sleep they've slipped into and that the child can then get the support he needs for both to work together."[15]

Another principal theme is embodied in the dialectic of existentialism—signified by the motifs of the tramp, the wind, the road, the railway track, the Sartrean mud of Serpentina's pond, and destiny—symbolized by Sirius, the Dog Star, and personified by the mystic Frog. The existential theme illuminates that the mouse and child are responsible for their actions, that they must face the consequences of having broken away from their cultural conditioning and the social expectations placed upon them.

The protagonists, though, only seemingly forge their own path through the harsh, chaotic world that confronts them. Having broken out of their original mode of being by breaking the rules of clockwork, their lives are controlled by a greater, metaphysical force, destiny, and they still continue to do "what one is wound to do." And though they no longer dance in a circle and move forward once the tramp has repaired them, they now unwittingly walk around the circumference of a much larger circle, the world. As in the first chapter, in which the tramp impersonates the mouse and child's motion of dancing together in a circle, so too do the mouse and child go on to replicate his lifestyle, as "tramps," outsiders, vulnerable to the machinations of a corrupt society and forced to participate in the schemes of others. Despite this passivity, their existence is central to other beings. Their destiny is enmeshed, interconnected with all of those that they encounter in what Frog articulates as a "pre-ordained design."

But this is to talk only and specifically of some of the thematic properties of Hoban's novel, which one cannot assume will be present in the animated movie. All of the issues discussed here so far are, however, to be found in the film, although much greater emphasis was given to certain themes, and in particular those regarding morality, existentialism/destiny, and the positive values of home, security, family, and kinship.

The multilayered soundtrack provides *The Extraordinary Adventures* with a form of non-diegetic subtext. The film has music for nearly every scene; the longest period without any music at all lasts approximately two minutes. Of the five songs written for the film, the child's song "Tell Me My Name" is the most prominent, and apart from the issue of morality, it encapsulates the prioritized themes. The first two verses are played during the establishing scene. The very first graphic image is that of the night sky, with the waxing moon and the stars. The camera "pans" down into the town below (figuratively moving from the macro to the micro, the universal to the specific). From there it contrasts images of the toy shop and of the mouse and child being wound up to dance in the window with images of the tramp and his dog venturing through the town and stopping to peer into the toy shop window:

> *Wind in the trees, leaves on the water*
> *Tell me my name, what am I here for?*
> *And knowing—*
> *As I walk under the umbrella of the sky*
> *I wonder why, and who am I*
> *I must be someone*

> *Stars overhead, silently glowing*
> *Tell me my name, where am I going?*
> *There must be—*
> *Out in the world, it somehow seems I have to learn*
> *Someone who'll smile, and know my name*
> *And who will take me home*

The child's delivery of these verses is deliberately tentative and noticeably off-key, thus accentuating his anxiety, immaturity, and innocence. The lyrics highlight the child's preoccupations with identity and belonging, his resignation to the journey ahead, and his recognition that only experience "in the world" can provide solutions. The song represents two leitmotifs of the novel that are not highlighted elsewhere in the diegesis of the film—the wind and the stars, and specifically Sirius, the Dog Star. The first line—"Wind in the trees, leaves on the water" echoes the cause-and-effect nature of the narrative. These references to the wind and the stars predicate that these are omniscient forces; the questions that the child raises in the song are directed at the wind and the stars, as if he believes that his destiny is somehow guided by or manifested in them. The opening bars of the song are performed on a treble glockenspiel, emulating the sound of a musical box, thus evoking the atmosphere of a child's nursery and reinforcing the fact that the child is in his infancy.

The final two verses, played over the concluding scene and credits, in which the tramp is seen moving away from the town along the railway track, are a response or resolution to the child's initial metaphysical, existential, and domestic anxieties:

> *Wind in the trees, leaves on the water*
> *This is my name, my name is laughter*
> *And always—*
> *As I walk under the umbrella of the sky*
> *Warm in the sun*
> *I know that I have become someone*
>
> *Stars overhead, silent and endless*
> *No-one's alone, no-one is friendless*
> *I think of that wondrous world*
> *That I no longer have to roam*
> *And close the door*
> *Knowing my name*
> *And knowing this is home. (Lyrics by Gene Lees)*

These verses are performed with confidence and are more accurately pitched. They connote the child's self-assuredness, now that he has completed his arduous journey. His fundamental preoccupation with "home" is emphasized by the placing of this word at the end of the second and final verses.

Once it has taken up an instrumental leitmotif, the song becomes the main theme for the film and an integral part of the narrative. It is the child's theme tune, an aspect of his character and a signifier for his desires and motivations. The film does not need to repeatedly express the child's needs, as the non-diegetic music does this, and the lyrics and their sentiments, though absent, are now repeated by implication. The simple diatonic melody of this tune—performed on strings, accordion, and pedal steel guitar in soft, mellifluous tones—is played at pertinent moments; it dictates the desired atmosphere of the scenes, underpins action and dialogue, and subliminally reveals that the child's hopes are gradually becoming realized.

The other musical motif attributed to the mouse and child is a syncopated rhythm, performed with beaters on a conga drum, and this is played at intermittent junctures during the mouse and child's journey. In the novel, Frog removes a nutshell drum from the corpse of a shrew, and the child keeps the drum for the remainder of the story. The drum serves to signify that the child has assimilated the territorial values of the shrews—values that he will put into practice when the assembled community fights for the doll house. In a figurative sense, the child adopts the role of drummer boy because he is the central motivating force behind the reacquisition of this territory. In the animation, the drum, accentuating their clockwork motion, becomes non-diegetic. This instrument, being the most fundamental of all musical instruments, here seems to hint at the primal nature of their quest, of the primal act of journeying through space and time, and of fulfilling a destiny.

DeLuca argues:

> To the mouse's child they [the inhabitants of the toy shop] are wonderful: they imprint on his imagination the American dream: a mother, a family, a big house, community—or, as the animals later teach him to call it, territory. Yet if Hoban satirizes many aspects of the dream, he never mocks the child's hopes.[16]

The Extraordinary Adventures champions not only the aspirations of the child, but the American Dream and the quintessential Middle American values of democracy, equality, fairness, righteousness, and respectability. These notions become the very answer to the child's desires. As opposed to the novel, the film not so much satirizes the American Dream as revels in it. It is hence appropriate that the narrative of the film concludes with

A still of the mouse, his child, and Manny Rat from *The Extraordinary Adventures of the Mouse and His Child*. Courtesy of the British Film Institute.

the wedding ceremony of the mouse and the elephant. To set this event at Christmastime and to depict the establishment of the doll house as an academic center (as the novel does) would cloud the sentiment that the film wishes to put across—that the heterosexual domestic environment, the locus of the family, should be the bastion of these Middle American ideals.

The film amplifies the moral dichotomy of the protagonists and antagonist in a number of ways. Manny Rat, as the mouse and child's *bete noire,* is portrayed as a figure to be ridiculed and despised. In a traditional, cartoon style, the drawings exaggerate this antihero's malevolence by accentuating his unkempt appearance, his pronounced teeth, and crooked snout. In contrast, the mouse and child no longer physically deteriorate as they had previously in the novel. They remain in pristine quality—wholesome and clean-cut—despite their harrowing experiences. With their rounded faces and ears and their matching suits they look more like a soft toy than a clockwork windup. Peter Ustinov's exaggerated delivery in the voice-over of Manny Rat is that of a despotic English aristocrat and contrasts with the timidity of the father's voice. Manny's asides to the "camera" are of a comic nature, a spoof of the vaudevillian shows in which the antagonist would confide in the audience, only to stimulate a Pavlovian-style "boo-hiss" response. The dump in the film epitomizes the antithesis of the American Dream—a dark, shadowy refuge that houses the discarded consumer goods of society, the unwanted vices. The film sends up Manny's cronies in the song-and-dance routine "Scat Rat"—and we are encouraged to laugh at their antics, their debauchery and hedonism, but ultimately, to despise them and their "boss" for profligacy.

One scene in particular that highlights this moral dichotomy is the one in which Manny smashes the mouse and child with a boulder. This connects with one of the film's final events, when the child, in an act of forgiveness, gives the defeated, toothless, and now impotent rat the good luck charm. In the novel, Manny comes close to destroying his victims, but is denied his wish; "a dog shall rise . . . a rat shall fall" is the Frog's prophecy, though the novel allows Manny no victory (except for temporary ownership of the doll house), only a "fall" and a conversion. Arguably, the reason that the film wishes for Manny to temporarily demolish the mouse and child—other than for dramatic effect—is that it heightens Manny's malevolence and strengthens the viewer's sympathy with the protagonists. Concludingly, the child's forgiveness, in the face of such adversity, is made all the more compassionate.

To reinforce these moral messages, Manny's own reactions to both of these acts, his act of destruction and the child's humane gesture, are of shock, possibly guilt that he himself could be so mercilessly violent, and utter dismay that the child could be so magnanimous. Furthermore, Manny's reactions are given as subjective shots, direct to camera, as if he is imploring the viewer for forgiveness as well. Within the moral framework of the film, the child's desires are realized not so much because this is his fate, but because this is his reward for his courage, benevolence, persistence, and his upholding of democratic values.

Instead of Manny being converted in the film, Muskrat is. The assembling community—Frog, the kingfisher, and the seal—take the broken parts of the mouse and child to be repaired by the self-absorbed Muskrat, who eventually cooperates. Muskrat is hence present at the wedding ceremony; he is an accepted member of the new community. But not Manny Rat—he can be forgiven, but curiously and paradoxically, there is no place for an "Uncle" Manny in their utopian democracy.

If one is to interpret the tramp as a deity figure, his final words to the occupants of the doll house in the novel and the film—"Be happy"—are thus God's blessing of the American Constitution and the American Dream. The closing "frame" of the film's narrative, of the tramp walking off down the railway track, coupled with the second half of the song "Tell Me My Name," gives a closure absent in the novel, leaving no room for ambiguity or open interpretation: the child's dream—that of the American Dream—is now fulfilled.

The *Time Out* review of the film proposes that, "Hoban won't thank directors Wolf and Swenson for laying naff hands all over the finale of his whimsy, and turning it into a homily." Indeed, with the novel's parodic elements of the doll house removed, the denouement is a patriotic, self-gratifying "homily."[17]

STYLE: IMPLIED READER AND AUDIENCE

Hoban has said that since childhood he has greatly admired English writers, and that one of his intentions for *The Mouse and His Child* was to write it in the style of an English novel; the text is even prefaced with a stanza from "Look Before You Leap" by the English poet W.H. Auden. In an interview,[18] Hoban expressed a preference for Dickens, Conrad, and Wilde, though with his work the greatest resemblances are to writers such as Tolkien, Carroll, and Grahame. With Tolkien, he shares the sense of the epic landscape; with Carroll, the philosophical dimensions, the oddball humor, and the quirky characters; and with Grahame, among other similarities already mentioned, a painterly evocation of the milieu: "The interior of the bank was chill and dim and hushed; the acorn-cup tallow lamps did little more than cast their own shadows and catch the glint of frost and mica on the earth walls." "Below them winked red embers through the broken skeletons of umbrellas and carcasses of old shoes, while flames flew up in wrecked birdcages, singing where silence long had been."

And indeed, these poetically descriptive passages could quite easily derive from an English novel of the last hundred or so years. And it is Hoban's poetic language that provides the novel with much of its flavor and ambience. Yet this is not replicated in any way by the film. In *The Extraordinary Adventures,* for whatever reason, no priority is given to translating the atmosphere derived from Hoban's poetic prose, and overall, emphasis is given more to action and emotion.

The Mouse and His Child is most bathetic—interweaving humor with tragedy, profundity with the absurd, the surreal with the mundane. Hoban shocks, amuses, endears, and stimulates intellectual thought in turns. For a work that tells of such harrowing experiences—murder, exploitation, slavery, and war—there is much comedy. Hoban's humor involves puns:

> "Didn't Uncle Frog once say that the bottom was strangely close to the top?" said the child.
> "This one isn't," said the father. "We're in very deep water."

> "And relying as we must upon the element of surprise," said Frog, "we cannot afford a single wrong move from the very first moment we show our hand."
> "Exactly," said the father. "The elephant of surprise. Element," he corrected himself.

Double entendres:

> "Last up the ladder were a scattering of selected social climbers."

Tongue-in-cheek descriptions:

> "The knock-about look of her black eye-patch and the pirate-style kerchief, lent the whole establishment a raffishly patrician flavour that was irresistible."

And satirical commentary on reactions to modernist drama:

> "We don't want none of your modern filth around here!"
> "Get that phoney rabbit out of here! . . . Bring on the chickadees!"

The novel could not be categorized as a popular form, but the film is very much mainstream entertainment, and does bear some Disney trademarks. The Disney influence is most evident in the caricature quality of the illustrated characters, the use of popular songs to express character motivations. In addition, the "Scat Rat" song-and-dance routine is highly reminiscent of the "King of the Swingers" scene from Disney's *The Jungle Book* (1967); however, this could be interpreted as a conscious intertextual reference. Yet in some respects the film has a certain graphic individuality—in particular, the opening shots of the toy shop and the sequence in which the child counts the infinite number of dogs on the Bonzo label.

Umberto Eco has said that "every story involves one or more archetypes" and that as a result, *Casablanca,* as a compound of narrative formulas, "is not one movie. It is 'movies'."[19] Stylistically, *The Extraordinary Adventures* is, to an extent, an amalgam of animation genres and Disney features, and—with its emphasis upon visual, slapstick humor—reminiscent of the comic "American cartoons." Hence, to borrow from Eco's comment, *The Extraordinary Adventures* is not one American cartoon, it is "American cartoons." And indeed, the most striking differences between these two forms of Hoban's text are in style and tone. For, as what originated as a quasi-"English" novel—one that carries echoes of Tolkien, Carroll, and Grahame—has become very much an "American" cartoon feature film.

Due to the novel's sophisticated nature—its satirical elements, metaphysical and existential dimensions, its arcane literary references, wry humor and allegorical associations—it is often referred to as being a "dual address" text, one that is appreciated by both child and adult readers, and "read" on different levels of meaning. It is, and always has been, published as a children's novel, even though it is a demanding and challenging work that requires a high level of literacy. The issue of the novel's ideal reader has caused much debate among children's literature critics since publication. The English children's author Jan Mark even claims that "Hoban is not a children's writer—he's a philosopher,"[20] but clearly, this is a gross simplification. Regarding the novel, Hoban admitted that he "didn't make any concessions for a younger reader either in vocabulary or in what [he] was putting into it."[21] And the fact that Hoban considers the text as belonging to "an existential nowhere"[22] between the two categories of child and adult books certainly does not help publishers in knowing how to categorize it.

Galef recognizes that among the contributing factors to the novel being marketed for child readers are (a) Hoban was already an established children's author, and thus it would be convenient to market this work similarly, and (b) there is "the apparent simplicity of the work's composition."[23] And perhaps another contributing factor is that adult readers in the main prefer mimetic texts and would not choose to read an anthropomorphic work that has two clockwork mice as its central protagonists.

The denouement of the novel has been criticized for being too conservative and idealistic. Hoban has retorted with, "I believed that the winning of a doll house was truly a victory and I believed that victory and I believed that victory might be a permanent thing. That's why the book is a children's book. Now I know that the winning of a doll house may be a proper triumph for clockwork mice in a story but for human beings in real life it won't do."[24] Sensibilities since the 1960s, when Hoban's work was published, have developed to the extent that utopian idealism in children's texts is now considered inappropriate and untruthful. There is a growing trend among contemporary writers to give a comparatively more candid representation of modern existence in their fictions. Anne Fine, quoting Susan Sontag, argues that "the most useful you can do is to introduce the child to the complexity of things. Say it is difficult, make them better equipped to make their way in life."[25]

Yet both the novel and film undeniably represent "the complexity of things" and they both conclude that final solutions are possible. The animation has a didacticism that the novel does not. Through the first-person narration, it speaks more directly to its audience—the 'I' of the song "Tell Me My Name" translates more easily to the perspective of the child viewer. The simplification of the denouement wraps up the events more neatly and the film's message—that marriage and the American Dream are the panacea to society's ills and a child's emotional needs—is, as a result, emphasized. Such simplified notions, coupled with the sentimentality that coats these ideals, might have been acceptable in the late 1970s when the film was produced, but could now appear somewhat outdated.

Aidan Chambers proposes that style is "the term we use for the way a writer employs language to make his second self and his implied reader and to communicate his meaning." He believes that it is more than "sentence structure and choice of vocabulary," and that it "covers the writer's use of image, his deliberate and unaware references, the assumptions he makes about what a reader will understand without explication or description, his attitude to beliefs, customs, characters in his narrative—all as revealed by the way he writes about them."[26]

Self-evidently, Chambers's theory applies to a literary text and not an animated feature film, though it does help to consider this animation's ideal audience. *The Extraordinary Adventures,* being in a visual/aural medium, necessitates another form of literacy, a rudimentary filmic literacy—the ability to comprehend the various codes inherent to film and animation, which most children would have acquired by about the age of six. The animation does not require—as with the novel—advanced reading skills, an extensive lexicon (to understand such terms as "sepulchral," "phoenixlike," "profundity"), the capacity to make connections between the motifs, or the ability to retain a multiplicity of minutiae whilst following the discursive narrative through. To an extent, the film "shows" the viewer what the reader would have to decode and make sense of. By being able to observe the events and actions on screen, a viewer's understanding of the novel's more arcane terminologies—that is, those that are reproduced in the film's dialogue, and particularly the discourses of Frog and C. Serpentina—is not so paramount; and the esoteric nature of Frog's discourses even becomes a source of humor on occasion. However, the animation introduces some references that even young American children may well be unfamiliar with: "An actress in the Hollow Wood—a tin seal in Tinsel Town!" or "Didn't Lincoln start out in a log cabin?" or "Think of Einstein . . . think of Herbert Hoover!"

A number of the film's alterations suggest an implied child audience. The shift from the novel's third-person omniscient narration to the film's quasi-first-person narration in the song "Tell Me My Name" implies a child narratee, and makes it all the more accessible for a child viewer, who would be able to more closely identify with the young protagonist and his preoccupations; Bazalgette and Staples's definition of a children's film reiterates this in the following statement: "Children's films can be defined as offering mainly or entirely a child's point of view. They deal with the interests, fears, misapprehensions and concerns of childhood in their own terms. They foreground the problems of coping with adults, or of coping without them."[27]

The musical soundtrack is wholly sentimental in places—possibly too sentimental for adult sensibilities. The central musical theme too provides a warmth and reassurance to temper and counteract the darker elements of the film. The elephant in the toy shop scene is now maternal and compassionate toward the child, no longer bigoted and egocentric. The morality of the animation is even more clear-cut and unambiguous than in the novel and does not so easily allow for any open interpretation. Manny Rat's vehicle in the film—a toy sports car—serves to heighten his status over his subjects and to increase the appeal to a child viewer. And many of the bleaker moments of the novel, such as the shrew war and the father's despair and nihilism, have been minimized in the film to allow for optimism to prevail. The film chooses to derive its humor less from puns, satire, and esoteric allusions, and more from cartoon slapstick, visual gags, and comic delivery of the dialogue and music. This emphasis on visual humor again tempers the darker moments, as well as increases the accessibilty.

On the one hand, the animation, like the novel, is a dual-address work, and to make it otherwise would mean altering much more of the original narrative, and especially the arcane discourses of Muskrat and C. Serpentina. Thus, the film's implied or ideal audience is also ambivalent, though arguably, it is more for a child or early teenager rather than a late teenage or adult viewer. The latter notion has been supported by a group of pupils (11- to 12-year-olds from Ryeish Green School, Berkshire, U.K.) that assisted with the research for this study. On average, the pupils felt that the movie was intended for 7- to 14-years-olds, whereas the novel, which most of them confessed to struggling with, they deemed to be more suitable for older teenagers. The group—as a result of the film's humor, songs, and greater accessibility—strongly preferred the film to the book.

Hoban himself, however, clearly disapproves of the film adaptation of his novel. He has commented:

> With *The Mouse and His Child,* they did the usual thing—they said how they loved it, and then they got somebody to re-write it. I found the whole thing very disappointing, simply because it was so far below the standard that I had written to. . . . The animation itself is completely undistinguished. It's just a, sort of a general Disney-derived style. Now the book is not written in a general Disney-derived style. I would say if they had any artistic intelligence they would've tried for a style something like Arthur Rackham. Now if they had had a look at him, they'd have been better off. . . . Because the look of the thing is very down-market and, as I say, very undistinguished, and the look of it is as bad as the screenplay.[28]

Hoban has further remarked that the production company felt that they had to make the dialogue more "accessible" and "cinematic,"[29] and that the film subverted the novel. The film's dialogue is indeed comparatively more "accessible" (and more colloquial), though this is a necessary change if the film wishes to appeal to a younger audience. And, for example, the lyrics of the theme song "Tell Me My Name" may not be to the poetic "standard"[30] of Hoban's prose, but they are to be seen from a child's perspective, and thus the sentiment is expressed accordingly.

When asked which he preferred, the feature film adaptation of *Turtle Diary* or *The Mouse and His Child,* Hoban remarked, "Well, *Turtle Diary* is better—it's feeble and flabby compared to the book, but it doesn't subvert the book as much as the animation feature does."[31] Hoban's disapproval of *The Extraordinary Adventures* and his reaction that it was produced in a "sort of general Disney-derived style" could, in one respect, seem somewhat unjust. Hoban must have sold the film rights to the film's production company based in Hollywood—the epicenter of Western mainstream cinema—knowing that their intentions would have been to make the film commercially viable. An animation that faithfully reproduces much of the darker tones, the subtle, wry humor, and the philosophical dimensions of *The Mouse and His Child* would not be made within the commercial arena—certainly not in Hollywood. It would be more the product of a small independent company or an auteur. And any cartoon feature film created in Hollywood is more than likely to bear some resemblances to the Disney model—Disney's aesthetic is successful with audiences, and clearly, popularity is a major concern in the production of a mainstream film.

In the following statement, Douglas Street offers a useful and practical template to apply when evaluating a film adaptation of a children's book—"Ultimate success is dependent upon the perceptive preservation of original feeling and attraction in harmony with requirements necessitated by the new, cinematic setting."[32] So, by this definition, and considering the inherent commercial factors and the change in implied audience with the film, I would argue that *The Extraordinary Adventures* is a reasonably successful adaptation.

Whatever the implied audiences of the novel and the animation may be, one of the novel's strengths, as it is often said of many children's "classics," is that it is one that can be consumed from early teenage and throughout adulthood, generating a variety of meanings, responses, and pleasures with each reading. Alternatively, the animation has enabled the work to be enjoyed and appreciated by the age range that the novel has always been published for.

NOTES

[1]Russell Hoban, *The Guardian,* London, 20 February 1986.

[2]Russell Hoban, interview with James Carter at Hoban's home in Fulham, London, 28 September 1995.

[3]Ibid.

[4]Ibid.

[5]Russell Hoban, *The Russell Hoban Omnibus* (Bloomington: Indiana University Press, 1999).

[6]Russell Hoban, "Thoughts on a Shirtless Cyclist, Robin Hood, Johann Sebastian Bach, and One or Two Other Things." *Children's Literature in Education* 4 (1971): 23.

[7]Carter interview.

[8]Graham Hough, cited in Peter Green, *Kenneth Grahame, A Biography* (London: John Murray, 1959), p. 263.

[9]Brian Macfarlane, *Novel to Film* (Oxford: Oxford University Press, 1996), p. 12.

[10]William Boyd, *Novel Image.* London: Channel 4, 17 March 1995.

[11]Russell Hoban, "Thoughts on a Shirtless Cyclist, Robin Hood, Johann Sebastian Bach, and One or Two Other Things." *Children's Literature in Education* 4 (1971): 23.

[12]Christine Wilkie, *Through the Narrow Gate* (London: Fairleigh Dickinson University Press, 1989), p. 23.

[13]Ann Thwaite, "But Then Again, He Is That Sort of Toad." *Weekend Telegraph* (London), 13 November 1993.

[14]Margaret and Michael Rustin, *Narratives of Love and Loss* (London: Verso, 1987), p. 191.

[15]Geraldine DeLuca, "A Condition of Complete Simplicity—The Toy as Child in *The Mouse and His Child.*" *Children's Literature in Education* 19 (1988), p. 217.

[16]Ibid., p. 217.

[17]Beverley Pagram, *Time Out Film Guide* (London: Penguin, 1995), p. 486.

[18]Carter interview.

[19]Umberto Eco, "Cult Movies and Intertextual Collage," in David Lodge (ed.), *Modern Criticism and Theory* (London: Longman, 1988), p. 453.

[20]Jan Mark, lecture at the University of Reading (Berkshire, U.K.), 3 August 1994.

[21]Russell Hoban, interview by Christine Wilkie, *Through the Narrow Gate* (London: Fairleigh Dickinson University Press, 1989), p. 98.

[22]Russell Hoban, "Thoughts on a Shirtless Cyclist, Robin Hood, Johann Sebastian Bach, and One or Two Other Things." *Children's Literature in Education* 4 (1971): 23.

[23]David Galef, "Crossing Over," *Children's Literature Association Quarterly* 20.1 (1995): 31.

[24]Russell Hoban, interview in Lois Kuznets, *When Toys Come Alive* (London: Yale University Press, 1994), p. 230.

[25]Anne Fine, lecture at University of Reading (Berkshire, U.K.), 4 March 1995.

[26]Aidan Chambers, *Booktalk* (Stroud: Thimble Press, 1985), p. 38.

[27]Cary Bazalgette and Terry Staples, "Unshrinking the Kids." Cary Bazalgette and David Buckingham, *In Front of the Children* (London: BFI, 1995), p. 96.

[28]Carter interview.

[29]Russell Hoban, "Russell Hoban Reads Russell Hoban," ed. Alida Allison, *The Lion and the Unicorn* (Danvers: Johns Hopkins University Press, 1991), p. 101.

[30]Carter interview.

[31]Ibid.

[32]Douglas Street, *Children's Novels and the Movies* (New York: Frederick Ungar, 1983), p. xviii.

FILMOGRAPHY

The Extraordinary Adventures of the Mouse and His Child, prod. J. Murakami, dir. Fred Wolf & Charles Swenson. 83 min. Murakami Wolf Productions. 1977.

Emmet Otter's Jug Band Christmas, prod. Jim Henson. Jim Henson Productions. 1977.

The Jungle Book, dir. Wolfgang Reitherman., prod. Walt Disney. 78 min. Disney. 1967.

Turtle Diary, dir. John Irvin. 96 min. CBS. 1985.

Deadtime Stories for Big Folk, dir. David Anderson. Argos Films/BFI. 1990.

BIBLIOGRAPHY

Bazalgette, Cary and Staples, Terry. "Unshrinking the Kids," Cary Bazalgette and David Buckingham (eds.), *In Front of the Children.* London: BFI, 1995, p. 96.

Boyd, William. *Novel Image.* London: Channel 4, 17 March 1995.

Chambers, Aidan. *Booktalk.* Stroud: Thimble Press, 1985, p. 38.

DeLuca, Geraldine. "A Condition of Complete Simplicity—The Toy as Child in *The Mouse and His Child.*" *Children's Literature in Education* 19.4 (1988): 217.

Eco, Umberto. "Cult Movies and Intertextual Collage," David Lodge (ed.), *Modern Criticism and Theory.* London: Longman, 1988, p. 453.

Fine, Anne. Lecture at University of Reading (Berkshire, U.K.), 4 March 1995.

Galef, David. "Crossing Over." *Children's Literature Association Quarterly* 20.1 (1995): 31.

Grahame, Kenneth. *The Wind in the Willows.* London: Puffin Books, 1983.

Hoban, Russell. *Charlie the Tramp* (New York: Scholastic Books, 1966).

———. *The Court of the Winged Serpent.* London: Jonathon Cape, 1994.

———. *Emmet Otter's Jug Band Christmas.* Tadworth: World's Work Ltd., 1971.

———. *Frances* series. London: Picture Puffins.

———. *The Guardian.* London, 20 February 1986.

———. Interview by James Carter at Hoban's home in Fulham, London, 28 September 1995.

———. *La Corona and the Tin Frog.* London: Jonathon Cape, 1979.

———. *The Last of the Wallendas.* London: Jonathon Cape, 1998.

———. *The Lion of Boaz Jachin and Jachin Boaz.* London: Picador, 1974.

———. *Marzipan Pig.* London: Jonathon Cape, 1986.

———. *Monster Film.* London: MacDonald Young, 1995.

———. *The Mouse and His Child.* London: Faber & Faber, 1969.

———. *The Return of Manny Rat* (unpublished).

———. *Riddley Walker.* London: Jonathon Cape, 1980.

———. "Russell Hoban Reads Russell Hoban," Alida Allison (ed.), *The Lion and the Unicorn.* Danvers: Johns Hopkins University Press, 1991, p. 101.

———. "Thoughts on a Shirtless Cyclist, Robin Hood, Johann Sebastian Bach, and One or Two Other Things." *Children's Literature in Education* 4 (1971): 23.

———. *The Trokeville Way.* London: Jonathon Cape, 1996.

———. *Turtle Diary.* London: Picador, 1977.

Hough, Graham. Cited in Peter Green, *Kenneth Grahame, A Biography.* London: John Murray, 1959, p. 263.

Macfarlane, Brian. *Novel to Film.* Oxford: Oxford University Press, 1996, p. 12.

Mark, Jan. Lecture at the University of Reading (Berkshire, U.K.), 3 August 1994.

Pagram, Beverley. *Time Out Film Guide.* London: Penguin, 1995, p. 486.

Rustin, Margaret and Michael. *Narratives of Love and Loss.* London: Verso, 1987, p. 191.

Saint-Exupery, Antoine de. *The Little Prince.* London: William Heinemann, 1945.

Street, Douglas. *Children's Novels and the Movies.* New York: Frederick Ungar, 1983, p. xviii.

Thwaite, Ann. "But Then Again, He Is That Sort of Toad." *Weekend Telegraph.* London: Telegraph, 13 November 1993.

Wilkie, Christine. *Through the Narrow Gate.* London: Fairleigh Dickenson University Press, 1989.

From the Temple of Solomon to Zionist Ironies
What *The Mouse and His Child* Is Also About

STAFFAN SKOTT

The Mouse and His Child is the story of two animals that are not like other animals. They survive against all odds; though seemingly helpless and weak—they prove to be indestructible. Their story is, among other things, also the story of the Jewish people, from the beginning to the very present. Consequently, Art Spiegelman's *Maus I* (1986) is not the first book where mice have been used to illustrate the history of the children of Israel, but while Spiegelman holds up his distorting mirror in front of events from modern history, Russell Hoban's *The Mouse and His Child* is a subtle and ironic, disguised version of a well-known story of five thousand years or more.

Jewish history is so long and varied that one must be aware of the risk of constructing parallels and associations where the question might be one of mere coincidence. Still, the resemblances between adventures of the long-suffering mouse and his son and the history of the Jews are too many to be neglected.

In the book there is a constant contrast between the inanimate toys and the animals of flesh and blood—they participate in the same actions, cooperate, and help each other. But the mechanical animals are of course dependent on the living animals; similarly, Jews in the Diaspora often were not allowed to participate in society on equal terms. The mechanical animals nevertheless take important initiatives, even solving crucial strategical tasks at the end of the book, just as the Jews, when let out of the ghetto, have played an enormous role in modern culture and science, as well as the economic life of many countries.

The mechanical animals, we are reminded, do not eat and cannot be eaten, as living animals do. It may be tempting to introduce into the discussion Jewish dietary rules, but I think that would carry us too far away from the real contents of the book, especially since real toys do not eat and real animals do. The fact of the mouse and his child not eating and not being eaten is rather one of the more important ways of stressing the otherness of the mechanical toys. More important is the picture of the father and the son always together, just as loyalty within the family has been crucial for the survival of the Jewish culture.

Unlike Pinocchio and most animated toys in other children's books, the mouse and the child have, as it has been pointed out by scholars, no objective of becoming like the living animals; similarly the Jews have adhered to their religion and the teaching of their ancestors (one of the more important explanations of why the Jews have survived). Assimilation on a larger scale became a fact only in later times, beginning with the French Revolution.

A feature in tune with the balanced irony that permeates the entire book is that there is no one-sided focusing only on the misfortunes of the mechanical animals. Around them, living animals kill and eat and mistreat each other. The mechanical animals are not the only ones suffering and tormented in this cruel world, nor are the Jews the only human beings to be the unhappy victims of fate. But while many living animals in this book are killed and eaten, the mechanical animals persist and in the end gather in the much-desired haven of the doll house. Similarly, the Jewish people still exist as such and have not disappeared in the way many once strong nations have been extinguished. This is maybe the leitmotif of the book: the ability of the mechanical animals to survive, against overwhelming odds—just like the Jews have survived, by means of stubbornness, persistence, and pure wits. We know that it is the fate of toys to wear out, rust, or disintegrate and be thrown away. The mouse and his child and some other mechanical toys in the book nevertheless persevere.

Early in the book, the mouse and his son are the victims of a great accident, the breaking of the vase that leads to their demolition. Even after having been repaired, they cannot stay where they once were happy but are doomed to wander; they do not remain in the same place and do not move in circles anymore. Off they go into the cruel world, just as the Jews more than once have been forced to leave the promised land after historic misfortunes. The mechanical mice are carried away by a hawk, and they have to work for the cruel Manny Rat. This is a reminder of the Jews' slavery in Egypt or their captivity in Babylon.

Manny Rat represents throughout the book the exploiters and tyrants that during the millennia have tormented the Jews, as well as other peoples. In the end, Manny is defeated, his weapons, the teeth, being knocked out, yet still he makes one more last, horrible attempt to destroy all the animals. His attempt fortunately, but by chance, fails. It is Manny, the archenemy, who makes the toys self-winding, giving them almost real life, just as the modern era has given Jews greater possibilities than they ever had. At the same time, however, our century has been the period of the most ghastly destruction, with worse persecutions than ever, and genocide on an incredible scale.

The army of the fierceful shrews with their effective drill and formidable spears come and go as a comical picture of the great armies of antiquity, which crushed each other. The illustrations underline the amusing resemblance between these smallest of mammals and the powerful Roman legions.

For a long time, the mouse and the child stand on the bottom of a pond, and readers at this point in the narrative say to themselves: Well, here the writer is at a dead end; how will Hoban ever be able to get them up in the air again? Of course, he manages the feat in an elegant way. And the time the mechanical mice spend away from everything (except the philosopher Serpentina) is like the life of the Marranos of Spain, who were forced to disappear as Jews, pretend to be Christians, and practice their real religion in secrecy.

The beginning and the end of the book are bound together by the doll house. It is the most wonderful thing the little mouse has ever seen, and he dreams of it all through the book. In the end it is conquered from the evil rats, repaired, and furnished anew. To make the correspondence to Jewish experience even clearer, the mice encounter not only the first, magnificent doll house, but the second version of the doll house. The second version is not exactly the same as the first, just as, metaphorically, after the destruction of Solomon's Temple, there was a Second Temple. The Temple of Solomon has been rebuilt in modern times as the state of Israel, just as the mechanical animals make the doll house a new and different place to live when it has been conquered from the rats.

As in the Bible, Hoban's book has only one god, almighty and impossible to understand, the tramp, who repairs the broken toy mice and sets them out on their travel through life. In the end, he returns and looks upon what they have achieved while he was absent (as the God from Sunday School is absent in the lives of most modern Jews or Gentiles) and says: "Be happy."

The chapter where the mechanical animals conquer the wonderful doll house from the rats is a great piece of fantasy, reminding us both of Tolkien's and of Grahame's tales. If we read Hoban's story carefully, there is nothing that says that the doll house by any law belongs to either party, the rats or the toys. The toys take it by superior strategy from an enemy with far superior forces. The rats are thrown out on a train and carried off too far to be able to return. It is a cruel and actually impartial picture of what happened in Israel's War of Independence (though the book was published in the year of the Six Day War, it was, of course, written before this event).

As a disarming contrast, the most irresistible feature of Jewish culture in this marvelous book (a "masterpiece," as the Swedish critic Jesper Högström wrote as recently as May 1998) is of course the child's dream of a real mother (he really does not know what a mother is). When he finds her, she is a little bit pompous and pretentious, but still quite nice. The Yiddische Mama, object of much concern in many American novels, is in this case not only one-eyed, she is a one-eyed mechanical elephant. I do not know any other culture than Jewish or any other book than Hoban's that would dare to portray the madonna and matrona thus. But Groucho Marx would have liked it.

The Ponders; or Much-in-Little
Some Recurring Aspects of the Work of Russell Hoban

DENNIS BUTTS

> *"You've heard of Muskrat's Much-in-Little, of course?"* (The Mouse and His Child)

> *"It seems to me that what I thought amusing but arch could more accurately be described as a sly way of broaching things that come out more truly later."* *(Ian MacKillop, "Russell Hoban: Returning to the Sunlight")*[1]

As Russell Hoban's career as an adult novelist has continued its trajectory from *The Lion of Boaz-Jachin and Jachin-Boaz* (1973) to *Mr. Rinyo-Clacton's Offer* (1998), works as remarkable for their unswerving pursuit of the truth as for their wit, variety, and imagination, there has perhaps been a tendency to take the children's books for granted, at least between the appearances of *How Tom Beat Captain Najork and His Hired Sportsmen* (1974) and *The Trokeville Way* (1996).

Too often they have been briefly noted among a miscellany of other (illustrated) books for young children, with little more than a sentence or two of comment. *Ponders* is a good example, receiving little critical attention except for a thoughtful page in Christine Wilkie's book *Through the Narrow Gate: The Mythological Consciousness of Russell Hoban* in 1989. Yet an examination of *Ponders* reveals Hoban almost at his absolute best, observant, ironic, inventive, and deftly capable of introducing themes of mystery and depth even to his youngest readers in ways very few juvenile authors can approach.

These short tales of animal life in and around a pond remind us, of course, of the importance of water in Hoban's works. The aquarium and the sea in *Turtle Diary* (1975) and the pond into which the family are thrown in *The Mouse and His Child* (1969) are just two among many examples. There is a key passage in "Thoughts on Being and Writing" where Hoban asserts his belief in the need for some kind of submersion before humans can return to the light and humanity. Indeed he often uses the language of diving and reemergence from water to symbolize the need to lose one's own identity before returning to life refreshed and reintegrated.[2] Yet although there naturally is a good deal about water and diving in *Ponders,* and these stories do sometimes touch on matters of life and death, there does not seem to be any sufficiently sustained or serious treatment of this motif here to justify a psychological interpretation of it.

Hoban has also written many other children's stories about animals—badgers in the "Frances" series, moles in *The Mole Family's Christmas* (1969), tigers in *The Dancing Tigers* (1979), cats in *Flat Cat* (1980), and hedgehogs in *Jim Hedgehog and the Lonesome Tower* of 1990, as well as the richly endowed landscapes of such books as *The Mouse and His Child* and *Turtle Diary.* Though A. Joan Bowers is right to suggest that Hoban's treatment of animals veers toward the poetic treatment of Kenneth Grahame rather than the more objective naturalism of Henry Williamson, there are significant variations in Hoban's treatment between the different books.[3] One only has to compare the very childlike Frances with the much more adult symbolism of *The Dancing Tigers* to see this. But there is little doubt that Hoban's treatment of the size and apparent vulnerability of animals are powerful sources of empathy for his young readers.

Any reference to animal stories, particularly illustrated stories, inevitably invites comparison with Beatrix Potter, with whose work Hoban is clearly familiar. *The Tale of Jeremy Fisher* (1908), Potter's tale about a frog's frustrated fishing in a pond, is an obvious example. But the humorous and linguistic vivacity of *Ponders* also reminds one of the great American writer of animal tales, Joel Chandler Harris, whose hero Brer Rabbit has perhaps had an influence on such *Ponders* tales as *Charlie Meadows* and *Carrie Possum.*

The first *Ponders* stories—*Jim Frog, Big John Turkle* (1983), and *Charlie Meadows* and *Lavinia Bat* (1984) (published individually and later, with additional stories, as the book *Ponders*)—even have something of the same format as Beatrix Potter's animal tales, for they are small flat books, approximately 16.5 × 18 cm., with colored illustrations by Martin Baynton on almost every page. *Big John Turkle,* for example, consists of twenty pages including seven full-page illustrations as compared with twenty-six pages of text and twenty-six pictures in Potter's

The Tale of Tom Kitten (1907). *Big John Turkle* totals 632 words compared with 712 in *The Tale of Tom Kitten*. The resemblances are obvious.

But while neither writer makes many concessions in vocabulary—Beatrix Potter uses "elegant" and "affronted" while Hoban uses "periscope" and "oriental"—the main difference in form is that while Beatrix Potter shapes her narrative with each page representing a different event, Baynton's pictures (large or small) appear on every page, so that words and pictures flow more continuously.[4]

One important difference between Beatrix Potter and Russell Hoban's tales lies in the different worlds they portray. Both authors share a sense of place, but while Potter's tales, with Mr. MacGregor's garden and Jeremy Fisher's pond, were inspired by her knowledge of the English country scene, Hoban's tales of *Ponders* are no less based on his knowledge and detailed observation of life around the American pond in Wilton, Connecticut, where he lived for a time. The scenery of *Ponders,* with its tree-lined pond, and the lily pads, dragonflies, and floating logs, is beautifully realized.

Where Potter and Hoban most significantly differ, of course, is in the imaginative worlds that they inhabit, and here there is undoubtedly a major difference. Beatrix Potter is rightly praised because she is realistic—"an acute and unromantic observer"—in Grahame Greene's famous words.[5] And it is true that the threat of danger stalks through her pages, but there is also more than a hint of the precious, as John Goldthwaite has noted, even in such stories as *The Tailor of Gloucester* (1902) with its "little teeny weeny writing."[6] By comparison with Potter, Hoban's world is more realistic. Hoban's animals don't dress up in human clothes or befriend human beings. Though comic, Hoban's world seems less cozy, but more matter-of-fact. It is a world where frogs eat dragonflies and owls eat mice if they can catch them. It is a world where not only death but also sex appears, as Starboy Mole courts the mysterious Stella, and Lavinia Bat gives birth to a baby daughter. Although sharp and in a sense "timeless," Potter's tales have many elements that appeal to the nostalgia of the "heritage industry," while Hoban's tales, however arch they may occasionally appear, with Poverty Hollow and a rubbish dump nearby, are recognizably of the modern world.

Where the two writers are most alike, of course, is in their depiction of animal behavior combined with an ironic sense of human parallels. For these stories are not only fantasies for children but about children, in which the animal-characters think, feel, speak, and behave like young children in ways with which the young reader can identify. *Peter Rabbit* and *Tom Kitten* are enjoyed by young readers who see their own behavior mirrored there, and in *Ponders* Russell Hoban has also created a whole gallery of psychological personalities.

There is Jim Frog, the epitome of the insecure, lonely, and depressed little boy, who suddenly realizes that life is not as bad as he thought. John Turkle, the greedy and envious snapper turtle, is an ambiguous figure, while the cheerful and adventurous Charlie Meadows has more than a touch of Peter Rabbit's foolhardiness about him. Roland Waters, the pond-famous diving beetle, has the likable vanity of many small boys, while Grover Crow exhibits many of their sudden enthusiasms. Through his dramatization of the internal as well as the external biographies of the Ponders, Hoban cleverly manages to depict the states of minds of many children, their anxieties and hopes, their fears and joys.

The first four Ponders stories, *Jim Frog* (1983), *Big John Turkle* (1983), *Charlie Meadows* (1984), and *Lavinia Bat* (1984), though they have characteristics in common, can be read independent of each other. Jim feels that everyone hates him. He is too depressed even to eat a damselfly nymph or to enjoy Roland Waters's pond-diving. But when he manages to evade Big John Turkle's greedy grasp and reaches home, he suddenly remembers Roland's diving, and the memory makes him laugh. "You look as if you've been having a pretty good day," says his mother, and Jim Frog agrees. "Actually it hasn't been bad," said Jim, "not bad at all."[7]

What is being asserted, in other words, is the fun and even beauty of commonplace events in ways that remind us not only of Hoban's classic *How Tom Beat Captain Najork and His Hired Sportsmen,* but also of Robert Frost's well-known poem "Dust of Snow." There the poet, in wonderfully direct language, celebrates the way a depressing day for the poet is rescued by the simple act of a crow's knocking snow from a hemlock tree onto the poet's head.[8]

Big John Turkle again seems slightly inconsequential. Big John, a large green snapping turtle, spends an autumnal day searching unsuccessfully for food, and we see him humanized, grumbling, cursing, singing, not liking to be laughed at (by some mallards), hungry and lonely. In the end his day is saved when he rescues a broken willow-pattern cup-handle from Grover Crow's hiding place and takes it home for his winter hibernation. The ending is clearly ambiguous by human standards. Big John's predatory behavior may make us smile, particularly after he has called Crow's praise of the handle "a lot of flummery old flobbery."[9] But his realization that, if you can't get what you want,

Tom, from *How Tom Beat Captain Najork and His Hired Sportsmen,* is one of many Hoban characters who enjoys being alive. Illus. Quentin Blake.

you must settle for what you can get, seems only pragmatic. Big John's successful robbery of Grover Crow seems a long way from the more acceptable social didacticism of Hoban's early stories.[10]

If there is a connecting theme in the first four Ponders books, it is the cyclical passing of the seasons, for the autumn suggested by *Big John Turkle* is followed by the wintry landscape of *Charlie Meadows.* Charlie is a meadow mouse who has a newspaper round, though only with a scrap of a headline, which he delivers at night, despite his mother's warnings about the danger of the predatory Ephraim Owl. But Charlie likes being out at night in winter and enjoys skating on the frozen pond until one night Ephraim swoops on him. But the owl is so enchanted and then confused by Charlie's skating on the ice that in the end he decides to let Charlie escape his outstretched talons and flies away. The story inevitably reminds us of Peter Rabbit's being warned about Mr. McGregor, but there is also something magical and mysterious about Charlie's unexpected survival.

The cycle of seasons continues as winter gives way to spring in the tale of *Lavinia Bat,* when Lavinia wakes from her winter sleep to the noise of ponders in order to resume catching and eating moths. But Lavinia gives birth to a baby daughter, Lola, and discovers that she has to pass her bat-wisdom on to her daughter exactly as her winter-dreams had foretold. Lavinia remembers how her winter-dreams had urged her to "pass it on." "Ah!" said Lavinia, tuned into everything, "I've done that!" and her daughter grows into independence and freedom. [11] After the melancholy of autumn and dangers of winter, this is the most cheerful and optimistic of the early Ponders stories, with its positive affirmation of the rebirth and renewal of the life cycle. Despite winter and death, life and wisdom are passed on to the new generation.

The remaining four Ponders stories were first published by Walker Books in 1988, again with illustrations by Martin Baynton, in the collection that also reprinted the first four tales. But whereas the first four tales are linked thematically by the cycle of the seasons, the second group are connected by what might be called the Story of the Lock. This is a metal combination lock that is found in the pond and which affects the lives of Hoban's next four characters—Grover Crow, Starboy Mole, Joram Vanderstander, and Carrie Possum.

Combination locks that require a knowledge of the right combination to open them are fascinating objects, of course, and unlocking them might be interpreted as symbolizing the unlocking of other mysteries. But in these tales about the lock, Hoban seems rather to be referring to what Christine Wilkie has called "The perception of noumena through phenomena . . . to the essential mystery of things."[12] For what happens in these tales is that the animals react to the combination lock with an intensity which implies that the object means more than it literally is. It is a lock, but with a quasi-mythical status.

Thus, in the first story of this group, "Grover Crow," Grover finds a combination lock at the dump, and thinks it is a short-wave radio, though his cousin Woodrow disagrees. Between them they lift the heavy lock into the air with a piece of twine, but when Woodrow opens his mouth, the lock falls onto John Turkle's head. Big John rescues the lock from the bottom of the pond but passes it on to Starboy Mole, who is able to manipulate the combination of the lock with his tiny tentacles. Although Grover has enjoyed the lock as a simple object, it is Starboy who recognizes its mysterious qualities.

In the story of "Starboy Mole," we see the mole's continued fascination with the lock that he plays with and to which he even dances: " 'Thus do I dance with an open mystery,' he would sing. Then he would close the lock and do the same things with it closed, singing, 'Thus do I dance with a closed mystery.' "[13] Temporarily distracted by the special scent of a female mole, Stella Velvet, Starboy goes off to have tea with her, but he soon returns to the mysterious, almost numinous presence of the lock. "I really can't be away from it too long, it needs me," he says.[14] In this strange haunting tale of life underground, there are various mysteries, the mystery of the lock—how does it work?—the mystery of Stella—sexuality and love—and above all the mystery of the lock's power. It is almost as if in evoking the mystery of strange objects Hoban is pointing to the mystery behind life itself.

But Starboy's strange obsession does not last. In the next story "Joram Vanderstander," the tale of a great blue heron, Starboy sees the heron in flight and is captivated by a greater mystery. Now the lock seems unimportant and in a conversion as sudden as Toad's switch of enthusiasm from caravans to motorcars in *The Wind in the Willows* (1908), Starboy longs to fly. He hires Joram with a gift of earthworms, and when the heron spreads his wings with Starboy on his back, the mole enjoys an exhilarating flight. When Joram loops the loop, however, Starboy falls off the heron, plunging back into the pond.

But although Starboy rejects the mystery of the lock in favor of the mystery of flight, the lock is not forgotten, and in the last *Ponders* story "Carrie Possum," the lock reappears. Carrie Possum does not know what to do with herself. She lives near the dangerous region called Todman's

Farm, inhabited by a great hound called Old Gallows, and she has dreams that seem to summon her to a mystery. (She is actually hearing the ghost of Starboy Mole.) Though she tries to resist the call, one night she succumbs, and heads for Gallows Hill, where she finds the old combination lock. Old Gallows pursues her fiercely, however, until she collapses exhausted and the hound, thinking her dead, gives up the chase. Then Carrie goes home and uses the lock on a chicken-wire cage to make the Soulfood Snackery she has always wanted.

The four-part story of the lock concludes. The lock was found by Grover Crow, who passed it on to Starboy Mole, then rediscovered by Joram Vanderstander, and finally kept by Carrie Possum. It brings happiness to Carrie as it did to Starboy Mole, but only after she has a variety of experiences, including hearing ghostly voices and evading a bloodthirsty dog by feigning death. The story in many ways reminds the reader of Beatrix Potter's *Tale of Mr. Tod* (1912), with its violent comedy, and the use of the word "Tod" (which in German means "death") in Todman's Farm gives Hoban's tale a further somber resonance, despite the happy ending.

These tales of Ponders are apparently very slight. They contain much of Hoban's characteristic humor, such as when Starboy tells his mystery "How I myst you!", or when Joram Vanderstander, the great blue heron, says "I don't say I'm a *great* blue heron . . . but I think I'm a pretty *good* blue heron."[15] Puns and wordplay abound in all the stories. These tales also demonstrate that movement, noted by both Alida Allison and A. Joan Bowers, away from the gentle social didacticism of Hoban's early animal stories toward the harsher depiction of more adventurous freedom-seeking in the later books.[16] It is significant, for example, that Charlie Meadows, Starboy Mole, and Carrie Possum all take death-defying risks in order to fulfill their deepest aspirations. These stories, particularly the group about the combination lock, which Starboy Mole actually learns to manipulate, also demonstrate Hoban's continuing interest in mechanical objects, shown from his first children's book *What Does It Do and How Does It Work?* in 1959, including such memorable works as *The Mouse and His Child* and *La Corona and the Tin Frog* (1979).

Above all, however, beneath the surface of these playful and apparently lighthearted tales of pond life, often revealing detailed and acute observations of natural history, there are profound undercurrents dealing with birth, death, the cycle of the seasons and of life, and of the immanence of things. Some readers might object to loading these slight animal tales with such significance, but it is because *Ponders* combines amusing storytelling with deeper archetypal qualities that it is so uniquely Hoban. For when Jim Frog meets the damsel-fly nymph, something natural and yet truly miraculous does happen:

> When he looked back there was her empty skin split down the back and the damsel fly was out of it.
>
> She looked altogether different, she waved her new wings dry, then she flew away blue and glittering across the pond.
>
> "How did she do that ?" said Jim. "I wonder if I can do it." He climbed onto a lily pad and tried to jump out of his skin but his skin jumped with him.[17]

NOTES

[1]Russell Hoban, *The Mouse and His Child* (London: Faber & Faber, 1969), p. 89. Ian D. MacKillop, "Russell Hoban: Returning to the Sunlight," in *Good Writers for Young Readers,* ed. Dennis Butts (St. Albans: Hart-Davis, 1977), p. 58.

[2]"Thoughts on Being and Writing," in *The Thorny Paradise: Writers on Writing for Children,* ed. Edward Blishen (Harmondsworth: Kestrel Book, Penguin, 1975), pp. 66–67.

[3]A. Joan Bowers. "The Fantasy World of Russell Hoban." *Children's Literature,* Vol. 8 (New Haven: Yale University Press, 1980), p. 84.

[4]Beatrix Potter, *The Tale of Tom Kitten* (London: Warne, n.d), pp. 18, 49. Russell Hoban, *Big John Turkle* (London: Walker Books, 1983), pp. 5, 18.

[5]Grahame Greene, Beatrix Potter." *Collected Essays* (London: Bodley Head, 1969), p. 232.

[6]John Goldthwaite, *The Natural History of Make-Believe: A Guide to the Principal Works of Britain, Europe, and America* (New York: Oxford University Press, 1996), p. 289.

[7]Russell Hoban, *Jim Frog* (London: Walker Books, 1983), p. 18.

[8]See Robert Frost, "Dust of Snow," *The Poetry of Robert Frost,* ed. Edward Connery Latham (London: Jonathan Cape, 1971), p. 221.

[9]Russell Hoban, *Big John Turkle,* p. 12.

[10]Bowers, p. 84.

[11]Russell Hoban, *Ponders* (London: Walker Books, 1990), p. 35.

[12]Christine Wilkie, *Through the Narrow Gate: The Mythical Consciousness of Russell Hoban* (London: Associated University Presses, 1989), p. 17.

[13]Hoban, *Ponders,* p. 48.

[14]Ibid., p. 57.

[15]Ibid., pp. 57, 59.

[16]Alida Allison, "Living the Non-Mechanical Life: Russell Hoban's Wind-Up Toys." *Children's Literature in Education* 82 (1991), p. 84.

[17]Russell Hoban, *Ponders,* p. 9.

Thoughts on Two Hoban Poems, Some Picture Books, and a Few Obsessions

ALIDA ALLISON

Russell Hoban wrote this poem about London in the 1960s:

> "London City"
> *I have London, London, London—*
> *All the city, small and pretty,*
> *In a dome that's on my desk, a little dome.*
> *I have Nelson on his pillar*
> *And Saint Martin's-in-the-Fields*
> *And the National Portrait Gallery*
> *And two trees,*
> *And that's what London is—the five of these.*
>
> *I can make it snow in London*
> *When I shake the sky of London;*
> *I can hold the little city small and pretty in my hand;*
> *Then the weather's fair in London,*
> *In Trafalgar Square in London,*
> *When I put my city down and let it stand.*[1]

Hoban held in his hand a snowglobe, a miniature London housed within a tiny, transparent dome. The manufacture of such souvenirs is not new, but their metaphorical and millennial appeal is heightened as the cities we actually live in grow increasingly out of hand. Why the appeal? Because for the instant I hold the toy in my hand, the city becomes my little London, my wee world. The only change occurs when I shake my pet city, and, for a few seconds before it settles again, snow flies over

London. Without me, my toy is changeless, the city serene beneath its lid. It's comforting to control change, even over so small a domain.

But we ourselves do not live beneath a lid; we live in a world of unfolding events. Ideas, attitudes, and behaviors change; they have histories. What once seemed rational and right is in later days seen differently and perhaps regretted. Mid-century, countries and corporations routinely exploited territory—theirs and others'—as a means to develop their financial muscle. But in the late twentieth century, we confront the unsettling realization that the growth of industry and population has had an appalling price. These contrasting attitudes are displayed in two picture books published half a century apart: Virginia Lee Burton's 1946 *The Little House*[2] and Russell Hoban's 1993 *M.O.L.E.: Much Overworked Little Earthmover.*[3] While both books focus on a symbolic house overwhelmed by development, the most startling and dramatic difference between them is in how the authors reckon the price of human development will be fixed—and paid.

The Little House is about countryside being turned into curbside. At first, the smiling, personified house is surrounded by meadows and hills. Under the trees, children play and beyond them the horizon is open. But, eventually, development happens. Burton's colors darken and muddy; lines become jagged and jumbled. In brief, things get ugly. Building the cities most of us live in, let us remember, "disturbed," "disrupted," or "destroyed"[4] whatever was there before we started digging. Burton's little house undergoes disturbance and disruption in its struggle to survive but is ultimately rescued from destruction. The great-grandaughter of the original owner materializes *deus ex machina* to arrange for the transport of the little house far from the crowd. With post–World War II optimism and ease, the daughter simply arranges for the little house to be trucked out of town, and, using a lovely bit of fantasy, Burton depicts the whole city as stopping to let the Cinderella house pass by. It is relocated in a new pristine countryside. Happy again, surrounded by birds and children, the house is returned to its snowglobe state. This is a comforting conclusion—like Peter Rabbit, we made a mess of it, but we have been forgiven by Mother (Earth).

But doesn't applying a contemporary post-everything, pre-millennial reading to Burton's narrative—deconstructing the house, so to speak—reveal that its rescue and removal to undisturbed countryside is only a respite, a sham, one more instance of the delusion that there is always more space? Indeed, nowadays we would not be surprised to hear the house had been situated over a toxic dump or condemned because of radon. Even worse, isn't the sweet little house itself the first intruder in a new cycle of development, the first thistle among the native grasses? The entire process of expansion will repeat itself—but only finitely, for space will eventually disappear, as we now know. In fact, the basic assumption of this popular picture book—that there is always more room—is a reassuring panacea relied upon greatly throughout history. In *Darwin's Dangerous Idea,* philosopher Daniel Dennett calls endings that save the day, like Burton's in *The Little House,* "skyhooks."[5]

Fifty years after Burton's skyhook denouement, however, Russell Hoban's resolution to self-destructive civilization is bleaker. Perhaps humanity can come up with what Dennett calls a "crane"[6]—a culturally generated constructon—to extricate itself from its spreading cities. Perhaps not. In either case, as the century ends we no longer can count on skyhooks.

Hoban collaborated with illustrator Jan Pienkowski to produce the picture book *M.O.L.E.: Much Overworked Little Earthmover.* In this version of our undoing, history is played out in an instant from Eden to Apocalypse . . . and beyond. Hoban's cautionary tale is told not by a sympathetic human substitute like the little house, but by one of the ecologically displaced—human progress as seen from a mole's point of view. Thus, in contrast to the people present in *The Little House,* humans are absent from Pienkowski's illustrations. All you see of *homo sapiens* is Adam's heel as it comes crashing down on the mole's head and home, and the relationship only gets worse from there. Oblivious to anything but himself, Adam informs the mole that he will now name him. "Make it fast," the mole says, "I'm busy." But as the mole later enjoys a meal of earth, savoring its good "heart" and juicy worms, the noise starts: human noise. When the mole comes up for a look, he sees the first house. Baffled, he calls it "a hole *above* the ground . . . a crazy idea."[7]

From this point on in the book, as industrialization takes over, the pen-and-ink mole provides a running commentary but is increasingly marginalized outside Pienkowski's colorful, city-building scenes. While Pienkowski's painting of an idyllic village looks good to people, the bruised and battered mole in the bottom left shakes his fist at the horses pulling a coach. Turn just one page and the house is already dwarfed by towers and power lines. In the foreground, in front of the horrified mole, a "big shiny thing"—a car—runs down and flattens a hedgehog and a frog caught in its lights. Next page the earth is "shrieking," the sky is black, and the house is for sale. In the increasingly flavorless and unnatural earth, mole makes an almost fatal error; he chomps on an electrical cable he mistakes for a worm.

A bulldozer is described by the mole as a monster devouring the earth; it "eats empty space."[8] Gap-jawed watching this, the mole observes, "I knew all at once why Adam and Eve had been thrown out of the garden: human beings might start out with a few leaves to cover their nakedness but they end up wearing things that go KER-CHONK."[9]

As skyscrapers and traffic close in, Pienkowski's little house itself is condemned, something that never happens to Burton's house. Pienkowski paints no skyhook denouement for his symbolic human house, as does Burton for hers. Here, at the conclusion of their respective stories, the mid-century's vision and the late century's vision diverge: Burton's house survives—but Hoban's doesn't.

Near the end of Hoban's story, Noah appears to the mole in a dream to announce the flood, the recurrent, sometimes violent readjustment of nature's balance. Hoban afficianados will appreciate the actual exchange between Noah and the mole:

> . . . A little old man with a beard came up to me and said, "My name's Noah. See *Genesis 6, Verse 7.*"
> "What's that supposed to mean?" I said.
> "Find something that floats," he said. . . .[10]

Though in Hoban's book, destruction is global, it is not quite total. Mole survives, and so does a cockroach; they float on a brownish sea in a styrofoam fast-food box—adaptability is a survival strategy. The two creatures converse about luck and evolution while behind them in Pienkowski's painting the human house sinks. The rainbow that backdrops this millennial scene is not a promise to humanity of continuation, not this time. Humanity has blown it, and the promise of a biological future is made only to life as a process, not to one living form of life. Far from central to the universe, far from the apple of God's eye, humanity has turned out to be expendable. As the mole puts it, philosophizing as he gobbles up the cockroach, "Everyone wants to be special but life is hard."[11] This diminution of human significance can be stated thusly: we are the end product neither of evolution nor of divine intervention. Our solace is that we are part of the process . . . as long as we survive.

Would things be better if we vacated the planet? Does paradise preclude people? Are we fatally driven to "eat empty space"? Are baboons better behaved? Dolphins more democratic? Late twentieth-century science says not, informs us that orneriness and worse are characteristic of many species, not just us. We just do more damage. And we now know it. Thus conscious of our part, we ask, What can we do to avert catastrophe? Or, more to the point, What will we do?

Children's literature is one of the cranes we use with children to start them thinking. This process—thinking—has resulted before in the development by humans of cranes, cultural lifting devices. Dare we trust that our children will build cranes, will be our skyhooks? No; if evolutionary theory, ethology, biology, and chemistry have taught us anything, it's that we are all in this globe together.

Virginia Lee Burton's and Russell Hoban's artistic resolutions regarding out-of-hand human development differ greatly. But both express, through the vehicle of children's literature, one of the most portentous questions of our time. As the mouse child says in *The Mouse and His Child:* "there's nothing beyond the last visible dog but us."[12] He does not say "me"; he says "us." He and his father then extricate themselves from the muck by constructing a lifting device. Can we extricate the earth from the muck we've made of it, so well represented by our polluted, overgrown cities? Can the species that makes snowglobes and writes children's books extricate itself from the toxic dumps? As long as humans survive, we will be finding out.

"CRYSTAL MAZE"

"Think about it," Harry said: "infinite regress." Infinite regress: "Is that when more and more gets less and less?" asks the narrator.[13] In this poem from Hoban's 1997 poetry collection *The Last of the Wallendas,* Harry persuades the narrator, his apprehensive younger brother, to accompany him into the fun house at the fair. "It's just a hall of mirrors," Harry assures him, ". . . no big deal unless you lose your head." However, there is the danger, he continues, of being disappeared into the fourth dimension—just the kind of thing a brother would say to spook a younger sibling. But once inside the maze of mirrors, the narrator relates that:

> . . . *the hundreds and the thousands of me*
> *sometimes pulled me, sometimes shoved me*
> *into strange and spooky places*
> *where I saw all kinds of faces*
> *that were not my brother Harry and they*
> *certainly weren't me.*

Happy finally to be back outside, the younger boy exults, "Harry, we have done it. . . . But Harry didn't answer because Harry / wasn't there." After getting help from the ticket-taker in his search for his brother stuck inside the maze somewhere, the narrator must eventually go home alone, though the ride attendant does refund the price of the boys' tickets to the hall of mirrors: "it was the best that he could do."

> *When I came home all alone*
> *I heard both my parents groan—first my dad and then my mother*
> *said, "You've come home short one brother,*
> *which is more than somewhat careless, it's a silly thing to do;*
> *we think you'd best be grounded for a week or maybe two.*

When he looks in the mirror at home that night to brush his teeth, what he sees frightens him. He doesn't see his own reflection; he sees Harry staring back "homeward through the fourth dimension."

> *We change the mirror every week;*
> *we've called in mediums to seek*
> *my brother on whatever plane*
> *he is, to bring him back again*
> *but nothing helps. I've tried and tried*
> *to cross him over to this side*
> *but there he stays—though bright they shine,*
> *I'm brushing Harry's teeth, not mine.*[14]

I don't know of too many writers fond the death-of-the-author theory or the "intentional fallacy," though to varying degrees they concede that their books have their own lives and are open to multiple responses from readers. But Russell Hoban writes about what's going on in Russell Hoban's head—though he doesn't explain it, and that's what makes his writing interesting.[15]

He writes:

> . . . very likely any writer who's worth anything doesn't understand the whole thing, won't be able to identify all the elements that are coming to him. . . . That's my job as a writer, to make that space in which something can happen . . . if the words are right, something more comes to the reader than simply what the words say.

Readers are attracted to the lyricism and the humor of Hoban's writing, certainly, but also to the quality of his ideas and to the originality with which he expresses them. Hoban works hard at cultivating his mind and the "inner society" within it—his characters in all their archetypal and contemporary guises. And while Hoban has written in about every genre and none of his books is like the last, his obsessions have been consistent over the forty years of his literary career. In "Crystal Maze," many of these reappear; thus the poem offers itself as a springboard to discussing just a few of Hoban's ideas: infinite regress, the space between the dots, inner society, and chanciness.

In "Crystal Maze," one of Hoban's fascinations, infinite regress, is expressed as disappearing into another dimension in which we are still ourselves but not the selves we are accustomed to being. This defamiliarizing perspective appears notably in *The Mouse and His Child* on the Bonzo can, but Hoban has said he has been drawn to the idea since, as a child, he held up to his eye his favorite cereal box that depicted a scene of infinite regress, and stared and stared and stared.[16] The endless diminution of a flawlessly reproduced scene calls to mind the kind of death joke Lewis Carroll was so fond of, for example, Alice collapsing like a telescope. But just as a telescope opens as well as closes, infinite regress implies infinite expansion. For if we posit the selves we know as ourselves as staring at an ever smaller representation of us, we must also acknowledge that implicitly behind us, over our shoulders, so to speak, there is an infitine progression of increasingly larger images of ourselves. On the scale we're accustomed to knowing ourselves—in the mirror or as participants in the consensual reality through which we receive external verifications of our being—"we" disappear either way.

"Crystal Maze" is especially unsettling because of the objective confirmation of the weird; older brother Harry, the one who did the reassuring, has indeed disappeared. He is gone betwixt the interstices that appear in so many forms in Hoban's work—"the space between the dots" where the boundary of the coherent image is broken down into the discrete colored dots that compose its totality. But Hoban stares even further, to the breaking down of the discrete dots themselves and then to the revelation of the space between and surrounding them, a space as real as the dots. In *Turtle Diary* the representation of this space becomes the place between the panes of a train passing swiftly by, in essence the same place Hoban identifies in *The Mouse and His Child* as being Beyond the Last Visible Dog, or, in the quote above, the space the writer creates between and within the words. Hoban is the master of minding the gap. It is there, where our familiar selves are displaced from their usual footholds on reality, that what Hoban calls the "action" of our lives takes place, the real significant moments, as opposed to what he calls "story"—the mundane, one-damn-thing-after-another horizontal plane through which we customarily plod. In his essay "Footplacers, London Transport, Owls, Wincer Boise," musing over why some people walking on the sidewalk avoid the cracks and some step upon them, Hoban deconstructs the actual ground we rely upon by noticing for his readers even its essential neither-here-nor-thereness, in addition to its omnipresent, available, and vast potential—its "gapness":

> That one calls them cracks is significant; it betokens a recognition of a
> surface that might be broken through, a surface that keeps separate the
> overness from an underness in which move creatures of the other in
> ways not to be understood by us.[17]

The beautifully illustrated *La Corona and the Tin Frog* (1979) also employs the shift of perspective that opens a Hoban character to a different quality of experience. The tin frog must jump between the dots of the picture of La Corona he wants to enter, as Nick in *The Trokeville Way* similarly slips between the edges of the rational image of the jigsaw puzzle, as does Hermann Orff discourse with creatures from the deep on

Infinite regress appears in many of Hoban's works, from the poem "Crystal Maze" to the Bonzo Dog Food can in *The Mouse and His Child*. Illus. Lillian Hoban.

his computer screen in *The Medusa Frequency*. Like breadcrumbs on the path left along the way through the maze, bits of music and usually a painting or two also connect the character's experiences, as in the adult novel *Mr. Rhino-Clacton's Offer*. As if he were sculpting one of those Chinese ivory globes in which one intricate sphere revolves within many others, Hoban builds his intertwined worlds of significant connections, or "hookings-up." As Hoban's characters learn to move in the space between the dots, they learn to listen to the silences between the notes; they attend to whatever words the painting or the statue conveys to them. "Nothing strange about that," Hoban might say.

The protagonist leaps down and in, and this takes courage—that British characteristic Hoban admires. As a defining moment, this action is not flamboyant, not earth-shaking; rather it is inner-shaking. Hoban's characters are not autistic, however; the hookings-up definitely affect the character's existence in the outer world. Take, for example, *The Little Brute Family*, one of Hoban's funniest picture books. The littlest brute is overtaken one day by "a wandering good feeling," something outside her sphere of reality thus far in the story—a space between the dots. She takes it home where it catches on, transforming the lives of everyone in her family.[18] In Hoban's short stories "Dark Oliver" and "The Ghost Horses of Genghis Khan," both about children, the major event takes place in this psychomachian place but has its playing-out in the world of outer society. Oliver overcomes his particular bully (bullies show up in many Hoban stories); the boy in "The Ghost Horses of Genghis Khan" becomes closer to his father. In the stories "The Raven" and "The Man with the Dagger,"[19] the action is a definite event occurring somewhere in this nonpublic, nonconsensual space. Diving with the raven into the core of being ("The Raven"), making your own map (*The Lion of Boaz-Jacin and Jachin-Boaz*), flying with the dragon (*Ace Dragon, Ltd.*), finding your own black dog (*Riddley Walker*), drifting out of wakefulness but not being asleep (*Turtle Diary*), whatever the metaphor, in Hoban's books these actions have their rewards—because there is risk. Just ask Harry, the brother stuck in the crystal maze.

The risk is that you don't know what you'll find in there, inside, do you? Just as you can't choose your relatives, you can't choose your inner society. All you can chose is whether you want to meet whatever inhabits your interior space. All those nasty but catalytic characters like the Kraken, Mr. Rhino-Clacton, Harry Buncher, even Miss Fidget Wonkham-Strong are acknowledged denizens of Hoban's inner society, and to varying degrees, of ours. Ontology recapitulates narratology—inside the lively world of our minds exists a panoply of plots and characters; the richer the contents of the author's head, the more interesting the insides of the heads belonging to the characters he creates. "Everyone lives a life," Hoban writes, "that is seen and a life that is unseen. . . . What we actually do in what is called the real world depends greatly on how we live this unseen life. . . ."[20] Hoban's protagonists, from the Toms, Johns, and Franceses of his children's books, to the Kleinzeits, Neara H.'s, and Pilgermanns of his adult stories, live this risky inner life well. They realize and eventually acknowledge the inner existence of both beauty and betrayal, the heroic and the terrifying: Orpheus, Eurydice, and Medusa all dwell within.

In *La Corona and the Tin Frog,* the quintessential postmodern book, for example, there is not only its open-window ending, in which the characters balance on the sill at the moment of literally breaking through the frame, its humorous misreadings of language and sign—as between the incense burner and the crocodile, but also the sly, undercutting message at the story's actual end: that whatever that nasty little thing inside the monkey puzzle is, it will also pop through the frame. "Everybody can't be good," it says.

Hoban discusses his "inner society" as resource:

The characters in *La Corona and the Tin Frog* prepare to leave the frame of the story. Illus. Nicola Bayley.

The inner society has its ballrooms and bedrooms and kitchens, its shops and offices, its narrow alleys and its open places, its figures of authority and of rebellion, of usage and surprise, love and hate, should and should not, is and isn't. As is the outer society, some things are done and some are not.[21]

And as a release:

Now my inner society . . . has always had that shirtless shouting cyclist in it. I know him of old as I know myself. . . . so it isn't likely that I shall ever have to go out into the street and do that myself; he's always there to take care of it for me. There may, of course, come a day when I shall riotously put on a bowler hat and a neat black suit, buy a tightly furled umbrella, and mingle in wild silence with the brokers and the City. One never knows what will happen.[22]

The comment that "one never knows what will happen" develops in many of Hoban's works as chanciness. Recognizing this metaphysical uncertainty, Riddley Walker says to the dying boar he spears, "your tern now my tern later."[23] One mouse gets eaten by the owl in *The Marzipan*

Pig and the other mouse doesn't get eaten by the same owl. During Hoban's university lecture tour of southern California in 1990, he and I stopped for gasoline and went in the convenience store. Inside was a rack of bumper stickers with slogans such as "Laid back," "Cruisin'," and "Easy Does It." The one that Hoban chose to buy said "Shit happens."

Clearly, "easy does it" and "laid back" are not characteristics of Hoban protagonists. They're not cruising, they're crisising. Like Tom in *How Tom Beat Captain Najork and His Hired Sportsmen* or the littlest brute, they have real—if private arena—problems to solve. For both Tom and the littlest brute, the problem is: no love in the house. The ingenuity of the solutions Hoban devises is part of the pleasure of reading his stories. In *The Dancing Tigers,* the problem for the tigers hunted by the Rajah is one of life or death, or, rather, death under what circumstances. The unfeeling Rajah on his bejewelled elephant rigs his hunts against the tigers, and while he rides high listening to bad music and talking to the office, the tigers are mourning their dead. They can even sympathize with the one in the wrong: "Perhaps he sees the tragedy of the thing." That is, the Rajah is as much a denizen of our inner society as are the tigers; he is diminished by his betrayal of the existence of tigers.

But the unexpected happens—both to the king and to the tigers. For the king does not know—isn't capable of knowing—that the tigers dance. Triggered by music, in this case the uninspired light classics the Rajah plays as he and his hunters approach, the tigers move from acquiescence to their fate into definitive action:

> "I'm thinking of dancing him to death," said the elder. "Him and his trackers and his beaters, his mahouts and his servants, the whole ruddy lot of them."
>
> "Well, there it is," said all the tigers. "Why not? It's certainly no worse than hanging about and being shot down."

And then they dance; all night long the tigers dance. They dance moon, shadow, starlight, and "glimmers on the river" dances. They dance "(u)nder the hissing and the humming of the moon, under the racing clouds they danced. They danced the moon down low and pale into the morning."[24] And the Rajah is indeed danced to death. There is no explanation for the tigers' ability to dance. It is part of their being. Enough to say that, dancing, they occupy the space that Hoban's books take his readers into.

Where is this hissing, humming, flickering place wherein such things can happen? Anywhere, really, but reliably, such things happen inside Hoban's head, and that's what makes his books so interesting.

NOTES

[1]Russell Hoban, "London City." *The Pedalling Man and Other Poems,* illus. Lillian Hoban (New York: Norton, 1968).

[2]Virginia Lee Burton, *The Little House* (Boston: Houghton Mifflin, 1946).

[3]Russell Hoban, *M.O.L.E.: Much Overworked Little Earthmover* (London: Jonathan Cape, 1993).

[4]Lyall Watson, *Dark Nature: A Natural History of Evil.* New York: Harper-Trade, 1997.

[5]Daniel Dennett, *Darwin's Dangeous Idea* (New York: Simon & Schuster, 1996), p. 74.

[6]Ibid., p. 76.

[7]Hoban, *M.O.L.E.,* n.p.

[8]Ibid., n.p.

[9]Ibid., n.p.

[10]Ibid., n.p.

[11]Ibid., n.p.

[12]Hoban, *The Mouse and His Child* (New York: Harper & Row, 1967).

[13]Russell Hoban, *The Last of the Wallendas* (London: Hodder Children's Books, 1997), p. 11.

[14]Ibid., n.p.

[15]As Christine Wilkie writes in her essay in this book, it is difficult if not just misguided to attempt to separate the contents of Hoban's books from Hoban's biography.

[16]Hoban lecture, SDSU, 1990, video.

[17]Russell Hoban, "Footplacers, London Transport, Owls, Wincer Boise." *Granta* 5 (1982): 237–39.

[18]Russell Hoban, *The Little Brute Family.* (New York: Macmillan, 1966), n.p.

[19]"Dark Oliver," The Ghost Horses of Genghis Khan," "The Raven," and "The Man with the Dagger" appear in Russell Hoban, *The Moment under the Moment* (London: Jonathan Cape, 1993).

[20]Russell Hoban, "Thoughts on a Shirtless Cyclist, Robin Hood, Johann Sebastian Bach, and One or Two Other Things." *Writers, Critics, and Children: Articles from Children's Literature in Education,* eds. Geoff Fox, Dennis Butts et al. (New York: Agathon Press, London: Heinemann, 1976), p. 95.

[21]Ibid.

[22]Ibid.

[23]Russell Hoban, *Riddley Walker* (New York: Summit Books, 1981), p. 1.

[24]Russell Hoban, *The Dancing Tigers* (London: Jonathan Cape, 1979), n.p.

Russell Hoban as Seen from Germany

WINFRED KAMINSKI

I would like to begin by telling the truth: even now there is no intensive public discussion in Germany of Russell Hoban's literary work, either for children or for adults.[1] This lack is a real scandal, because it has been over thirty years since his books were first translated into German. The difficulty of discussing his work is made clear by the fact that only one of his books is currently available on the booksellers' shelves: *Das Kleine Meerwesen*[2] (*The Sea-Thing Child,* reissued with illustrations by Patrick Benson). This seems to me surprising and disappointing.

We cannot accuse his German publishing houses of not being capable of promoting Hoban's work. Although the companies have rather different literary reputations, all of them are well known and usually successful with their productions. To name just a few publishers: Diederichs Verlag (Munich), S. Fischer (Frankfurt a.M.), and Rowohit (Reinbek b. Hamburg) carry his adult titles, while his children's books are carried by Otto Maier (Ravensburg), Sauerlander (Aarau, Frankfurt a.M.), and Loewe (Bindlach).

And so the question is what the reasons could be which make Russell Hoban's success in Germany, if not completely impossible, at least problematic. Is it because of his subject matter? Perhaps he tells stories of matters and people that are not commonly written of in Germany, or is it because of style or genre? Perhaps his style doesn't appeal to young German readers? Could one of the reasons be the breadth of the literary genres in which Russell Hoban works, so that his German readers do not recognize him in all his diversities and disguises?

THE PUBLISHER'S VIEW

To begin this study of Russell Hoban's works, I wrote to the publishing houses which currently have his books on their backlists or have had those books in the past. I was rather excited to receive their responses. Rowohit Publishers answered at once that they had no materials concerning Hoban's books and had none of his titles available. But they encouraged me to contact the Munich publishers Eugen Diederichs, who were the first to bring Hoban's books to Germany. This house, however, is no longer independent, and they told me it was not possible to consult their archives. The editor of Loewe publishing (Bindlach), who published the children's book *The Marzipan Pig,* wrote to me: "The books are ambitious and obviously not suitable for children, so that they haven't been accepted by the booksellers." This is the first hint of the direction in which our minds should go when considering the position of Hoban's books in the German children's books field. He is characterized as "ambitious" and as "not suitable for children."

THE VIEW OF GERMAN CHILDREN'S BOOKS CRITICS

The explanation of the Loewe editor relates to *The Marzipan Pig* and cannot easily be applied to Hoban's other work; however, critic and educator Jutta Gruetzmach (Berlin) judges Hoban's Frances books, which were reissued in Germany in 1990 by Sauerlaender, rather highly. As a reason for the long-term value—despite all questions—of his books, she proposes Hoban's ability to write intelligently of "the tiny problems of growing up." She recognizes how cleverly the writer presents children's vulnerability and egocentrism, as well as the patience of parents. The badger family of which Hoban tells us is accessible to children, and the parents react to Frances's egocentrism "without any violence." All in all, this particular critic seems to view Hoban's books as a contribution to "Gemuetsbildung."[3]

Hoban's stories, critics say, do not describe the world as it is, but represent instead a model of how life should be. In this model, growing up, the process of overcoming the child's instinctive egocentrism, is not affected by overt warnings or punishment, but by the child's own insight, for which parents should wait patiently.[4]

Such an evaluation, which indicates that these books are indeed suitable for children, is a surprise, because it contradicts the editor's statement that was quoted earlier. A similar estimation of Hoban can be found in the "ekz-Informationsdienst" (Library Information Service), an important publication of the German public library system.[5] Here the Frances stories are called "classics" and the "little books" on children's anxieties, children's table manners, and jealousy are appraised as sensible and harmonious "educational compendiums." These judgments must mean that the books are suitable for children! These critics praise Hoban's books for qualities that were not recognized by the booksellers.

If we look at the reputation of *The Marzipan Pig* among German critics, however, we immediately see a difference between the way that story is received and the way the Frances stories are judged. The literary critic Claudia Toll cites *The Marzipan Pig* as one of the few examples of tales which are loved by children and adults alike.[6] She admires the "strangeness" as well as the "surprising ways," and she especially enjoys the lack of a simplistic solution at the end of the story. But for Anna Wagner-Meyle, on the other hand, this "tragicomical story" of failing communication and disappointed illusions is much too enigmatic. She compares this book to Hans Christian Andersen's fairy tales, but descries the "melancholic poetry" of *The Marzipan Pig* as destructive of the illusions that Andersen's stories foster.[7]

This same depreciation of Hoban's story occurred in *Librarian's Magazine,* in which one critic is afraid that Hoban's humor is beyond children's understanding.[8] And as a last negative vote, I cite the literary educator Sigrid Lichtenberger (Saarbruecken). She believes that the story's animism and anthropomorphism are not well-suited to the cognitive level of the children at the age that would otherwise match the book's reading level.[9] In addition, she writes that *The Marzipan Pig* contains too much reflection and too little action. All of this leads to her conclusion that children wouldn't enjoy this story at all.

My juxtaposition of the evaluations of the Frances books and *The Marzipan Pig* shows that neither excellent illustrators, such as Garth Williams and Quentin Blake, nor such fine translators as Rolf Inhauser or Cornelia Krutz-Arnold are enough to guarantee the success of these extraordinary books in the long run. The ideas of the writer and of the many different individuals engaged in the publication of the book quickly come into conflict with limiting educational concepts regarding the kind of material that is appropriate for children.

A WRITER UNDER PUBLIC DISCUSSION

The quarrels discussed earlier do not exist within the criticism of Russell Hoban's adult novels. To the contrary, the very quality that seems more or less suspect to German critics of children's books is precisely the quality that is highly approved: ambition. No matter who presents and discusses Russell Hoban, the sophistication of his work will usually be underlined. Critical discussion of *Kleinzeit,* for instance, emphasizes that the novel is not just a simple hospital story, but one in which the author retells and renews the myth of Orpheus, bringing into existence an enigmatic, complex, but also humorous book.[10] Russell Hoban's idea of the "vanishing of the individual into myth and language" is experienced as "hyper-slapstick" and his black humor makes his hospital a reborn Kafkaesque "Castle."[11] The author manages, the reader is told, to use a language of laconic simplicity to turn omnipotent horror and omnipresent demands into literature.[12] For the German novelist Ludwig Harig, *Kleinzeit* is a fairy tale about a human being who is afraid because objects that are usually inanimate take on life and speech.

Hoban's Frances books were reissued in Germany in 1990. From *Bread and Jam for Frances.* Illus. Lillian Hoban.

Without hesitation, the German critics also recommend Russell Hoban's *The Medusa Frequency.* They find it interesting that the writer allows us to perceive that for a long time it has not been only men who invent and live in stories, but ancient stories that look for, find, and live in mankind.[13] This opinion stems from the presence of the Orpheus myth in the novel, and the book itself is estimated as a genuine scurrilous comedy, a "comedy of vanishing imagination."

In the beginning of my little essay, I mentioned that Hoban's writing is ambitious but unacceptable for children. By now it should be clear that assessments of his work for adults are totally different from assessments of his children's books. The epithet "ambitious and playful" is understood as a positive remark. Hoban's novel *The Medusa Frequency* is valued as a fanciful modern colportage-Kunstlerroman without any illusions and the hero Herman Orff as another "Ulysses" of our century.[14] Another novelist considers Russell Hoban one of the most interesting contemporary artists and acknowledges *The Medusa Frequency* to be a text of Rabelaisian dimensions.[15]

PLAYING WITH STRANGE ELEMENTS

An overview of the different kinds of Russell Hoban's works allows us to realize important parallels and particularly interesting repetitions of characteristic elements and motifs. In his book *The Lion of Boaz-Jachin and Jachin-Boaz,* we discover the moment of exchanging roles, the search for a father, and the problem of "social coupling." The element of the father and son story is also common to *The Mouse and His Child,* which is also an example of a kind of "mechanical coupling" and a travel story, as well. Hoban here goes back to the tradition of E.T.A. Hoffmann's fantastic tales (bringing objects and toys to life) and alludes on the other hand to Kenneth Grahame's story. But in Hoban's work we don't have a neat and fine children's world. Instead we find a world of laughter and sorrow, a world full of fighting and violence, a world where there is life and death. In *The Mouse and His Child,* Hoban tells us a "depressing odyssey." Barbara Herkommer-Korfgen, a specialist in Anglo-American literature, describes *The Mouse and His Child* as a hybrid of children's literature, with a happy ending on the one side and an adult catastrophism on the other.[16] She judges this children's book as a "*Wind in the Willows* of the post-Buchenwald generation."

The retelling or deconstruction of familiar stories was also attempted by Hoban in *Kleinzeit,* partly by introducing the Orpheus myth, but especially by taking advantage of the Hofmannian denial of the border between living beings and inanimate objects. Whether Hoban accuses humanity of lacking an understanding of the natural world as in *Turtle Diary,* or makes use of the old motif of wandering, of being on the road, as in *Riddley Walker,* all of these travels lead us through a world of general disaster. It is symptomatic of Hoban's difficult reception in Germany that *Riddley Walker* has not yet been translated into German. This may be due to the enormous verbal challenge of the text and language, but it may also be due to the extreme story that Russell Hoban tells.

In Hoban's *Pilgermann,* which is also untranslated, we read once more of extreme situations, but they are different from those in *Riddley Walker. Pilgermann* is not a vision of the future, but a look into the historical past, in which the author once again talks about the Jewish experience of being different, of being a stranger. Pilgermann is a "Wandering Jew," an Ahasuerus, who undertakes a physical and metaphysical journey. In this novel, Hoban takes us back into the age of crusaders, and he offers his hero Pilgermann as a searcher for God, inviting us to take part in his "inner journey."

Wherever Russell Hoban tries to direct us, be it the future, the past, or contemporary London, all his heroes and heroines are similar to the "homo viator." There is little difference between his adult heroes and the mouse and his child. The mouse and his child are travelers, too, and are on their way in a world that doesn't show a friendly face. Their world shows a face that shocks us, but which nevertheless draws our gaze and compels our attention.

Russell Hoban's novels for children and adults are not comforting at all. Very often the discomfort hides behind literary, historical, or everyday allusions and quotations, behind poetic play. And the one specifically human quality, our language, cannot be taken for granted any longer. The experience of the science fiction novel *Riddley Walker* shows that we are not allowed much more than a corrupted or degenerate language. To me it seems to be this element, this irritation in the center of his books, which makes it difficult for Hoban's works to be accepted by the German book market. His novels are extremely sophisticated. And, in contradiction to such philosophical bestsellers for children as Jostein Gaarder's *Sophie's Welt* or Mora K. and Vittorio Hoesle's *Des Café der Toten Philosophen* (1996), which say that life makes sense, Russell Hoban's books maintain an insight of misery on a world scale, an insight that shouldn't or couldn't be denied without making all of us into liars.

NOTES

[1]An exception would be the doctoral dissertation of Barbara Herkommer-Korfgen, *Das Muster in Bewegung: Die Romane Russell Hobans* (Peter Lang Vertag, Bertn et al., 1995).

[2]Russell Hoban. *Das Kleine Meerwesen*. Illus. Patrick Benson. Munich: Bertelsmann Verlag, 2000.

[3]Jutta Grutzmach, after the manuscript 1990.

[4]Ibid., op.

[5]Monika Wolter in *Ekz-Informationsdienst* (Reutlingen 8. 1990).

[6]Claudia Toll, "Suber Reigen," *Eselsohr, Informationsdienst fur Kinder- und Jugendmedien* 9, no. 5. Also see same author *Spielen und Lernen* 4 (1989): 76.

[7]Anna Wagner-Meyle, "Die Neue Mucherei: Zeitschrift fur die Offentichen Buchereien." *Bayern* 3 (1989).

[8]Ingeborg Dietrich, *Der Evangelische Buchberater* 1 (1989).

[9]Sigrid Lichtenberger after the manuscript 1988.

[10]Matthias Thibaut, "Alles & Nichts." *Frankfurter Rundschau vom* 30.8 (1989).

[11]Bernd Klahn, "Orpheus auf der Intensivsation." *Basler Zeitun von* 3.11 (1989).

[12]Wolfgang Steuhl, "Auch Gorr mub mit der Zeit Gehen." *Frankfurter Allgemeine Zeitung* 19.3 (1992): 27.

[13]Thomas Klingenmaier. "Der Kpof im Kuhlschrank." *Hannoversche Allgemeine Zeitung* 19.3 (1992): 27.

[14]Wolfgang Steuhl. "Konkurs einer Muse." *Frankfurter Allgermeine Zeitung* 11.5 (1991).

[15]Ulrich Horstmann. "Orpheus im Kuhlschrank." *Die Zeit* 29.3 (1991). I should mention that this novel has also been criticized sharply. See Thomas Feibel, "Die Tiefe im Flaschrelief." *Frankfurter Rundschau* 29.6 (1991).

[16]Herkommer-Korfgen, 1995.

Post-*Mouse,* Postmodernist, Hoban, and the *fin de siècle* Culture of Childhood

CHRISTINE WILKIE-STIBBS

When we think of Russell Hoban we probably think of *The Mouse and His Child*[1] and *Riddley Walker.*[2] These two Hoban fictions have attracted something of a cult following and have positioned Hoban as a radical and subversive writer of both children's and adults' fictions. Their qualities of ludic wordplay, ironic humor, reflexivity, dissonance, pastiche, and unconventional narrative style have become the hallmark of Hoban's writing.

Hoban is also famous for his stories about little furry animals, not least among which are the Frances stories, and for the short stories collected in *Ponders*[3] (featuring, for example, Big John Turkle, Jim Frog, and Charlie Meadows) and others. Critics,[4] generally, have examined these and other Hoban works in the strain of humanist philosophy, for their numinous qualities of depth and interiority, and for their narrative and subjective quests for wholeness and truth. But, returning to Hoban several years after my research into his earlier fictions,[5] I find that by concentrating on these humanist aspects of the works and neglecting to focus on their other, discursive, qualities, we might have critically displaced them. So, I want to begin here with a short focus on *The Mouse and His Child* and *Riddley Walker,* because I believe it was in these two books that Hoban began to develop the kinds of narrative style and discursive features from which all his subsequent "post-*Mouse*" writing stems. By focusing on these and some of his "post-*Mouse*" fictions—*Jim Hedgehog and the Lonesome Tower,*[6] *Monsters,*[7] *The Court of the Winged Serpent,*[8] and Hoban's recent adolescent novel, *The Trokeville Way*[9]—I want to position Hoban as a radically postmodernist writer whose fictions reflect, and speak to, the end of twentieth-century psychic and material culture of childhood.

Like *Alice, The Wind in the Willows,* and *Watership Down,* Hoban's *The Mouse and His Child* sits, not unsurprisingly, ambivalently at the interface of adult and child fiction. But, surprisingly, it is this obviously subversive book that gave Hoban recognition as a classic writer of children's fiction in the 1970s. *The Mouse and His Child* is the episodic story of two clockwork mice and their epic quest for "self-winding," with all the political implications in that phrase of nationhood and of the struggle for territory and self-determination (significantly, in this respect, Hoban is a Jewish American who has made his home in England). The story features, for example, "The Last Visible Dog," which is a picture on the label of a can of BONZO dog food, imaging infinity in the regressive image within an image of itself and diminishing to limits of the visible. The narrative also features C. Serpentina and the "Caws of Art Experimental Theatre Group," in a performance of "The Last Visible Dog a tragi comedy in three acts," an obvious pastiche of Beckett's *Happy Days,* with the characters Furza and Wurza emerging from two tin cans at stage left and representing the "Isness of TO BE"; also, Muskrat, who speaks in Carrollian-style chop logic, in veils and baffles, and in the incomprehensible quasi-algebraic formulae that are his "Much-in-Little" thinking in the realms of pure thought: "Them times Us equals Worse," "Key times Winding equals Go," "Why times How equals What," and et ceteras. We can perceive in these playful narrative features the beginnings of Hoban's unseating the stability of words and their meanings and undermining the linearity of plot.

Riddley Walker is one of Hoban's unambiguously adult fictions, although its central character, Riddley Walker, from whom the book takes its title, is a twelve-year-old boy who speaks two thousand years after a nuclear catastrophe. The work is written in a fractured, debased, vernacular English, full of neologisms, aphorisms, and earthy colloquialisms, representing the detritus of a destroyed culture and sensibility. The language of *Riddley Walker* is a ventriloquial collage of fragments that constantly allude to misunderstood and misquoted signs, titles, and cultural texts, evoking postmodernism's displacement of signs and the collapse of meanings: *"inputting," "programming," "datter," "eqwations," "Puter Leit," "pirntowt."* Riddley Walker is effectively defined by his name: he walks and aspires to be a Riddler; he is presented less as an originator of the language than as a product and victim of it. He is an eerier forerunner of postmodernist paradigms that have irrevocably dissolved the monadic subject by pronouncing it as nothing more than the *effect* of language: "The postmodernist subject," Victor Burgin tells us, "must live with the fact that not only are its languages arbitrary, but it is itself an 'effect' of language, a precipitate of the very symbolic order of which the humanist subject supposed itself to be the master."[10]

These are just a few of the many examples that manifest the postmodern possibilities of Hoban's writing, and it is to the discourses of postmodernism that I now turn.

In poststructuralist theory and aesthetics, Roland Barthes[11] and Michel Foucault[12] have declared the death of both the Author-God and the transcendental subject. Barthes has described the literary text as "A multidimensional space in which a variety of writings, none of them original, blend and clash,"[13] and he has proclaimed the reader as "the space on which all the quotations that make up a writing are inscribed without any of them being lost."[14] This is the textuality in which authors, readers, and texts are inscribed in an infinite semiosis that Hoban has already unwittingly reified in his image of "The Last Visible Dog," as the recursive play of signifiers in the system of signs. In Fredric Jameson's definition of the postmodern condition,[15] words and actions have been severed from their meanings, signifiers have been severed from signifieds, and signs have been split from their referents; syntactical time has broken down, leaving a succession of empty signifiers and absolute moments of perpetual presence. In such a condition, language, Jameson says, has become an infinite play of signifiers without origin or connection:

> The sign separates itself from the referent liberating the signifier from the signified, or from meaning proper. . . . This play is no longer of a realm of signs, but of pure or literal signifiers freed from the ballast of the signifieds; it is the realm of the autonomous play of signs when the ultimate final referent to which the balloon of the mind was moored is now definitively cut.[16]

Baudrillard is concerned with the circulation of nonreferential images in what he has described as a late twentieth-century culture of "simulacra," where the imitation (the copy) both replaces and determines the "real" in a phenomenon he has called "hyperreality."[17] Similarly, Kroker and Cook, in their work *The Postmodern Scene*,[18] have captured the essence of the cultural melee of late twentieth-century life and living, describing postmodernism as "catastrophe that has already happened."

They present an image of the social and topological landscape of post-modernism that is every bit as refracted and fragmented as Riddley Walker's "Inland." In it, the saturation of media messages as a circuit of self-referential codes, not meanings, has been captured in their concept of "hypercommunication," in which the electronic soundtrack of TV, rock music, and other mediums of mass communication's information and sensory overload have been redefined as "panic noise": "a hologram providing a veneer of coherency for the reality of an imploding culture."[19] They perceive the postmodern subject not as just a fractured, but a fractal, self, living on the edge between violence and seduction, between ecstasy and decay. The postmodern subject is seen as an empty sign across which run "indifferent rivulets of experience neither fully localized nor fully mediated."[20] In the postmodern scene, computers reify memory, and money is conceived as symbolic exchange in an endless circulation of electronic displays of the computer monitor.[21] Cyber-pets act as surrogates invoking real emotions and real affections equally in adolescent boys and seven-year-old girls, and cinematic images such as we have seen in *Titanic* and its *pretension to the real* are caught up in their own game of perfecting the model of the myth. But the myth, much less the model, no longer relates to a historic reality, a phenomenon described by Baudrillard as an "endless enwrapping of images" that refer only to other models and become sites of the *disappearance* of representation.[22] This is the model of the *fin de siècle* textuality and culture I want to draw upon in which childhood is irrevocably implicated. And within these theoretical issues and textual spaces I shall explore the Hoban texts I have identified for their postmodernist privileging of the spatial over the temporal, their inscription of characters as narrative signs and as agents of visual and verbal game-playing in the slippage from signifier to signifier. In these Hoban texts, as in the model of the aesthetics and culture of postmodernism I have described, the depth model of modernism gives way to narratives of refracted surfaces, to simulational worlds with no pretension to depth, and the effacement of boundaries between the image and the "real," and between the "real" and the imaginary.

Monsters (1989) is a picture-book cameo that plays upon the Baudrillardian blurring of boundaries between the image and the real, and, ultimately, on a quite literal effacement of boundaries between art and life. Quentin Blake's fiber-tip illustrations of voracious, death-inducing, and devouring monsters simulate a "real" child's drawings in their character of the child's attention to detail, in their line, in the style of their "coloring in," and in their characteristic, random outbreaks of computer-game-induced violence; these monsters fire "guided missiles, lasers, bows and arrows, spears, clubs and rocks." They represent the real by posing as the drawings of young John, whose insatiable passions for drawing monsters is real enough:

> "Don't you ever get tired of drawing monsters?" she (his mum) said. "Not really," said John. "Monsters are my favorite thing to draw." "Still," said Mum, "there are so many other nice things to draw. There are houses and trees and birds and animals." "Monsters are animals," said John. "I mean real animals, like dogs and cats," said Mum, "or even lions and tigers if you like." "Monsters are real," said John.

When his mother and father finally refer John to a psychiatrist in an attempt to cure him of his addiction, the image becomes more real than the real. His life-sized paper drawing of a monster, the simulacra, comes alive, leaving unanswered questions about psychic reality and psychic constructions of "the real," effectively reifying Baudrillard's claim that: "Art is everywhere, since artifice is at the very heart of reality."[23]

> "No more drawings?" said Mum. "Drawings?" said John, as the door behind him slowly opened, "Who needs drawings?"

The Court of the Winged Serpent (1994), is another narrative interrogation of the real, this time between dreaming and waking. This picture book, illustrated by Patrick Benson in a series of discontinuous frames and in heavily cross-hatched images, gives an immediate sense and feel of the ephemeral nature of the dream-scape in which the story happens. The narrative features another John, who, like the dreaming Max in Maurice Sendak's *Where the Wild Things Are*,[24] has jungle dreams, and who, also like Max, crosses treacherous jungle terrain to reach the dark point of his dream in the court of the "tremendous winged serpent with glittering emerald-green scales." Here, his dream-self meets his waking-self as double who is carried off by the green serpent. The emerald key that unlocks the serpent's door becomes the transitional object as John's dream-self wakes in his everyday life (or is it still the dream? And how are we to know the difference?), clutching the key in his hand and declaring his need to rescue his waking-self from the dream.

The trick of this narrative is the way in which it plays upon readers' expectations for fixed points of certainty that continually elude them.

The real and the imaginary, in the shape of the dream-world and "real world," are confused in an endless flow of uncertainties, thus challenging and deconstructing the very notion of reality, representing it as no more than what Baudrillard describes as an "'aesthetic hallucination of reality"[25] that "de-realises" the real.[26]

> "You can't eat real John," said John. "You're just a dream." "But I can eat you," said the serpent as it breathed its terrible breath on dream John.

The serpent, too, is another point of uncertainty, ambivalently placed between dreaming and reality, posing postmodernist, ontological, questions about the status of his existence in relation to an objective "truth," or "reality," and seeking confirmation through another point of uncertainty by addressing his question to *dream* John. Dream John confirms the postmodernist realization of unstable identity by announcing that the serpent's existence depends on the whim of real John as the last bastion of the pre-computer age dreamers, to dream him:

> "Everybody dreams me!" it said. "I'm everybody's bad dream." "No you're not," said dream John. "Real John is the last of the winged-serpent dreamers. . . . The world has changed since you were young. The only place you hear of winged serpents nowadays is in computer games." "What's a computer game?" said the serpent. "You see what I mean?" said dream John, "You're completely out of touch. Nobody takes winged serpents seriously anymore and nobody dreams them." "Except real John," said the serpent. "Real John dreams me." "He won't if you eat him," said dream John.

In moments like these, Hoban plays up premodernist myths of legitimation and totality against postmodernist inscriptions of the subject in a set of mutable and discontinuous narratives.

Jim Hedgehog and the Lonesome Tower is the sequel to *Jim Hedgehog's Supernatural Christmas,*[27] with a similar mix of punning wordplay and metafictional uncertainty. *Lonesome Tower* operates on the promiscuous, postmodernist inmixing of narrative styles and codes, moving between conventional typeface and bold uppercase, the effacement of boundaries between high art and popular culture: between on the one hand, well-worn, traditional fairy-tale and gothic clichés, and, on the other, Hoban's heavy-metal fan hero, Jim Hedgehog, and his music; and the collapsing historical (fairy tale) time into an indiscriminate, contemporary present and an indeterminate "no-place" contemporary landscape.

Jim Hedgehog is presented as every bit the contemporary, adolescent boy hero, except in a single narrative moment when, in his moment of fear in the Lonesome Tower, the illusion is broken. He reverts to his animal status in a collapsing image of his hedgehog spikes, the spikiness of his heavy metal gear and his hairstyle:

> What if it's something huge and really dreadful? he thought. All I can
> do is roll up in a ball and make myself as spiky as possible. (47)

The myth of the "Lonesome Tower" is embedded in many conventional fairy-tale and gothic clichés. Among these are an abandoned and weeping maiden locked in a high tower who is rescued by a questing male; a haunted castle that stands "dark and lonely on the mountain"(43–44), looking "empty and deserted" (44), with "portcullis," "cobwebs and dust," a "hooting of an owl," the "squeaking of bats," and images of the gothic storm expressed through Jim's feet, which "seemed to crash and thunder as they went rolling down the mountain"(44). These narrative features represent a deliberately postmodernist pluralization of narrative codes. They dissolve into the nonreferential status of the signifier and into the slippage of meaning between signifier and signifier. For example, "Lonesome Tower" is also the name of a piece of music, with or without words; it also might the title of an album, or a cassette, or it might be the name of a group, or a building.

> "Is Lonesome Tower the album or the group?" said Jim. "It's part of a
> building," said Mr Strange. "What's the group?" said Jim. "It's a
> thing," said Mr Strange. "Why doesn't it say Itsa Thing on the cas-
> sette?" said Jim. "Cheap Cassette," said Mr. Strange.

"Itsa thing Live" emerges as a motif of shifting identity and the postmodernist definition of self that is fluid, multiple, and subject to rapid change. "Itsa Thing" might be subject or object, singular or plural: "'IT ISN'T THEY, IT'S IT,' said Mr. Strange"(38), functioning first as the "real" heavy metal, "panic noise," rock band; it then metamorphosizes into the lonesome maiden of the tower whom Jim sets out to rescue. In "Itsa," all the narrative themes converge as the fairy-tale maiden of the "Lonesome Tower," turned heavy-metal rock star, is tutored by Jim's newly acquired knowledge of music from his mother's lessons. The maiden goes on to sing her "lonesome tower" song in a voice like "five thousand tomcats and ten thousand bees and two or three hurricanes"(58).

The Trokeville Way (1996) could be read at one level as the collected memoirs of adolescent fantasies recollected in old age. But for my purposes it simulates perfectly the Baudrillardian scene. *The Trokeville Way* is the story of a psychic trip into a watercolor of that name "glued to a backing and jig-sawed into a puzzle" (8). The painting is therefore, de facto, an image, a flat surface. It is an image that becomes more real than the real as the fragmented narrative moves across the disjointed pieces of the puzzle and inscribes psychic fragmentation in the bewildering loss of spatial orientation. This is symptomatic of what Jameson has called the postmodern "hyperspace."[28] And, like Jameson's analysis of Andy Warhol's "Diamond Dust Shoes,"[29] *The Trokeville Way,* as both narrative and picture, is characterized for its qualities of depthlessness.

In *The Trokeville Way* the syntax of narrative breaks down, characters emerge as a set of signs and then dissolve into the textual play of signifiers, and image and experience feature as nonreferential abstractions that can best be described as a "bad trip": the "schizophrenic submersion" in the "hyperspace" characterized by its ability to "(d)islocate the human capacity to organise its immediate surroundings perceptually and cognitively, or to map its position in a mappable external world."[30] It is as if Hoban has taken seriously Baudrillard's reminder that "It no longer needs to be rational, since it is no longer measured against some ideal or negative instance."[31]

There is a map of Trokeville that appears, real enough, at the front of the book. But the places marked on it refer to no actual or even fictional territory, but rather to the *images* that appear in the picture. The reader is thus caught up not in a system of meanings but in the play of illusion, a polysemous textuality that refers only to itself and is infinitely mutable. Along the Trokeville Way the detritus of a commodity landscape litters the ground as a signifier of postmodern ennui: "all kinds of rubbish: rusty tin cans, a rotting car seat, used condoms, crumpled empty cigarette packets, a broken suitcase full of pulpy letter with rain-blurred handwriting, a lady's shoe and soggy newspapers from years ago" (51). In this hyperreal hyperspace, language is not so much a system of communication as a system of sounds that massage the narrative and move it from place to place. And there is music, functioning as the postmodernist definition of "panic noise" in the continual replay of a piece called "Libertango," and Debussy's "Reverie," and "Clair de Lune," invoking nostalgia as a compensatory device because the reality principle is under

"Trokeville is the place where things happen, or seem to happen." Illus. Russell Hoban.

threat. And in another exhibition of linguistic innovation of the type we saw in *Riddley Walker,* Hoban performs the postmodernist trick of liberating the sign from its referent by inventing a new set of signifiers to evoke the conceptual spaces of the narrative: the "Troke" of Trokeville is eventually revealed to be a corruption of "trick" and "stroke," puzzle is "juzzle," just as the maze is "mise"; the wood is "the little would WOULD," and bridge is " the old brudge": a bridge with a grudge. Each marks a position along the Trokeville Way.

And so, armed with this new set of signifiers, the reader takes a trip down the Trokeville Way with Nick, the hero of the show: a latter-day Holden Caulfield for his manifest erotic, pubescent, male fantasies. He has recently escaped from a graphic beating-up by his enemy Harry Buncher (most of Hoban's fictions are unequivocally male, and unapologetically macho) and is now perceiving the world with hallucinogenic intensity through turbocharged mind and vision: "everything seemed sharper and more detailed than usual; . . . had more color than before" (3).

Everything in *The Trokeville Way* is surface, including Nick's mind that is reified in the narrative in uppercase print and acts as a sounding board for all of Nick's imaginary and projected futures, for example:

> "YOU COULD HAVE DONE BETTER AGAINST BUNCHER; HE'S EASY TO HIT."
>
> "I know."
>
> "THEN WHY DIDN'T YOU?"
>
> "I was afraid of making him mad, that's why I backed away."
>
> "SO WHEN ARE YOU GOING TO STOP BACKING AWAY FROM BUNCHER? THIS YEAR, NEXT YEAR, SOMETIME, NEVER?"
>
> "Sometime, I said. All right?"

We have met this device before in an earlier Hoban novel titled *Kleinzeit.*[32] Thus, Nick is inscribed as the depthless and decentred postmodern subject, located on the edge between the violence of his lived experience and the seductions of his psychic fantasies, a subject of refracted surfaces across which experiences pass: he is acted upon rather than proactively acting. He meets Moe Nagic (No Magic) a former illusionist, and buys from him the juzzle that is the watercolor-turned-jigsaw puzzle—part picture, part puzzle—that marks the start of his gyroscopic mind trip into the alternative reality of Trokeville:

> "doing the Troke." "You've got to get into the picture." says Moe Nagic. "You get into the picture and you'll wish you were out of it."

"Why?" "Life is like that, isn't it. You get into something and you wish you were out of it." (20)

In the depthless surface of the juzzle, the Trokeville Way becomes something of a postmodern *Pilgrim's Progress,* where signifiers of every male fear and fantasy appear and dissolve in adverbs of time and are reproduced in a circuit of mere names, simulating the effect of characters. They are: Zelda, Moe Nagic's lover of fifteen years previously who deserted him for Charlie; Charlie, her new boyfriend; Cynthia, the young version of Zelda who is Nick's fantasy lover; Nick's mother; and Harry Buncher. Each of these signifiers of character invokes in Nick experiences of "momentary intensity" that are depersonalized substitutes for feelings in the postmodernist subject. Instead, feelings feature here as another set of signifiers, this time in the adjectival mode: rage, eroticism, sympathy, disappointment, and fear, and they operate only as pieces of information across which the subject we call Nick traverses on the Trokeville Way. These postmodernist "momentary intensities," Jameson suggests, "are free floating and impersonal and tend to be dominated by a particular kind of euphoria,"[33] and Neville Wakefield adds that they "are quickly overlaid by successive events like phosphorescence sparkling in the wake of the signifiers of emotion."[34] In this image of transience, Wakefield describes precisely the succession of superficial ephemera that substitutes for feelings in this novel. This sucession effectively undermines any pretension to emotion in the reading subject who is inscribed equally, and by default, in the textuality of both *The Trokeville Way* and the postmodern scene.

There is an ending to *The Trokeville Way* in which Hoban willfully dodges the postmodernist open ending in a well-played cliché: Nick wakes up in a hospital bed to find it had all been a dream; but, he insists, it had been a dream with a difference!

There is a paradox in all this. While in this chapter I have been promoting Hoban as a postmodern writer and invoking the poststructuralist death of the author, it won't have gone unnoticed that the chapter (as my title implies) has been as much about the historical Hoban as his writings. This is symptomatic. Because, seemingly inescapably, Hoban operates as the classic, premodernist cult of the undead author who is tenaciously and egocentrically alive both in and out of his fictions, and who steadfastly refuses the semioticians' diagnosis of him as a mere signifier in the system of signs. Inside his fictions he exists in a clear and distinctive narrative voice, and in narrative disguise in recurring idiosyncratic themes, tropes, and topoi, drawing unapologetically on the biographical details of his life. In *The Trokeville Way,* for example, he appears, like John Fowles as the novelist-as-impresario, as his young self in Nick, and as his old self in Moe Nagic:

> He was wearing faded Denim trousers with holes in the knees, worn-out trainers, and a dirty white T-shirt. I guessed he was sixty or so: medium height, grey hair, bald on top, a face that might have been handsome once (7).

Already in this chapter I have given some biographical details of Hoban, and this too is symptomatic: it is seemingly impossible to talk about the *fictions* of Hoban without somehow including him as the historical, living author. Almost every commentary on Hoban's works carries some biographical detail. Unusually for a writer, he has been repeatedly interviewed, on radio, on TV, in newspapers, and in magazines, to explain the "meaning" and mysteries of his writing, and his work in other media.[35] And these commentaries have influenced the humanist interpretation of his works: of course there is depth and interiority if what you are talking about is the workings of your own mind! The same side-shot picture of him appears on the book jackets of almost every book he has written for both adults and children: Hoban the author is not only infinitely present and alive, but he is also patently, infinitely ageless, and postmodernly timeless.

NOTES

[1]Russell Hoban, *The Mouse and His Child* (New York: Harper & Row, 1967; London: Faber and Faber, 1969).

[2]Russell Hoban, *Riddley Walker* (London: Jonathan Cape, 1980; New York: Washington Square Press, 1982).

[3]Russell Hoban, *Ponders,* illustrated by Martin Baynton (London: Walker Books Ltd., 1989).

[4]See, especially, Marie McLean, "The Signifier as Token: The Textual Riddles of Russell Hoban." *AUMLA,* Journal of Australian Universities Language and Literature Association 70 (November 1988): (211–219). See also, Valerie Krips, " 'Mistaken Identity':' Russell Hoban's *Mouse and His Child,*" *Children's Literature* 21 (1993): 92–100. Krips attempts to place *The Mouse and His Child* in terms of the Lacanian split subject, but, I find, ultimately, her essay plays safely within humanist criticism.

[5]See Christine Wilkie, *Through the Narrow Gate: The Mythological Consciousness of Russell Hoban* (Cranbury, NJ: Associated University Presses, 1989).

⁶Russell Hoban, *Jim Hedgehog and the Lonesome Tower.* Illustrated by John Rogan. (London: Hamish Hamilton Ltd., 1990).

⁷Russell Hoban, *Monsters.* Illustrations by Quention Blake (London: Gollancz, 1989).

⁸Russell Hoban, *The Court of the Winged Serpent.* Illustrated by Patrick Benson (London: Jonathan Cape Ltd., 1994).

⁹Russell Hoban, *The Trokeville Way* (Jonathan Cape Ltd., 1996).

¹⁰Victor Burgin, *The End of Art Theory: Criticism and Postmodernity* (London: Macmillan, 1979).

¹¹Roland Barthes, "The Death of the Author," in Stephen Heath (ed.), *Image, Music, Text* (London: Fontana/Collins, 1977).

¹²Michel Foucault, "What Is an Author?" *Screen,* 20, no. 4 (Spring 1979): 13–33.

¹³Roland Barthes, *Image, Music, Text,* p.146.

¹⁴Ibid., 147.

¹⁵Fredric Jameson, "The Cultural Logic of Late Capitalism," in *Postmodernism, Or The Cultural Logic of Late Capitalism* (London: Verso, 1991), pp. 1–54.

¹⁶Frederic Jameson, "Periodizing the 60s," in S. Saynes et al. (eds.), *The Sixties without Apology* (Minneapolis: University of Minnesota Press, 1984), pp. 178–218.

¹⁷Jean Baudrillard, *Simulations* (New York: Semiotext(e), 1983); see also "Simulacra and Simulations," in Mark Poster (ed.), *Jean Baudrillard: Selected Writings* (Stanford: Stanford University Press, 1988); and "The Evil Demon of Images and the Precession of Simulacra," in Thomas Docherty (ed.), *Postmodernism: A Reader* (London: Harvester Wheatsheaf, 1993).

¹⁸Arthur Kroker and James Cook, *The Postmodern Scene, Excremental Culture and Hyper-Aesthetics* (Basingstoke: Macmillan, 1988), pp. i–vi. All references to, and paraphrases of, Kroker and Cook's work, here and subsequently in this chapter are taken from these pages.

¹⁹Ibid.

²⁰Ibid., v, vii.

²¹Ibid.

²²Jean Baudrillard, "The Evil Demon of Images and the Precession of Simulacra," p. 194.

²³Jean Baudrillard, *Simulations,* p.151.

²⁴Maurice Sendak, *Where the Wild Things Are* (Harmondsworth: Penguin Books, 1970).

²⁵Jean Baudrillard, *Simulations,* 148.

²⁶W. F. Haug, *Commodity Aesthetics, Ideology Culture* (Cambridge: Polity Press, 1986), p. 123.

²⁷Russell Hoban, *Jim Hedgehog's Supernatural Christmas.* Illustrated by John Rogan, (London: Hamish Hamilton Ltd., 1989).

[28]Frederic Jameson, *Postmoderism or, The Cultural Logic of Late Capitalism,* pp. 117–18.

[29]Fredric Jameson, *Postmodernism,* pp. 8–10.

[30]Ibid., p. 44.

[31]Jean Baudrillard, "Simulacra and Simulations," p. 167.

[32]Russell Hoban, *Kleinzeit* (London: Jonathan Cape, 1974; New York: Viking Press, 1983).

[33]Fredric Jameson, "The Cultural Logic of Late Capitalism." *New Left Review* 146 (July/Aug. 1984): 64.

[34]Neville Wakefield, *Postmodernism: The Twilight of the Real* (Winchester: Pluto Press, 1990), p. 64.

[35]There is, for example, a stage version of *Riddley Walker* (1986), and a theater piece titled "The Carrier Frequency" (in cooperation with the Impact Theatre Company), 1984). Hoban is currently working with "Status Quo" on material for a demo CD with some songs from his sci-fi novel, *Fremder* (Jonathan Cape, 1995).

BIBLIOGRAPHY

Barthes, Roland. "The Death of the Author," in Stephen Heath (ed.), *Image, Music, Text.* London: Fontana/Collins, 1977.

Baudrillard, Jean. "The Evil Demon of Images and the Precession of Simulacra," in Thomas Docherty (ed.), *Postmodernism: A Reader.* London: Harvester Wheatsheaf, 1993.

———. "Simulacra and Simulations," in Mark Poster (ed.), *Jean Baudrillard: Selected Writings.* Stanford: Stanford University Press, 1988.

———. *Simulations.* New York: Semiotext(e), 1983.

Burgin, Victor. *The End of Art Theory: Criticism and Postmodernity.* London: Macmillan, 1979.

Foucault, Michel. "What Is an Author?" *Screen* 20, no. 4 (Spring 1979): 13–33.

Haug, W.F. *Commodity Aesthetics, Ideology Culture.* Cambridge: Polity Press, 1986.

Hoban, Russell. *The Court of the Winged Serpent.* Illustrations by Patrick Benson. London: Jonathan Cape Ltd., 1994.

———. *Jim Hedgehog and the Lonesome Tower.* Illustrations by John Rogan. London: Hamish Hamilton Ltd., 1990.

———. *Jim Hedgehog's Supernatural Christmas.* Illustrations by John Rogan. London: Hamish Hamilton Ltd., 1989.

———. *Kleinzeit.* London: Jonathan Cape, 1974, New York: Viking Press, 1983.

———. *Monsters.* Illustrations by Quention Blake. London: Gollancz, 1989.

———. *The Mouse and His Child.* New York: Harper & Row, 1967; London: Faber and Faber, 1969.

———. *Ponders.* Illustrations by Martin Baynton. London: Walker Books Ltd., 1989.

————. *Riddley Walker.* London: Jonathan Cape, 1980; New York: Washington Square Press, 1982.

————. *The Trokeville Way.* Jonathan Cape Ltd., 1996.

Jameson, Fredric. "The Cultural Logic of Late Capitalism." *New Left Review* 146 (July/Aug 1984).

————. "The Cultural Logic of Late Capitalism," in *Postmodernism, Or The Cultural Logic of Late Capitalism.* London: Verso, 1991, pp. 1–54.

————. "Periodizing the 60s," in S. Saynes et al., *The Sixties without Apology.* Minnesota: University of Minnesota Press, 1984.

Krips, Valerie. "'Mistaken Identity': Russell Hoban's *Mouse and His Child.*" *Children's Literature* 21 (1993): 92–100.

Kroker, Arthur and Cook, James. *The Postmodern Scene, Excremental Culture and Hyper-Aesthetics.* Basingstoke: Macmillan, 1988.

McLean, Marie. "The Signifier as Token: the Textual Riddles of Russell Hoban," *AUMLA,* Journal of Australian Universities Language and Literature Association 70 (November 1988): 211–219.

Sendak, Maurice. *Where the Wild Things Are.* Harmondsworth: Penguin Books, 1970.

Wakefield, Neville. *Postmodernism: The Twilight of the Real.* Winchester: Pluto Press, 1990.

Wilkie, Christine. *Through the Narrow Gate: The Mythological Consciousness of Russell Hoban.* Cranbury, NJ: Associated University Presses, 1989.

The Way of *The Trokeville Way*

MARGARET BRUZELIUS

> *"Weare going aint we."*
> *"Yes weare going."*
> *"Down that road with Eusa."*
> *"Time and reqwyrt."*
> —OPENING CHANT FOR THE "EUSA SHOW,"
> *RIDDLEY WALKER*

One of the great pleasures of reading is the moment of starting the narrative machine: the gears engage, the wheels begin to turn, and the machine starts rolling; the reader is obliged only to follow the words down the page. Generic fiction, based as it is on well-known gambits, accentuates this familiar pleasure by reminding us that we have gone down this road before: we have seen this butler, or this Los Angeles, or these aliens, or ones very like them, and we welcome these familiar characters and look for the small refreshing differences. The appeal of the generic is the appeal of the mastered machine—not only will the merest touch engage the gears, but this machine is guaranteed not to take us anyplace that we don't want to go. To the cry of modernism, "Make it new!" the huge readership for generic fiction responds, "Play it again, Sam": the defining wish of the twentieth century's major aesthetic movement has been refused by a public that has resolutely resisted its demand. And, indeed, some of the most enduring (and read) modernist texts, such as *The Turn of the Screw* and *Heart of Darkness,* combine mastery of generic convention—the ghost story, the adventure yarn—with a destabilizing, modernist sensibility.

No matter what form it uses, postmodern fiction foregrounds the mechanics of the narrative machine, a practice that partly explains its fondness for highly codified modes (detection in all its forms, thrillers, adventure). Postmodern fictions include not only an awareness of emplotment—of narrative machinery *as* machinery—but also a consciousness of the arbitrariness of emplotment—of the fact that any of the elements of a plot can be vectored within other, equally powerful conventions. *The Turn of the Screw* and *Heart of Darkness,* while full of highly self-conscious echoes of past fictions, nevertheless depend for their effect on an ultimate surrender to the generic mechanism, however expanded and elaborated. In contrast, Italo Calvino's *If on a Winter's Night a Traveler,* while also indebted to generic fiction, emphasizes the facticity of narrative itself (while also seducing us with the pull of narrative pleasure). In postmodern fictions the narrative is always aware of its antithetical other lurking at the corner: tragedy can meet farce, indeed probably is farce, at the same time as it remains tragedy.

In *The Trokeville Way,* Russell Hoban's most recent young adult fiction, Hoban has composed a model postmodern novel for the young. The self-awareness that he gives his narrator marks this novel as postmodern in the most exact sense of that mode: it is self-reflective, jokey, parodic, and yet effective. Like *Through the Looking Glass, Trokeville* is the story of a child's voyage through a different world and of what he found there. It illustrates Hoban's mastery of the adventure genre: the plot of exotic journey, return, and coming into adulthood that was reinvented for the secular novel by Scott.[1] (This is a framework Hoban has used before to extraordinary effect in *Riddley Walker* and *The Mouse and His Child.*) But it is Hoban's virtuosic display of the mechanics of romance—his ability to effect the romance plot despite the novel's self-consciously knowing tone about the nature of the story being told—that makes this novel both quirky and powerful. (This may be especially true for the young readers for whom it is marketed, who are intensely familiar with every variant of this genre in both fantasy and science fiction.) *Trokeville* makes available to younger readers both Hoban's acutely postmodern awareness of the factitiousness of stories and the peculiar alertness to the life of things and language that characterizes his adult fictions. Published in 1996, the same year as the adult book *Fremder,* it is, like that science fiction novel, an exploration of a highly familiar genre, in this case the "coming of age" novel. What sets it apart in this crowded field is Hoban's ability to present his story both as story and as experience of the real. The devices that he uses—the well-worn romance plot itself; our hero Nick's world-weary tone; his interior dialogue with his mind (which always replies to him in capitals and quite literally seems to have a mind of its own); the effervescent play with language; the ironic acceptance with which characters in Nick's life inhabit both his dream and his real world—combine to insist on the novel simultaneously as artifact and as real, lived experience. Hoban refuses to hierarchize the plots of the romance versus the real; rather, with a postmodern awareness of the importance of artifice in everyday life, he makes us realize how they bleed into and transform each other.

Trokeville's effect can be summed up by the effect of the song that becomes its leitmotif, "Libertango," whose lyric is "Strange—I've seen that face before, / Seen him hanging round my door. . . ." Hoban uses this song not only because it is strange—Nick describes it as "a spooky, shadowy sounding thing" (6)—but because within the novel it is familiar: Nick's father owns it on a Grace Jones CD; it is part of the noise of everyday life that becomes profoundly significant in the story. Moreover, the lyric of the song itself emphasizes the moment when the familiar becomes oddly different, and thus perceptible in a new way, "Strange, I've seen that face before. . . ." Nick freshly perceives the music of "Libertango" when he hears it played in a new context, just as the reader newly perceives the familiar coming of age plot in Hoban's variation. But more than that, Hoban shows us that this familiar plot is itself strange and capable of a transforming energy. Like a magician who carefully disassembles his trick for the audience, then performs it at speed and astonishes them anyway, Hoban reminds us that the romance plot is familiar and even stale, and then seduces us with it.

The romance conventions that Hoban marshals are familiar not only from their earlier incarnations in his writing, but historically in the tradition inaugurated in the nineteenth century by Scott, elaborated by Verne, Dumas, Stevenson, Kipling, and others, and continued in modern fantasy fiction and films such as *Star Wars*.[2] Since *Trokeville*'s strategy depends on our recognition of this familiar plot as part of Nick's mental landscape, it is worth briefly rehearsing the classic adventure plot. First, of course, these are the quintessential "coming of age" novels for boys. Despite efforts to imagine female heroes (Le Guin's *Tehanu* and McKillip's *The Forgotten Beasts of Eld* come to mind), the genre remains dedicated to the success of young men: from Scott's Waverley to Le Guin's Ged (in *Wizard of Earthsea*), adventure celebrates the accession to young man's adulthood.[3] Despite the fact that these young men are "our heroes," they are usually depicted as vacillating and uncertain: they stumble into their adventures, and their progress is marked by frequent calamity. (Stevenson's Jim Hawkins in *Treasure Island,* whose multiple truancies finally lead to the unravelling of the pirates' plot and the return of the treasure seekers to England is a splendid example of the hero's gift for doing the wrong things that turn out to be right.) Adventure heroes tend to be self-reflexive and *un*heroic, acted on rather than acting: their journey through the exotic space is not the result of their will to power but rather the result of a series of unforeseen accidents.

The passage into adulthood is literalized in adventure as the traversal of an exotic space dominated by a powerful hypermasculine figure such Verne's Captain Nemo, Dumas's Count of Monte Cristo, or Stevenson's Long John Silver. Although these characters are the most memorable characters in such novels—who remembers that it is Aronnax who is the hero of *20,000 Leagues under the Sea*?—it is important to realize that they are never the heroes and are never allowed back into the frame world, the world in which the narratives begin and end that is also, implicitly, the world of the reader. These hypermasculine men represent an unbridled will to power that must ultimately be rejected by the young man. The threat to the hero presented by these demonic figures (usually because they represent the temptation of a profoundly asocial energy) is counterbalanced by the support of a guide or friend. This is perhaps the most miscellaneous group of characters, who can be of any sex or class: Ned Land, the harpooner, and Conseil, the manservant, represent two such helpers for Aronnax in *20,000 Leagues under the Sea*. The exotic landscape through which the hero travels always contains a crucial, formative space (an extinct volcano, a cave behind a waterfall, the central ocean at the center of the earth in Verne's *Journey to the Center of the Earth*), often described in highly eroticized terms as a female body, which the hero must enter. This space is the farthest and most dangerous point of his itinerary; having survived his encounter with it, he begins to make his way back to the frame world. The final element of the exotic world is the frequent presence within it of an attractive but "unsuitable" young woman. Her "unsuitability" may be because she is of the wrong class or kind (the immortal Ayesha for the merely mortal Leo, in Rider Haggard's *She*), or on the wrong side (the Jacobin Flora MacIvor for the primly Whiggish Waverley).

Despite the obvious artificiality of the exotic worlds of romance, writers of adventure invest considerable energy in making their worlds seem real and internally coherent. From the editorial machinery Poe elaborates to attest to the truth of his tales; to Verne's stupefying expositions of machinery—submarines, rockets, balloons; to science fiction's pseudo explanations of weird worlds, adventure insists on the reality of the fabulous. The romance is not a genre that brandishes its own artificiality before readers, but rather seduces them into a seamlessly created exotic. It is here, precisely in romance's central, factitious claim to the "real" that

Hoban is most radical in his claims. The title of this novel, *The Trokeville Way,* plays on a portmanteau word, the troke, a combination of a trick and a stroke. But it also a trope—a well-worn trick that represents the topos of romance. When you successfully combine a trick and a stroke you are in Trokeville: the place where things happen. What Hoban asserts is that the unreal place where things happen—the trick/stroke/trope where the story is—is the real. Trokeville is completely polymorphous; not a particular place, but a state of mind that can happen to anyone at any time. Hoban's writing by definition refuses the hierarchization of the imagined as somehow a lesser subset of the real; rather, he asserts in *Trokeville* as in his other writings that we apprehend the real through our relation to stories.

Trokeville* is narrated by Nick Hartley, twelve at the beginning of the novel (as is Riddley, who also narrates his own story in *Riddley Walker*). Nick is an English schoolboy at the edge of adolescence. Like every hero of adventure, he is more acted upon than acting: tormented by the class bully Buncher (the hypermasculine figure), intrigued by his friend Tom's big sister Cynthia (the unsuitable love), and beginning to negotiate his place in the adult world. At the opening of the tale Nick is knocked unconscious in a fight with Buncher, comes to with a sense of heightened awareness, buys a magical jigsaw puzzle that depicts an old bridge over a river from an itinerant musician and ex-magician named Moe Nagic, learns how to enter the puzzle world—the "juzzle"—and spends the rest of the story engaging and disengaging from it.[4] What separates Nick from the ordinary hero of adventure fictions and makes him indelibly postmodern is his doubled consciousness of himself as part of a story, as an artifact of narrative. Like the reader, Nick loses himself in a fictional world—the world of the jigsaw puzzle—but also like the reader, he retains the consciousness that allows him to comment on the story in which he participates.

The jigsaw puzzle that Nick buys becomes the exotic world that is essential to romance. Like many such worlds, it is both near and far, the world beside the everyday world that is always there for the hero of adventure. When Nick buys the juzzle (jigsaw + puzzle) from Moe Nagic, a busker who plays the concertina, Moe explains what entering the juzzle world is like: "while this [his first exploration of the juzzle world] was happening, I knew I was standing on a bed in our room in Mrs. Whitby's Seaview Hotel. I wasn't out of touch with reality—I was in touch with *two* realities" (16). Moe shows Nick how to enter the juzzle world (he is clearly a helper figure), but also makes clear to him that "there's no magic, remember? The whole thing is a mind trip. It's a level of reality that you get to with your mind and it's your mind that determines whom and what you encounter. I feel morally obliged to tell you one thing, though—you get into that picture and you'll wish you were out of it" (20). Moe's explanation of the experience of entering the juzzle world— being in touch with two realities—parallels the reader's experience in reading, when we are both here, in a chair, and there, somewhere in the world of the book. Like Nick, we can enter and exit the juzzle world more or less at will, it is a "mind trip." But Hoban insists, even while he emphasizes the factitiousness of narrative, that it is also transformative, and not necessarily only in a benign way: "you get into that picture and you'll wish you were out of it."

Once Nick takes the picture home he enters it a few times, first only briefly, until he finally commits to the fantasy and explores the picture in depth. In the course of this exploration he comes across all the figures I have enumerated as central to adventure. First, of course, is Buncher, Nick's nemesis, who is presented as both hypermasculine and grotesque. Before Nick enters the juzzle world, he encounters Buncher "swinging his conker" and surrounded by a "really depressing smell that took the heart out of you before anything even started" (1).[5] When Nick shatters Buncher's conker, a fight is inevitable, a fight that Nick knows he will lose precisely because he lacks the manic rage that Buncher embodies: "I knew I was going to lose, the same as I'd lost the other two fights with him. . . . Not because he was bigger . . . but because I could never work up as much rage as he had in him all the time. He was like a boiling pot with its lid jumping up and down. . . . He was so *serious* about the whole thing" (2). In the "juzzle" world Buncher continues to intimidate Nick because he is "more developed": Nick says, "I couldn't help noticing that some of the other boys of my age . . . were more developed than I was. Buncher, at thirteen, with his hormones and his pong, looked pretty much like a man already" (64). Buncher confronts Nick in the juzzle world twice—once Nick throws him into the river and once he knocks him out with the flat side of a shovel (in the final resolution of the book Nick is finally able to defeat Buncher on the "real" playground as well). It is important to note, as is typical in romance, that the forces the hyper-masculine figure represents need to be defeated, but not entirely repudi-ated. Buncher's rage is the force that Nick must himself master both in the juzzle world and in the "real" world, nor would Nick ever have en-tered the juzzle had it not been for the concussion he receives in the opening fight.[6] In not only beating Buncher, but also seeing he is taken care of when injured, Nick shows that he has mastered the use of Buncher's rage, but not allowed it to engulf him.

Like most romances, Hoban's contains an unsuitable erotic choice for the hero, Cynthia Jeffreys, whose final dismissal of Nick signals the end of his encounter with the exotic world. In a manner reminiscent of Hoban's other fictions, especially *The Medusa Frequency,* Hoban links Cynthia to other women in Nick's world as representations of an always already lost love choice.[7] The flickering of a white dress, the piece of clothing by which Nick first recognizes Cynthia in the juzzle world, re- veals in turn Cynthia, Violet (Nick's mother), and Zelda (both the busker Moe's lost love and Cynthia's mother). Nick himself identifies Cynthia with the beggar maid in Burne-Jones's painting of *King Cophetua and the Beggar Maid,* whose "face always seemed full of terror and mystery and sadness" (27). Nick's progress through the juzzle is described as his search to find Cynthia, but once he finally finds her Hoban has Cynthia herself declare herself out of Nick's reach: "I'm more than a year older than you, Nick, and I've got a boyfriend. . . . You're very sweet . . . and I really like you but that's how it is" (103). When she gives Nick a good- bye kiss (which reminds him of the kiss he received from her mother, Zelda), he is ejected from the juzzle world and finds himself coming to in the hospital, while the image of Cynthia's face is transmuted into that of Lavinia Metcalf, S.R.N.

The topography of the juzzle world also contains the necessary transformative space, the mise (maze) which Nick traverses. Hoban ex- plicitly associates it with female energy—the mystery of sex that Nick is beginning to live. Hoban connects the mysterious female body and the mise by making a joke: "The look of the mise reminded me of a long-ago family outing in Dorset when we visited Maiden Castle and saw great earthen ramparts. . . . Dad had said they made him think of female geni- talia . . . I asked who the Genitalia were; I thought they might be an Iron Age tribe" (77–78). On his way into the mise Nick identifies Cynthia's face with the warm smell of the earth in a moment of illumination, "I closed my eyes and it seemed as though the moonlight was in my head and in the moonlight I saw Cynthia's face, her great luminous eyes full of a mystery that I'd never understand . . . as young as I was, I knew that it wasn't meant to be understood, all I could do was offer myself to it" (79).[8] (Once he reaches the center Nick sees the full moon in "the great dark circle of the mise" [96], a final confirmation of its connection to femaleness.) As is typical of such transformative spaces, it is here that

Nick first realizes that he is in danger and that the "mind trip" that the juzzle represents may not hold together: "I could see the headline: MIND LOSES BOY" (83). Only after he has traversed the mise and survived the danger can Nick finally meet Cynthia and begin the journey home.

Hoban has clearly constructed a story that uses all the traditional elements of the adventure yarn. But it is his self-conscious sense of emplotment—of two realities existing at the same time—that informs *The Trokeville Way* and marks it as postmodern. Nick's doubled consciousness of the reality of the the juzzle world and his "real" world parallels the reader's own doubled consciousness as he or she reads *and* the double consciousness that Moe describes when he first enters the juzzle world *and* the doubled consciousness of the people who exist both inside and outside Nick's mind trip in a vertiginous proliferation of levels of story. As readers, we know that we are in Nick's plot, as mind says at one point, "THIS IS WHAT THERE IS," but we are also aware that "this is what there is " only for the moment. Outside the moment there are other stories; the one we are in now is contingent, if also seductive. What distinguishes *Trokeville* is, as always in Hoban, the sense that fiction and meta-fiction collude (collide) to create new possibilities—multiple layers of story that exist simultaneously and that can be glimpsed through the endless play of language. Hoban amplifies the fundamental sense of contingency and strangeness produced by this double consciousness with his masterful play with voice, both in Nick's narrative and in his dialogue with his mind; with music as a device that moves the reader from one narrative level to another; and with language.

Like characters in other Hoban novels—Herman Orff in *The Medusa Frequency,* Kleinzeit in *Kleinzeit,* Riddley in *Riddley Walker*—Nick is always aware of himself as being *in* and *of* story, both shaped by and shaping his plot. The sense that every story contains multiple layers is suggested first by the ironic distance created by Nick's tone, a self-consciousness shared by the other characters who discuss with Nick their phantasmatic appearances in his dream world. Hoban's opening pages (narrated by Nick) emphasize him as a familiar character, a literary commonplace not only to the reader but to himself, a bored child stuck in school: "I was leaning against the brick wall of the schoolyard, smelling the tomato sauce on my tie and thinking of all the school lunches still ahead of me. . . ." (1). (If the game of conker that precipitates the opening fight of the novel is not familiar to American readers, the free-floating hostility of the playground and despair over school lunch will be.) Nick never abandons this flattened, ironic tone, which works both to normalize the strangeness of the story he tells and also to mark his consciousness of himself as part of a story, if not quite the story that he thought he was in. When he brings the juzzle home to his room, Nick's description of his surroundings suggests the multiplicity of narratives in his life, many suggested as musical possibilities:

> From my brother David's room I could hear the sound of Gaye Bykers on Acid and from downstairs "Clair de Lune" drifting up from Mom's piano. . . . on the patchwork bedspread she'd crocheted were my worn-out teddy bear and frazzled crocodile and four or five other old friends, all looking at me as if from long ago. The guitar I'd got for my birthday was leaning against the wall . . . my flute was on top of the chest of drawers, and my flute certificates were on the wall along with Iron Maiden, Morgoth and Sepultura posters. I'm listening to a Bartòk quartet as I write this and the time when I had ears for that other music seems a long way back. (24)

The time confusion created by this passage—it begins as a description of the present moment when Nick begins to enter the juzzle and ends with the present moment of the writing (listening to Bartòk) after the juzzle experience is over—encapsulates the fluidity of narrative line in Hoban; anything can lead you anywhere in any dimension. But this strangeness is normalized by the unemphatic irony of the narration, which takes as its premise the inherent doubleness of experience, full of the detritus of other stories just as the juzzle is full of garbage: Nick describes himself as "start[ing] up the hill again, through the dead leaves, the soggy newspapers and used condoms, and the rest of the rubbish" (69).

Nick's self-conscious tone implies that this narrative just happens to be the one that contains its characters at the moment, but that it has no exclusive right to them: there are always other, simultaneous narratives to slip in and out of. Early in the book, after Nick first sees her in the juzzle, Cynthia Jeffreys remarks to him (in the real world) that he was in a dream she had that directly mimics Nick's juzzle experience. When he reenters the juzzle Nick encounters his mother, who tells him that "there's nothing unusual about spending a good bit of your time lost in the wood and the rest of it doing whatever you ordinarily do" (76) and also meets his father. (The only character who seems to be upset to find himself in Nick's mind is Buncher, who is always presented as crude.) In addition to these characters Nick meets his history teacher, Zelda, a previous lover of Zelda's, and a dweeby boy who had once been his classmate.[9] While these people occasionally ask Nick why he is wandering around in his pajamas, they otherwise display no astonishment at their current position and fade in and out of his presence like the Cheshire Cat. When Nick finally meets Cynthia she says to him, "I know this is some special kind of reality . . . and I think I'm here because you like me" (102). Cynthia's matter-of-fact acceptance of her presence in Nick's dream is part of the ironic flattening of the romance narrative: Cynthia treats it as simply another happenstance.

The distance achieved by Nick's ironic tone is amplified by his many (and frequently hilarious) conversations with his mind, an independent and testy entity that gives him a hard time: "ACTION TALKS, BULLSHIT WALKS, OKAY?" (58) it says to him at one fraught moment. Readers of other Hoban fictions will recognize his animation of the inanimate. (While it seems peculiar to name mind as an inanimate object, we do not usually think of our minds as hectoring us in an independent voice.) Kleinzeit is addressed by Hospital; Hermann Orff (*The Medusa Frequency*) by Orpheus's head that metamorphoses into a head of cabbage, a half grapefruit, and a soccer ball. In *Trokeville,* Nick's mind represents the same eruption of address from an unexpected quarter, and its speech is always set in capitals, which gives the effect of yelling on the page. When he first confronts Buncher, his nemesis, Nick recounts the fight almost as a spectator: "HERE WE GO AGAIN, said my mind. I heard a sigh coming out of me" (2). The impression is of a hapless narrator stuck between mind and me, condemned to fight with fools like Buncher. When Nick enters the juzzle world, Moe Nagic warns him that "The whole thing is a mind trip" (20); what Nick finds out is that mind is a cranky, contrary place, full of stuff that it does not know what to do with. As Nick traverses the juzzle, he converses more and more with his mind, only to discover that his mind knows different, but does not necessarily know more. At one point he seeks reassurance from it that he will be able to get "home" only to hear, "ARE YOU STUPID OR WHAT? . . . I KEEP TELLING YOU, THIS *IS* HOME. I'M STUCK IN THIS MODE AND I DON'T KNOW ANYTHING ELSE UNTIL YOU GET US THROUGH IT. YOU WANT ME TO PUT IT MORE SIMPLY THAN THAT?" (58). When Nick accuses his mind of "making it up," it replies, "NOBODY TELLS ME ANYTHING. ALL I KNOW IS WHAT HAPPENS—PEOPLE COME INTO IT AND PEOPLE GO OUT OF IT AND THIS IS WHAT THERE IS" (69).

Mind represents an entirely disembodied and arbitrary reality principle within the dream world of the romance: at one point *in the juzzle* it says to Nick, "WHAT CAN I TELL YOU? THIS IS REALITY" (103).

When Nick becomes unnerved by his experience with the juzzle, he asks his mind, "Whose side are you on?" to which mind replies, "I'M ALL THERE IS, I'M THE WORLD THAT LIVES IN YOUR HEAD." When Nick presses for reassurance, mind snidely replies, "HOW ABOUT LESS TALK AND MORE ACTION?" (30). Its constant emphatic pronouncements provide another source of ironic meta-commentary on the story—"NICE WOMAN, YOUR MOTHER" (76)—while insisting on the fundamentally opaque nature of experience: "YOU KEEP NAGGING ME FOR ANSWERS. DO YOU REALIZE THE EFFORT IT TAKES TO KEEP THIS WHOLE THING TOGETHER WHILE YOU BUMBLE AROUND IN IT? ANSWERS ARE NOT MY BUSINESS. I'VE GOT THE WHOLE WORLD IN ME BUT I DON'T KNOW WHAT ANY OF IT MEANS, ALL RIGHT?" (97). The distancing accomplished by Nick's ironic tone is completed by mind's tetchy commentary: all it can do is promise an ungovernable elsewhere centrally located within consciousness, not recuperate that consciousness for meaning. (There is at times a flavor of an author refusing even to admit that there may be a moral to the story in mind's cranky replies.)

While mind is a recalcitrant and ungovernable reality that erupts in Nick's head (although not contained by it), music is a bridge between narrative levels, as in the description quoted earlier where Gaye Bikers on Acid, "Clair de Lune," and Bartòk express the concurrent stories present in Nick's house. Hoban uses music, particularly the tune "Libertango," a tune that marks the entrance of the familiar strange, as a way to access the various levels of narrative without privileging one over the other. Nick first hears Moe Nagic playing the tune on his concertina when he buys the juzzle. Hearing the tune does not merely remind Nick of being at the circus; it brings him into the circus: "A kind of darkness came into the light and I could see the bright spangled figures high up in the riggings of the tent . . ." (7). But "Libertango" is not only the key to the circus; it is also a real song in the frame world, sung by Grace Jones on a CD owned by Nick's father: "Strange—I've seen that face before, / seen him hanging round my door, / like a hawk feeling for the prey, / like a night waiting for the day" (7). The lyric to the song, emphasizing as it does both repetition and threat, "I've seen that face before . . . like a hawk feeling for the prey," suggests both the déjà vu of the romance plot and the ever present threat (and promise) of romance's strange eruption into the everyday: as Moe says of the tune. "It's got mystery, the music, it's got magic—it takes you out of the everyday sameness into a place where anything can happen" (12). When Zelda, Cynthia's mother, reads the newspaper that contains Moe Nagic's obituary, she hums "Libertango," which she associates with her former life of magic, possibility (and risk) that she abandoned when she abandoned Moe. As Nick proceeds through the juzzle he hears "Libertango" repeatedly. At first it seems to mark the connection between the juzzle world and the real world—the fact that time has not passed in the "real" world when he is in the juzzle—but then becomes the mark of his willingness to engage strangeness as he decides to enter the mise. At the end of the novel, "Libertango" is superseded by the Debussy pieces "Reverie" and "Clair de Lune," both of which are associated with domestic spaces (Nick has heard both his mother and Cynthia practice them). When Nick is finally firmly in the everyday, he himself begins to practice both tunes with his new girlfriend, Felicity. As "Libertango" marks the eruption of the strange, "Clair de Lune" marks the return of the everyday.

As always in Hoban, language itself is a motivating force, with words metamorphosing into new words and revealing hidden connections: Moe Nagic says, "There's no magic but there's Moe Nagic" (11). When Moe gives Nick the juzzle, he makes clear that he has given its geographical features "off-straight" names to reflect their weird nature: the wood is the "little would," the maze is the mise, the bridge is the brudge (explained as a "bridge with a grudge" [15]). As is frequent in romance, significant names reveal the story's allegorical overtones: the little wood is the place of those whose desires have not been strong enough to sustain their dreams: Nick meets both of his parents there. The mise in Moe's description of the picture is linked in Nick's daydreams about Cynthia to the "wild surmise" in Keats's poem "On First Looking into Chapman's Homer," and finally to Nick's desire for Cynthia, "my blue Pacific! My wild surmise—where is it?" (97).[10] (Although his naming of desire as an it, as opposed to a she, suggests the way in which his desire is incommensurate with its object.) At the end of the novel Nick plays flute with his new girlfriend, Felicity, whose name suggests at least one object of the Trokeville way. The final and most important bit of wordplay is, however, the troke—the trick and the stroke that gets you into Trokeville. Trokeville is, as Nick's mind unhelpfully tells him, "WHEREVER YOU ARE WHEN YOU DO THE TROKE," for Nick in the end it means taking the initiative and picking a fight with Buncher himself. When he beats him, Nick's mind says, "TROKEVILLE" and he replies, "It's a good place to be" (115).

Hoban's narrative suggests that plots literally transfigure us, since they move us into new realms of figuration, new modes of apprehending the world. After his experience in the juzzle Nick takes charge of his story in the real: when he meets Buncher for the final fight he repeats to Buncher the words that his mind had used to him, "Action walks, bullshit talks" (no longer in capitals since Nick is saying them). After the troke, Nick starts a new story for himself in a last chapter named "Felicity." Even though Nick no longer inhabits the world of the juzzle (he has, in fact, given the juzzle away), his encounter with it has taught him not just how to beat Buncher, but how to approach life. On the last page he writes, "Those strange mental powers I had when I was involved with the juzzle are long gone but I'm more in touch with the lower level of reality than I used to be. And I'm certainly more aware of the strangeness of everthing that I ever was before" (117).

Adolescence is, in our culture, traditionally a time of transition from the aimless plotlessness of childhood to the time-driven plots of the adult world. It is therefore a time in which the multiplicity and arbitrariness of the plots available to us are acutely apparent, a fact that Hoban has taken advantage of before in his most famous novel, *Riddley Walker* (also the story of a twelve-year-old boy). At the end of that novel, Riddley, who has been raised as a soothsayer, a "connexion man," leaves behind his original community and creates a small itinerant troupe who trek around his ruined world performing a Punch-and-Judy show. Riddley describes the power that the puppet show has when he puts the figures on his hands: "You put your head finger in the head you put your arm fingers in the arms then that figger looks roun and takes noatis it has things to say. Which they wont all ways be things *youwd* think of saying o no them wood heads the hart of the wood is in them and the heart of the wud and all" (the novel is written in a post-apocalyptic argot devised by Hoban) (204). Riddley takes over the Punch-and-Judy show as a participant in the mystery of storytelling itself: once he puts the "figgers" on his hand, he says the words that the show requires, not the things that he himself would think to say. As with the Eusa show, the other great performance in Riddley, once you "go down that road" you must continue to set one foot before the other, even if you do not exactly know where you are going, it is "time and reqwyrt." In his final emphasis on the power of the momentary yet necessary solutions offered by narrative, Nick repeats Riddley's lesson, leaning into the story of the moment in the full awareness of its arbitrariness, and in trust that it will see him through.[11]

In the classic versions of adventure/romance, the exotic other world, even though it is often very close to the "real" world, is nevertheless walled off from the frame world. The exotic world in which adventure is possible is abandoned; the world of the real begins: Aronnax cannot return to the *Nautilus* through the maelstrom; the map of Treasure Island is carefully concealed; Monte Cristo's island is emptied of treasure and he himself sails for the Orient. Hoban suggests to us instead that the story— even as old and worn a story as this one—is wherever we are. Moreover, stories have purposes beyond our knowing to which we are bound whether we recognize them or not. Nick, entering the juzzle world, recognizes that he is in the grip of a tale whose entire meaning will continue to elude him. He consciously offers himself to the tale when he enters the juzzle as he offers himself to the mystery of the mise within the juzzle, in the awareness that he can neither control nor fully understand it and that it may not be the tale he expects. (In a similar vein, Fremder Gorn realizes that he is part of a story that he cannot control at the end of *Fremder:* "At this moment that might well be the beginning of the end of my life I was looking for high tragedy but I seemed to have become the rear half of a Jewish pantomime horse" (181).) Hoban's trope for this pervasive arbitrariness of plot is mind. The reified mind that speaks to Nick shows us that the strangest story is where we are when we tell the stories that we cannot help always telling: Trokeville is where we are because we are always capable of doing the troke. It is through this melding of the generic and the ordinary, the necessary and the arbitrary, that Hoban inflects the romance for the postmodern: "it's a good place to be."

NOTES

[1]Hoban has written movingly of his love for such fiction in "With a Choked Cry" from *The Moment Under the Moment.*

[2]The modern adventure novel is a secular modern subset of the much larger tradition of the romance, with its roots in ancient myths and legends. For the purposes of this article I am using adventure and romance interchangeably.

[3]Le Guin has remarked on the persistence of the masculine hero in her talk about her own work, *Earthsea Revisioned,* which begins, "In our hero-tales of the Western world, heroism has been gendered: The hero is a man" (5).

[4]The construction of a picture world into which a character enters is reminiscent not only of Carroll's *Through the Looking Glass* but also of M.R. James's short story "The Mezzotint" (from *Ghost Stories of an Antiquary*), where a newly purchased print displays for its purchaser a grisly story of revenge.

[5]Conkers is a game played with varnished chestnuts fastened to a string. The idea is to hit and break your opponent's chestnut.

[6]Moreover, at the end of the novel Nick is playing the flute with Buncher's sister, named Felicity, appropriately enough. In contrast, Moe Nagic is unable to reclaim his "girl" Zelda from the rich man she marries because he is unable to

summon the necessary rage. When Nick asks him, " 'What kind of trick or stroke is the troke anyhow?' " Moe replies, " 'I believe it's the trick or stroke that gets you to Trokeville. . . . I've seen it from a distance like Moses looking at the land of Canaan but I never got there' " (21).

[7]In *The Medusa Frequency* Hoban creates a haunting image of Hermann Orff's lost love as a series of linked figures—Vermeer's Girl with a Pearl Earring, Eurydice, Medusa, Persephone, her modern stand-in, Melanie Falsepercy, Luise Himmelbett—all of whom merge in and out of each other.

[8]In *Treasure Island,* just as Jim hears the pirates plotting mutiny, he is flooded by light in the apple barrel in which he is hiding, another moment of illumination in the transformative space at a critical juncture in the story.

[9]All of these people represent other plots that Nick has neglected. The history teacher, Mr. Vickers, remarks on this by commenting on Nick's singular failure of the imagination in his exam answer on the reign of Charles I: "In the eleven years that Charles ruled without Parliament things went from bad to worse." Mr. Vickers reproaches Nick (in an acute imitation of the elaborate tone adopted by some teachers) with "slackness of character" since "an intensely interesting period in our history failed to stir you to more than fifteen words." He ends by exhorting Nick, "Pay attention, Hartley: do better" (81–82).

[10]Mr. Vickers repeats this loaded word when he says to Nick " 'What am I doing here? I should have thought you might have *surmised* that I am talking to you' " (81). His use of "surmise" in the banal context of teacher's speculation on a wayward student suggests yet another vector of narrative in the plot.

[11]He is also aware of the way in which he does not conform to generic expectation: "In books and films boys who fight each other often end up friends but that didn't happen with Harry Buncher and me" (117).

BIBLIOGRAPHY

Carroll, Lewis. *Alice's Adventures in Wonderland and, Through the Looking Glass and What She Found There.* New York: Oxford University Press. 1982.

Dumas, Alexandre. *The Count of Monte Cristo.* ed. David Coward. New York: Oxford University Press, 1990.

Hoban, Russell. *Fremder.* London: Jonathan Cape, 1996.

———.*Kleinzeit.* London: Picador, 1974.

———. *The Medusa Frequency.* London: Picador, 1987.

———. *The Moment Under the Moment.* London: Jonathan Cape, 1992.

———. *The Mouse and His Child.* New York: Harper & Row, 1967.

———. *Riddley Walker.* Blomington and Indianapolis: Indiana University Press, 1998.

———. *The Trokeville Way.* New York: Knopf, 1996.

James, M.R. *Ghost Stories of an Antiquary.* New York: Dover Publications, 1971.

Jones, Grace. *Nighclubbing.* New York: Island Records, 1981.

Le Guin, Ursula. *Earthsea Revisioned.* Cambridge: Children's Literature New England; Cambridge England, Green Bay Publications, 1993.

———. *Tehanu, the Last Book of Earthsea.* New York: Bantam, 1991.

———. *Wizard of Earthsea.* New York: Bantam Spectra Books, 1984.

McKillop, Patricia. *The Forgotten Beasts of Eld.* New York: Atheneum, 1974.

Stevenson, Robert Louis. *Treasure Island.* ed. Emma Letley. New York: Oxford University Press, 1985.

Verne, Jules. *A Journey to the Center of the Earth.* trans. William Butcher. New York: Oxford University Press, 1998.

———. *Twenty Thousand Leagues under the Sea.* trans. William Butcher. New York: Oxford University Press, 1998.

Works by Russell Hoban
Publications in Chronological Order

SHORT STORIES

"Dream Woman." *The Fiction Magazine*. October 1985, rpt. in *The Moment under the Moment*. London: Jonathan Cape, 1992.

"Dark Oliver." *The Observer Magazine*. 30 July 1989, rpt. in *The Moment under the Moment*.

"The Man with the Dagger." *Granta* (25) 1989. Also, *Best Short Stories* 1990. William Heinemann Ltd., rpt. in *The Moment under the Moment*.

"Schwartz." *Encounter*, March 1990, rpt. in *The Moment under the Moment*.

"My Night with Leonie." *Sphinx*, Spring 1992, rpt. in *The Moment under the Moment.*.

"The Ghost Horse of Genghis Khan." *BBC Radio* (4), 6 April 1992, rpt. in *The Moment under the Moment*.

"Telling Stories." *BBC Radio* 4, 15 March 1993. *Telling Stories 2*, Coronet 1993.

"The Devil's Kitchen." *Granta* 42, 1993.

"The Mantris Woman." *BBC Radio* 4, 14 June 1993.

"Call Girl." *BBC Radio* 4, 27 February 1995.

"Be Jubilant, My Feet." *The Mail on Sunday*, 3 March 1996.

"Partly Now, Partly Remembered." *BBC Music Magazine*. March 1996.

"Cuts." *Metropolitan*, Winter 96/97.

"My Peepshow Love." *Metropolitan*, Autumn 1997.

"Like a Circle in a Spiral." *BBC Radio* 3, *BBC Music Magazine* 1998.

NOVELS

The Mouse and His Child. New York: Harper & Row, 1967; London: Faber and Faber, 1969.

The Lion of Boaz-Jachin and Jachin-Boaz. New York: Stein and Day, 1973, rpt.in
   The Russell Hoban Omnibus. Bloomington: University of Indiana Press,
   1999.
Kleinzeit. New York: Summit Books, 1974.
Turtle Diary. New York: Random House, 1975, rpt. *The Russell Hoban Omnibus*
Riddley Walker. New York: Summit Books, 1981, rpt. Bloomington: Indiana Uni-
   versity Press, 1998.
Pilgermann. New York: Summit Books, 1983, rpt. *The Russell Hoban Omnibus.*
The Medusa Frequency. London: Jonathan Cape, 1987.
Fremder. London: Jonathan Cape, 1996.
The Trokeville Way. London: Jonathan Cape, 1996; New York: Knopf, 1996.
Mr. Rinyo-Clacton's Offer. London: Jonathan Cape, 1998, rpt. *The Russell
   Hoban Omnibus.*
Angelica's Grotto. London: Bloomsbury, 1999.

PICTURE BOOKS FOR CHILDREN

What Does It Do and How Does It Work? Illus. Russell Hoban. New York:
   Harper, 1959.
The Atomic Submarine. Illus. Russell Hoban. New York: Harper, 1960.
Bedtime for Frances. Illus. Garth Williams. New York: Harper, 1960; London:
   Faber and Faber, 1963.
Herman the Loser. Illus. Lillian Hoban. New York: Harper & Row, 1961;
   Kingswood, Surrey: World's Work, 1972.
The Song in My Drum. Illus. Lillian Hoban. New York: Harper & Row, 1962.
London Men and English Men. New York: Harper & Row, 1963.
Some Snow Said Hello. Illus. Lillian Hoban. New York: Harper & Row, 1963.
A Baby Sister for Frances. Illus. Lillian Hoban. New York: Harper & Row, 1964;
   London: Faber and Faber, 1965.
Nothing to Do. Illus. Lillian Hoban. New York: Harper & Row, 1964.
Bread and Jam for Frances. Illus. Lillian Hoban. New York: Harper & Row,
   1964; London: Faber and Faber, 1966.
The Sorely Trying Day. Illus. Lillian Hoban. New York: Harper & Row, 1964;
   Kingswood, Surrey: World's Work, 1965.
Tom and the Two Handles. Illus. Lillian Hoban. New York: Harper & Row, 1965;
   Kingswood, Surrey: World's Work, 1969.
The Story of Hester Mouse Who Became a Writer. Illus. Lillian Hoban. New
   York: W. W. Norton, 1965; Kingswood, Surrey: World's Work, 1969.
What Happened When Jack and Daisy Tried to Fool the Tooth Fairies. Illus. Lil-
   lian Hoban. New York: Scholastic, Four Winds Press, 1965.
Goodnight. Illus. Lillian Hoban. New York: W. W. Norton, 1966; Kingswood,
   Surrey: World's Work, 1969.

Henry and the Monstrous Din. Illus. Lillian Hoban. New York: Harper & Row, 1966; Kingswood, Surrey: World's Work, 1967.

Charlie the Tramp. Illus. Lillian Hoban. New York: Scholastic, 1966.

The Little Brute Family. Illus. Lillian Hoban. New York: Macmillan, 1966.

Save My Place. Illus. Lillian Hoban. New York: W. W. Norton, 1967.

The Stone Doll of Sister Brute. Illus. Lillian Hoban. New York: Macmillan, 1968; London: Collier-Macmillan, 1968.

A Birthday for Frances. Illus. Lillian Hoban. New York: Harper & Row, 1968; London: Faber and Faber, 1970.

Ugly Bird. Illus. Lillian Hoban. New York: Macmillan, 1969.

Best Friends for Frances. Illus. Lillian Hoban. New York: Harper & Row, 1969; London: Faber and Faber, 1971.

Harvey's Hideout. Illus. Lillian Hoban. New York: Parents' Magazine Press, 1969; London: Jonathan Cape, 1973.

The Mole Family's Christmas. Illus. Lillian Hoban. New York: Parents' Magazine Press, 1969; London: Jonathan Cape, 1973.

A Bargain for Frances. Illus. Lillian Hoban. New York: Harper & Row, 1970; Kingswood, Surrey: World's Work, 1971.

Emmet Otter's Jug-Band Christmas. Illus. Lillian Hoban. New York: Parents' Magazine Press, 1971; Kingswood, Surrey: World's Work, 1971.

The Sea-Thing Child. Illus. Brom Hoban. New York: Harper & Row, 1972; London: Gollancz, 1972.

Letitia Rabbit's String Song. Illus. Mary Chalmers. New York: Coward, McCann & Geoghegan, 1973.

Dinner at Alberta's. Illus. James Marshall. New York: T. Y. Crowell, 1973; London: Jonathan Cape, 1977.

How Tom Beat Captain Najork and His Hired Sportsmen. Illus. Quentin Blake. New York: Atheneum, 1974; London: Jonathan Cape, 1974 (Whitbread Award).

Ten What? A Mystery Counting Book. Illus. Sylvia Selig. New York: Scribner's, 1975; London: Jonathan Cape, 1974.

Crocodile and Pierrot. Illus. Sylvia Selig. New York: Scribner's, 1977; London: Jonathan Cape, 1975.

A Near Thing for Captain Najork. Illus. Quentin Blake. New York: Atheneum, 1976; London: Jonathan Cape, 1975.

The Twenty-Elephant Restaurant. Illus. Emily Arnold McCully. New York: Atheneum, 1977.

Arthur's New Power. Illus. Byron Barton. New York: T. Y. Crowell, 1978.

The Dancing Tigers. Illus. David Gentleman. London: Jonathan Cape, 1979.

La Corona and the Tin Frog. Illus. Nicola Bayley. London: Jonathan Cape, 1979.

Ace Dragon Ltd. Illus. Quentin Blake. London: Jonathan Cape, 1980.

Flat Cat. Illus. Clive Scrunton. New York: Philomel, 1980; London: Walker Books, 1980.

The Serpent Tower. Illus. David Scott. London: Metheun, 1981

The Great Fruit Gum Robbery. Illus. Colin McNaughton. London: Walker Books, 1981, rpt. as *The Great Gumdrop Robbery.* New York: Philomel, 1982.

They Came from Aargh! Illus. Colin McNaughton. New York: Philomel, 1981; London: Walker Books, 1981.

The Flight of Bembel Rudzuk. Illus. Colin McNaughton. New York: Philomel, 1982; London: Walker Books, 1982.

The Battle of Zormla. Illus. Colin McNaughton. New York: Philomel, 1982; London: Walker Books, 1982.

Jim Frog. Illus. Martin Baynton. New York: Holt, Rinehart & Winston, 1984; London: Walker Books, 1983.

Big John Turkle. Illus. Martin Baynton. New York: Holt, Rinehart & Winston, 1984; London: Walker Books, 1983.

Charlie Meadows. Illus. Martin Baynton. New York: Holt, Rinehart & Winston 1984; London: Walker Books, 1984.

Lavinia Bat. Illus. Martin Baynton. New York: Holt, Rinehart & Winston, 1984; London: Walker Books, 1984.

The Marzipan Pig. Illus. Quentin Blake. New York: Farrar, Straus & Giroux, 1989; London: Jonathan Cape, 1986.

The Rain Door. Illus. Quentin Blake. London: Gollancz, 1986.

Jim Hedgehog's Supernatural Christmas. London: Hamish Hamilton, 1989.

Jim Hedgehog and the Lonesome Tower. London: Hamish Hamilton, 1990 (shortlisted for the Smarties Prize 1990).

M.O.L.E. (Much Overworked Little Earthmover). Illus. Jan Pienkowski. London: Jonathan Cape, 1993.

Monsters. Illus. Quentin Blake. London: Orion, 1993.

The Court of the Winged Serpent. London: Jonathan Cape, 1994.

Monster Film. Illus. Toni Goffe. London: Macdonald Young Books, 1995.

Trouble on Thunder Mountain. Illus. Quentin Blake. London: Faber and Faber, 1998.

The Sea-Thing Child (revised). Illus. Patrick Benson. London: Walker Books, 1999.

Jim's Lion. London: Walker Books, 1999.

VERSE FOR CHILDREN

The Pedalling Man and Other Poems. New York: W.W. Norton, 1968; new edition with additional poems London: William Heinemann, 1990.

Egg Thoughts and Other Frances Songs. New York: Harper & Row, 1972; London: Faber and Faber, 1973.

Six of the Best (with five other writers). London: Puffin, 1989.

The Last of the Wallendas. Illus. Patrick Benson. London: Hodder, 1997 (shortlisted for the Signal Poetry Prize.)

ADDENDA

Animated Films: *Deadsy and Door.* Text and voice-over by Russell Hoban, animation by David Anderson.
Works on Film: *The Mouse and His Child*; *Emmet Otter's Jug-Band Christmas*; *Turtle Diary.*

ANTHOLOGIES

The Moment under the Moment. London: Jonathan Cape, 1992.
A Hoban Omnibus. December 1999, Indian UP.

SECONDARY SOURCES

Allison, Alida. "Russell Hoban: Excerpts from a Talk at San Diego State University." *Poets and Writers Magazine* 20(4) July/August 1992, 26–36.
———. "Russell Hoban Reads Russell Hoban at SDSU." *The Lion and the Unicorn* 1992.
———. "An Interview with Russell Hoban." *Dictionary of Literary Biography 1990 Yearbook.* Detroit: Gale Research Company, 1991.
———. "Living the Non-Mechanical Life: Toys as Metaphors in Russell Hoban's Books." *Children's Literature in Education* 22 (1991): 3:189–194.
———. "Orpheus, Eurydice, Medusa: An Interview with Russell Hoban." *Pacific Review* Spring 1991, 77–82.
———. "Russell Hoban." *American Writers for Children Since 1960: Dictionary of Literary Biography,* Vol. 52. Detroit: Gale Research Company, 1988.
Awl, Dave. "Head of Orpheus." http://www.suba.com/~dayvoll/rh/listserv.html.
Beard, Pauline Winsome. "A Riddling Thing: A Study of Time in Five 20th Century Novels." *Dissertation Abstracts International* 47 1986, 528–528.
Cowart, David. *History and the Contemporary Novel.* Carbondale: Southern Illinois University Press, 1984.
DeLuca, Geraldine. "A Condition of Complete Simplicity: The Toy as Child in *The Mouse and His Child.*" *Children's Literature in Education* 19 1988, 211–221.
Dipple, Elizabeth. "Russell Hoban: This Place Called Time." *The Unresolvable Plot: Reading Contemporary Fiction.* New York: Routledge, 1988, 160–181.
Dowling, David. "Russell Hoban's *Riddley Walker:* Doing the Connections." *Critique* Spring 1988, 179–187.
Galef, David. "Crossing Over: Authors Who Write Both Children's and Adults' Fiction." *Children's Literature Association Quarterly* 20(1) Spring 1995, 29–35.

Granofsky, Ronald. "Holocaust as Symbol in *Riddley Walker* and *The White Hotel.*" *Modern Language Studies* 16 Summer 1986, 172–182.

———. "Leap of the Lion: Russell Hoban." *The Contemporary Symbolic Novel. Dissertations Abstracts International* 47(2) August 1986, 165–238.

Gregory, Sinda and Larry McCaffery. "An Interview with Russell Hoban." *Alive and Writing: Interviews With American Authors of the 1980s.* Urbana: Univeristy of Illinois University Press, 1987.

Kincaid, Paul. "The Mouse, the Lion, and Riddley Walker: An Interview with Russell Hoban." *Vector* 124/125 April/May 1985, 5–9.

Krips, Valerie. "Mistaken Identity: Russell Hoban's *The Mouse and His Child.*" Children's Literature 21 (1993):97.

Kuznets, Lois R. *When Toys Come Alive: Narratives of Animation, Metamorphosis, and Development.* New Haven: Yale University Press, 1994.

Lake, David J. "Making the Two One: Language and Mysticism in *Riddley Walker.*" *Extrapolation* 25 (2) 1984, 157–170.

Laurence, Frank. "The Pack and the Lunch Box: Hemingway's Stylistic Influence on Russell Hoban." *Hemingway Notes* 6(1) 1980, 29–31.

Maclean, Marie. "The Signifier as Token: The Textual Riddles of Russell Hoban." *AUMLA: Journal of the Australasian Universities Language and Literature Association* 70 Nov. 1988, 211–219.

Maynor, Natalie and Richard F. Patterson. "Language as Protagonist in Russell Hoban's *Riddley Walker.*" *Critique Fall* 1984, 18–25.

McKillop, Ian. "Russell Hoban: Returning to the Sunlight." *Good Writers for Young Readers.* Dennis Butts, ed. St. Albans, UK: Hart-Davis Educational, 1977, 57–66.

Morrisey, Thomas J. "Armageddon from Huxley to Hoban." *Extrapolation* 25(3) 1984, 197–211.

Mustazza, Leonard. "Myth and History in Russell Hoban's *Riddley Walker.*" *Critique* Fall 1989, 17–25.

Myers, Edwards. "An Interview with Russell Hoban." *Literary Review* 28(1) Fall 1984, 5–16.

Punter, David. "Essential Imaginings: The Novels of Angela Carter and Russell Hoban." *The British And Irish Novel Since 1960.* James Acheson, ed. New York: St. Martin's, 1991, 142–158.

Robit, Earl. "The Fiction of Russell Hoban." *The Hollins Critic* 34(3): 1997, 1–12.

Rustin, Margaret and Michael. "Making Out in America: *The Mouse and His Child.*" *Narratives of Love and Loss: Studies in Modern Children's Fiction.* London: Verso 1987.

Schwenger, Peter. "Circling Ground Zero." *Publications of the Modern Language Society* 106 (2) March 1991, 251–261.

Schwetman, John W. "Russell Hoban's Riddley Walker and the Language of the Future." *Extrapolation* 26 (3) 1985, 212–219.

Swanson, Roy Arthur. "Versions of Doublethink in Gravity's Rainbow, Darkness Visible, Riddley Walker, and Travels to the Enu." *World Literature Today* 58(2) 1982, 27–39.

Taylor, Nancy Dew. "'. . . you bes go ballsy': Riddley Walker's Prescription for the Future." *Critique* Fall 1989, 27–39.

Wilkie, Christine. *Through the Narrow Gate: The Mythological Consciousness of Russell Hoban.* Cranbury, NJ: Associated University Press, 1989.

Contributors

James Addison is Professor of English at Western Carolina University, where he regularly teaches "Fairy Tales and After" and "The Golden Age of Children's Literature: Folk and Fairy Tales in Britain," to both undergraduate and graduate students. He holds the B.A. and M.A. from Clemson University and the Ph.D. from the University of Tennessee. He has been selected for four NEH Summer Seminars, including the influential 1989 Seminar "Fairy Tales and the Emergence of Childhood" with U.C. Knoepflmacher at Princeton University. Sparked by this seminar, he has given nine papers on fairy tales at national conferences, such as SAMLA and ChLA, and had articles accepted for the *Cambridge Guide to Children's Books*. He serves on the Article Award Committee of the Children's Literature Association. Most recently, he has been examining fairy tales in the context of Sufism.

Alida Allison is Associate Professor of English and Comparative Literature at San Diego State University, where she directs the Children's Literature Circle and its web site at http://www-rohan.sdsu.edu/dept/english/childlit/index.html. *Isaac Bashevis Singer: Children's Stories and Childhood Memoirs* was published in 1996.

Margaret Bruzelius is a lecturer in the Program for Degrees in Literature at Harvard University. She is currently working on a book on modern and postmodern forms of the romance, particularly adventure fiction, and its relation to the novel.

Dennis Butts teaches children's literature on the graduate level at Reading University in England and is a past president of the Children's Books History Society. He has written widely on various aspects of nineteenth-century literature and children's books, including studies of Barbara Hofland and Robert Louis Stevenson. He edited Frances Hodgson Burnett's *The Secret Garden* and E. Nesbit's *The Railway Children* for the Oxford University Press's World Classics.

James Carter is a freelance English teacher and writer. He teaches Creative Writing and Children's Literature on the BA.Ed. degree course at Reading University, where he recently completed an M.A. in Children's Literature. Carter's publications include poetry for children as well as *Talking Books* (Routledge, May 1999)—a collection of interviews with contemporary children's authors.

Winfred Kaminski is currently a professor of Language and Literary Education at the University of Applied Sciences in Cologne, Germany. For ten years he was on the staff of the Institute for Children's Book Research at Frankfurt University. He received his doctorate from Frankfurt University.

Jamie Madden is working on an advanced degree in English at San Diego State University, where she also teaches literature and composition.

Maria Nikolajeva is a Professor of Literature at Stockholm University and Associate Professor of Literature at Abo Academy University in Finland, where she teaches children's literature and literary theory. She has written and edited several books on children's literature, among them *Children's Literature Comes of Age: Toward the New Aesthetic* (1996) and *From Mythical to Linear: Time in Children's Fiction* (1999), in addition to publishing many articles in journals and essay collections. She was the President of the International Research Society for Children's Literature from 1993 to 1997.

Carole Scott is Dean of Undergraduate Studies and a member of the English and Comparative Literature Department at San Diego State University. She has published articles in *Children's Literature, Children's Literature Association Quarterly,* and *The Lion and the Unicorn,* in Australia's Papers and Orana, and in collections of essays published in South

Africa, Sweden, the United Kingdom, and the United States. She is currently co-authoring a work on picture books with Maria Nikolajeva.

Staffan Skott is the author of twelve books, mainly on Russian history and culture and also the translator into Swedish of many Russian literary works, including all of Chekhov's full-length plays and literature by Gogol, Solzhenitsyn, and others. For the past two decades, he has worked for Sweden's largest morning newspaper, *Dagens Nyheter.*

John Stephens is Associate Professor in English at Macquarie University, Australia, where his main teaching commitment is children's literature, but he also teaches and supervises postgraduate research in medieval studies, post-colonial literature, and discourse analysis. He is the author of *Language and Ideology in Children's Fiction; Retelling Stories, Framing Culture: Traditional Story and Metanarratives in Children's Literature* (with Robyn McCallum); two books about discourse analysis; and around sixty articles about children's (and other) literature. His primary research focus is on the relationships of texts produced for children (especially literature and film) with cultural formations and practices. He was President of the International Research Society for Children's Literature from 1997 to 1999.

Martin Teitel is the Executive Director of the Council for Responsible Genetics and Editor of *GeneWatch Magazine.* He is the author of numerous articles and books on environmental and human rights issues. Teitel has a Ph.D. in Philosophy from the Graduate School of the Union Institute. His most recent book, co-authored with Kimberly A. Wilson, is *Genetically Engineered Food: Changing the Nature of Nature* (2000).

Christine Wilkie-Stibbs lectures in English and directs the M.A. program in Children's Literature Studies at the University of Warwick, U.K. She received her Ph.D. from the University of Cardiff. Her publications include *Through the Narrow Gate: The Mythological Consciousness of Russell Hoban* (Cranbury, NJ: Associated University Presses, 1989), and several articles in refereed journals on children's literature. Additionally, she has given papers at international venues.

Index

Credits